Self-esteem at Work

Research, Theory, and Practice

Joel Brockner
Columbia University

Lexington Books
D.C. Heath and Company/Lexington, Massachusetts/Toronto

Quote on page 12 is reprinted with permission from Morris Rosenberg, *Conceiving the Self,* Copyright 1986, Robert E. Krieger Publishing Company, Malabar, Florida.

Table 6–1 on page 127 is reprinted with permission from the *Journal of Vocational Behavior,* 15, Phyllis Tharenou, "Employee Self-esteem: A Review of the Literature," Copyright 1979, Academic Press.

Table 6–2 on page 129 is reprinted with permission from the *Journal of Vocational Behavior,* 15, Phyllis Tharenou, "Employee Self-esteem: A Review of the Literature," Copyright 1979, Academic Press.

Figure 8–1 on page 199 is reprinted with the permission of Alice Eagly.

Figure 8–2 on page 204 is reprinted with the permission of Robert Ziller, *The Social Self,* Copyright 1973, Pergamon Books, Ltd.

Figure 8–3 on page 227 is reprinted with the permission of Joseph McGrath.

Library of Congress Cataloging-in-Publication Data

Brockner, Joel.

   Self-esteem at work.

   Includes index.
   1. Work—Psychological aspects. 2. Self-respect.
3. Psychology, Industrial. I. Title.
HF5548.8.B686   1988   158.7   84–48747
ISBN 0–669–09755–1 (alk. paper)

Published simultaneously in Canada
Printed in the United States of America
International Standard Book Number: 0–669–09755–1
Library of Congress Catalog Card Number 84–48747

The paper used in this publication meets the minimum requirements of
American National Standard for Information Sciences—Permanence of
Paper for Printed Library Materials, ANSI Z3.48–1984. ∞

89 90 91 92 8 7 6 5 4 3 2

To my father, Irving Brockner, my sons, Eliot H. and Dustin J. Brockner, and the memory of my mother, Helen Brockner— four special people who have taught me much about both self-esteem and work.

Contents

Figures and Tables

Foreword

Arthur P. Brief
Benjamin Schneider

What sort of people are most likely (a) to slack off in response to negative feedback from their boss, (b) to imitate the style of their superiors, and (c) to survive poorly the layoff of their co-workers? For over a decade, Joel Brockner, through his research on self-esteem, has sought answers to these and related questions. Now, in *Self-esteem at Work,* he brings together results from his extensive program of research and integrates them with a broad range of others' theories and findings. The book, importantly, is more than a mere catalog of findings; it represents an attempt to articulate the many ways by which self-esteem interacts with various situational factors to affect job attitudes and behaviors. As a theory-building effort that focuses on a personality construct, the book stands alone among contemporary works in organizational behavior.

Current approaches to understanding organizational behavior are dominated by situationists. The situationist perspective focuses attention on features of the work environment as determinants of job attitudes and behaviors. Indeed, we have learned that the ways in which goals are set, performance is appraised and fedback, rewards are administered, and the like are predictive of how people think, feel, and act at work. In all of this, however, it seems the individual has lost his or her identity as an active agent, as an agent with a personality that disposes particular responses to the environment.

This neglect is attributable at least in part to the way personality frequently has been studied by students of organizational behavior. This or that personality construct appears to have been operationalized in any given study more as an afterthought rather than on the basis of a well reasoned, a priori, rationale of why the specific personality variable is expected to be salient in the situation under investigation. For personality to take its rightful place in understanding organizational behavior, theory driven research is required in which personality attributes are not arbitrarily lifted off a shelf just to be included to see if there is an effect. *Why* a particular personality construct is important and *how* it is likely to behave must be specified. Brockner's book moves us toward the sort of theory that is required.

We hope *Self-esteem at Work* will come to be accepted as a model of how personality constructs should be approached by those interested in applied settings. That is, the book goes beyond research and theory to show how managers might use the insights presented about self-esteem to promote both individual and organizational effectiveness. Thus, for both conceptual and practical contributions we are pleased to add Brockner's book to our Series.

Preface

As implied by its title, this book is about how employees' self-esteem "matters" in the workplace. Self-esteem influences individuals' work behaviors and attitudes in two fundamental ways. First, employees bring to their work settings different levels of self-esteem, which, in turn, relate to how they act, feel, and think while on the job. Second, as a general rule, individuals need to feel good about themselves; thus, much of what workers do and believe is in the service of enhancing, preserving, or restoring their self-esteem. Self-esteem refers both to an individual difference variable as well as a motivational process, which in different though related ways may help us to understand, explain, and manage human behavior in work organizations.

I have several goals—some short-term and others long-term—in writing this book. More immediately, the book is designed to integrate theory and empirical research across different subdisciplines in the behavioral sciences. Personality, social, and clinical psychologists have long recognized the significance of self-esteem to the human condition. To a lesser, though still significant extent, students of industrial psychology, organizational behavior, and management also have explored self-esteem, particularly its relationship to employee behavior. To date, however, there have been few attempts to integrate the primarily theoretical contributions of personality and social psychologists with the largely applied concerns of organizational psychologists and practicing managers. This book, therefore, seeks to build several bridges: between subdisciplines in the behavioral sciences; and between theory, research, and (managerial) practice.

Over the longer haul, I hope that this book will put self-esteem on the map as an important topic of inquiry among organizational scholars. There is ample evidence that employees' self-esteem, usually in conjunction with characteristics of their work settings, is an important predictor of their job behaviors and attitudes. And yet, self-esteem hardly has been embraced by organizational scholars, or at least not nearly as much as by their brethren in personality and social psychology.

The marginal role of self-esteem in extant organizational research may reflect a more general ambivalence felt by many about the role of personality in work organizations. As discussed in the first chapter, much (though certainly not all) personality research in work organizations has not elucidated the theory or practice of managing people. However, to conclude that employees' personalities don't matter simply would be premature, even in light of previous empirical evidence that has not made a convincing case for the role of personality. Thus, a second long-term goal of this book is to give personality more generally a better name among organizational scholars.

The primary intended audience is composed of those interested in learning more about the role of individuals' self-esteem in the workplace, be they the advanced undergraduate, graduate student, or the professional scholar. Another audience consists of self-esteem theorists and researchers, even those not especially concerned with the implications of self-esteem for individuals' work behaviors and attitudes. Secondary intended audiences include organizational practitioners (for example, managers, consultants) who should find the applied implications of the theory and research relevant to their daily work: managing (or helping others to manage) human forces in work organizations. Finally, those with a more general interest in personality processes — especially as they relate to behavior in organizations — should be intrigued by this book.

I am especially pleased and excited to take this opportunity to thank the many people who assisted me in writing this book. I suppose I can divide them into two categories: those who provided support on the task versus the socioemotional aspects of the undertaking. I know that I benefited greatly from the comments of several esteemed colleagues on previous versions of the manuscript. They include Bob Dipboye, Phyllis Tharenou, and especially the editors of the "Issues in Management" series, Ben Schneider and Art Brief. In addition, my research assistant, Rocki Lee DeWitt, and the word processing department at Columbia Business School — Maxine Braiterman, Maureen Gelber, and Colette Neven — performed their tasks so quickly and efficiently that sometimes I was forced to get back to work on the book much sooner than I might have otherwise preferred! Other task facilitators to whom I am grateful are Bruce Katz, Bill Hamilton, and Susan Sitkin, editors at Lexington Books, and the Columbia Business School, who supported the writing of this book with several faculty research grants.

I am delighted to report that the primary source of socioemotional support was provided by my wonderful wife, Audrey Brockner. I am not sure which is harder: writing a book, or living with someone who is writing a book (and journal articles, and book chapters, and . . .). In any event, Audrey proved, as always, that she was more than equal to *her* task. Other very special and supportive people include Edmund Payne, Eve and Charles Poret, Channe and Penn Melnick, and my father-in-law, Dr. Harvey Jacobs. To all of you, a heartfelt thanks.

1

Introduction

One of the most significant personality dimensions along which employees differ from one another is the trait of self-esteem. As discussed throughout this book, high self-esteem individuals (high SEs) differ from their low self-esteem counterparts (low SEs) in the ways that they think, feel, and, perhaps most importantly, behave. Moreover, such differences between high and low SEs manifest themselves before and during their entry into work organizations. For example, individuals' self-esteem is predictive of their occupational choices (for example, Korman 1966) and job searching tendencies (Ellis & Taylor 1983). In addition, workers' self-esteem affects the impact of the organization's socialization practices on their adjustment to the organization (Jones 1986).

Perhaps most noteworthy are the variety of ways in which employees' self-esteem relates to their work behaviors and/or attitudes *after* they have attained the status of full-fledged organizational members. For example:

1. Two individuals receive the exact same negative feedback during their annual performance appraisal discussion with their superior. In the months subsequent to the appraisal, one employee exhibits a marked increase in work motivation and performance, whereas the other shows a sharp decline.

2. Two managers work for the same supervisor; as a result they are constantly exposed to their supervisor's leadership style and work values. One of the manager's work behaviors and attitudes are very similar to those of his or her supervisor. The other manager exhibits a leadership style that is virtually unrelated to that of the supervisor.

3. Two individuals are part of the same work group, in which members must work interdependently in order to accomplish their tasks. On certain days the interaction among the group is supportive, whereas on other days it is much more nonsupportive. The performance of one of the two group members is much more influenced by the degree of supportiveness of the group than is that of the other. Indeed, on days when the group is supportive, the former person performs very well; but, on days when the group is nonsupportive, the former person's performance suffers to a great extent.

4.   Two employees work in the same stressful environment, in which their work roles are both ambiguous and conflicting. Nevertheless, the work performance and job satisfaction of one person is invariably greater than that of the other.

5.   Two individuals are survivors of a recent layoff at a large organization. For a variety of reasons, most employees who survived the layoff have begun to work harder than they did prior to the layoff. Nevertheless, of the two individuals in this example, one is exhibiting a much greater increase in work performance than is the other.

6.   A quality circle program has been developed in an organization so that group members can analyze and solve work-related problems. The overseers of the quality circle program note that there are consistent differences between groups in their productivity; some groups often generate useful suggestions for improvement to management, whereas others do not.

In these six examples, there are countless ways to explain the differences in work behaviors and attitudes exhibited by the individuals (or groups) in question. And yet, empirical research has demonstrated that workers' self-esteem is one of the determinants (or at least predictors) of the differences. Thus, relative to low SEs, high SEs are: more apt to work harder in response to significant negative feedback (for example, Brockner & Elkind 1985); less likely to imitate the managerial styles of their supervisors (Weiss 1977, 1978); less likely to perform differently as a function of the supportiveness of their work group (Mossholder, Bedeian & Armenakis 1982); less negatively affected by chronic stressors, such as role ambiguity and conflict (Mossholder, Bedeian & Armenakis 1981), and acute sources of stress, such as layoffs (Brockner, 1988); and more likely to be productive in quality circles (Brockner & Hess 1986).

In spite of this rather impressive array of differences between high and low SEs in their work behaviors and attitudes, it must be emphasized that the role of self-esteem in particular and personality in general has been viewed with much skepticism among organizational scholars and practitioners. For example, Mitchell (1979) has suggested that personality should be relegated to secondary status in the organizational setting, because its impact on work behavior often is far less than that of situational factors (such as the nature of the task, the formal and informal organizational arrangements, and extra-organizational considerations). In parallel fashion, managers may choose to ignore personality differences among subordinates, perhaps reflecting managers' belief that subordinates' work behaviors are more influenced by the situational factors denoted already.

Two other developments in the psychological literature—one pertaining to personality in general and the other tied more specifically to self-esteem—have fueled organizational scholars' and practitioners' doubts about the utility of self-esteem in elucidating human behavior in organizations. First, although researchers often expected individuals' personality to determine (or at least be predictive of) their behavior both inside and outside of organizations, many empirical studies have revealed that personality variables either were weakly or not at all related to the outcome measures of interest (Guion & Gottier 1965; Mischel 1968). Of course, this is not to say that personality never has been shown to be predictive of employees' work behaviors (for example, Schneider & Schmitt 1986). Nevertheless, much more often than personality researchers would have predicted, the relationships between personality and the key outcome variables have been disappointingly small.

Second, the self-esteem literature is alive, but perhaps not well. Wylie (1979) concluded from her exhaustive review of the self-esteem literature that nonsignificant or weak results often emerged even when theory and conventional wisdom predicted strong trends. This gloomy assessment applies equally well to the organizational research on self-esteem (for example, Tharenou 1979).

If previous research has shown personality, in general, and self-esteem, in particular, to be unpredictive (let alone not determinant) of employees' behavior, then the skepticism of organizational scholars and practitioners would appear well justified; indeed, in light of the rather dismal empirical state of affairs just described it is reasonable to ask why anyone would want to read (or write) a book about the role of self-esteem within organizations.

The potential for personality, in general, and self-esteem, in particular, to help explain human behavior within organizations is great. The fact cannot be argued that much (though not all) previous research has yielded statistically unenlightening, and hence often disappointing, results. However, such findings are not necessarily diagnostic of the true role of personality in organizational behavior. Indeed, as demonstrated in the earlier examples, self-esteem has been shown (on some occasions) to be an important predictor of employees' work behaviors and/or attitudes.

This book is an attempt to identify the various ways in which employees' self-esteem does add insight into both the theory and practice of human behavior in organizations. In order for the role of self-esteem in the organizational context to be more fully appreciated, we will need to consider: how personality variables in general may be conceptualized more profitably by those interested in work organizations, and the nature of self-esteem in particular. The latter task will be discussed in chapter 3. The former task is addressed now.

The Relationship of Personality to Organizational Behavior

In a recent review article, Weiss and Adler (1984) noted that personality research often has not enlightened our knowledge of individuals' behavior in organizations. Perhaps most glaring, as mentioned previously, low (or nonexistent) statistical associations between personality and behavior frequently have been obtained. There are probably numerous methodological reasons for such nonsignificant results, for example, invalid measures of the personality dimension and/or the criterion variable(s), and inadequate sample sizes. However, as Weiss and Adler (1984) suggested, the disappointing results of prior research probably are more reflective of a conceptual rather than methodological failing. Many researchers have failed to justify—on theoretical grounds—the expected role of the personality variable(s) that they have included in their studies. All too often, personality variables are included in empirical research projects for any or all of the following reasons: the instrument that assesses the trait dimension is readily available; the trait dimension has been investigated in previous research, sometimes even yielding significant results, but with little explanation of such results; and for exploratory purposes.

In none of these instances has the inclusion of the personality dimension been justified on a firm theoretical basis. It is not being suggested that researchers always must have a firm theoretical basis—that is, in which clear predictions about the role of the personality variable can be offered—to include the personality variable(s) in their studies. Indeed, some of science's most important breakthroughs have stemmed from exploratory research. What is being suggested is that the failure to provide a sound theoretical rationale for the inclusion of the personality variable probably will increase the likelihood of obtaining results that are either statistically nonsignificant, or, if statistically significant, not easily interpretable. Note, however, that such unenlightening outcomes are not necessarily revealing of the potential role of personality; that potential may have been realized had the researchers taken the time beforehand to think more carefully about the bases on which the personality variable was chosen for study.

Toward Theoretical Justification:
The Case of Self-esteem

But, what exactly does it mean "to theoretically justify the inclusion of personality variables" in studies of individual behavior in organizations? There are at least three ways to go about doing so.

Self-esteem in the Context of Existing Theory. One strategy is to start with an already-existing, well-grounded theory, and then specify how self-esteem is embedded within that theory. For example, personality variables in isolation, including self-esteem, often are poor predictors of job performance (Ghiselli 1973; Guion & Gottier 1965). Does this mean that personality variables have no relevance to job performance? Not necessarily. Rather, as Hollenbeck and Whitener (1985) have pointed out, it may be more useful to delineate the conditions under which a personality variable such as self-esteem does relate to job performance. Of course, to do so Hollenbeck and Whitener suggest that it is necessary to work from an appropriate theoretical base.

One fairly simple theory, originally proposed by Tolman (1935), is that job performance is a multiplicative function of ability and motivation. According to this viewpoint, self-esteem should correlate with job performance only to the extent that the former is related to ability and/or motivation. Although there may be some instances in which self-esteem may be related to ability to perform, it seems more likely that self-esteem will influence motivation. More specifically, the expectancy theory of motivation (for example, Vroom 1964) posits that motivation is a multiplicative function of the extent to which workers expect to succeed and desire to succeed at the task at hand. Many studies (for example, Coopersmith 1967; Lawler 1971) have shown that self-esteem is positively related to individuals' success expectations.

If the preceding theoretical analysis is correct—that is, if performance is a function of individuals' ability and motivation, and motivation is a function of individuals' expectation and desire to succeed—then it may be possible to specify the conditions under which self-esteem and performance will (and will not) be related. More specifically, self-esteem should be associated with work performance to the extent that individuals desire to succeed and possess the necessary level of ability. In a field study in 1987 Hollenbeck et al. explored the role of several individual difference variables in predicting the job performance of insurance salespersons (as measured by their sales commissions). Included were measures of the salespersons' ability (that is, an aptitude test developed by the Life Insurance Marketing and Research Association) as well as their self-esteem. Consistent with predictions, the salespersons' ability and self-esteem interactively combined to predict job performance. For the high ability workers, there was a strong positive correlation between self-esteem and performance. For the low ability salespersons, however, self-esteem was slightly negatively associated with performance. Such results suggest that the predictive power of self-esteem may be enhanced considerably when employed in combination with other theoretically derived variables.

The Use of Self-esteem to Compare Existing Theories. In the preceding discussion the role of self-esteem was analyzed within the context of several broader, well-established theories (the motivation × ability theory of performance, and the expectancy theory of motivation). The results reported by Hollenbeck et al. lent further support to these already well-grounded theories. Self-esteem also may be useful in the context of other theories, which are not as generalizable as the "motivation × ability" framework. That is, it is sometimes the case that different theories offer competing predictions of individuals' behavior in the organizational context. It may be that the inclusion of self-esteem will help investigators evaluate the relative merit of these different theories; that is, the obtained differences between high and low SEs may inform the investigator of whether one theory is more appropriate than the other in a given context.

For example, much research has explored the effect of positive inequity (that is, employees' perceptions of having received more than their just desserts) on work motivation. The classic finding, originally demonstrated by Adams (1965), is that positive inequity may cause individuals to increase their work motivation, presumably in order to redress the inequity or restore fairness. Several reviews of the equity theory literature (for example, Mowday 1979) have noted that very few studies have explored if and how individual differences between workers moderate their reactions to positive inequity.

Self-esteem appears to be one such relevant moderator variable. However, unlike in the previous discussion of self-esteem and work performance, a number of "mini-theories" may offer predictions.

Low Self-Esteem and Behavioral Plasticity. Brockner (1983) recently marshalled considerable evidence suggesting that low SEs are more behaviorally "plastic"—their work motivation and/or performance is more susceptible to influence by external cues—than are high SEs (see chapter 3). For now, suffice it to say that the subsequent work motivation of low SEs may be especially prone to influence by positive inequity. Relative to high SEs, low SEs may be especially apt to believe that they did not deserve to receive remuneration that was more than the "going rate." Consequently, low SEs may be particularly driven to increase their work performance in response to positive inequity.

Cognitive Dissonance Theory. An extension (Aronson 1968) of the original version of this theory (Festinger 1957) suggests that dissonance is aroused when individuals focus on cognitions that threaten their view of themselves as good, moral, and/or likable. According to this logic, the failure to redress positive inequity will be more dissonance-arousing for high than low SEs. In times of positive inequity, high SEs are apt to think, "I am a good person," and "Good persons play fair." Low SEs are less likely to hold the former cognition. As a result, not playing fair, that is, not working harder in response to overpayment, is less likely to elicit dissonance in the low than the high SEs. Thus, contrary to the behavioral plasticity analysis, dissonance theory posits that high SEs will be more likely to increase their work motivation in response to positive inequity than will low SEs.

Expectancy Theory. A third possibility is that positive inequity may implicitly convey to workers that they should or must perform at a very high level of productivity. If so, then subsequent effort may be a function of individuals' expectations of being able to meet such a difficult challenge. Previous research (for example, Sigall & Gould 1977) has shown that highly challenging tasks have directly opposite effects on the motivation of high and low SEs. Because of their positive expectancies for performance, high SEs respond by redoubling their efforts; due to their negative performance expectancies, low SEs tend to withdraw from the task at hand. This reasoning predicts an interactive effect of self-esteem and positive inequity on work performance of the following nature: *relative to a control condition,* high SEs will be more productive and low SEs will be less productive in response to positive inequity. Note that such a prediction is different from both the behavioral plasticity and dissonance-based predictions.

Several studies have explored the effect of self-esteem and positive inequity on work performance (Brockner 1985; Brockner, Davy & Carter 1985). In so doing, these studies have evaluated the relative accuracy of these three different theoretical accounts. Interestingly, the findings do not consistently demonstrate that one theory is superior to the other; in one study (Brockner 1985) expectancy theory received firm support, whereas in the other (Brockner, Davy & Carter 1985) the behavioral plasticity reasoning received strong support. Apparently, the interactive effects of self-esteem and positive inequity on performance are more complex than originally believed; that is, the moderating influence of self-esteem in response to positive inequity is, in turn, moderated by additional factors. Further thought and empirical research is needed to identify the conditions under which low or high SEs are more responsive to positive inequity. (This complex problem is discussed in chapter 5.)

Although these initial studies on self-esteem, positive inequity, and work performance demonstrate that further research is warranted, they are consistent with the thrust of this chapter (indeed, this book); namely, that by working from a reasonable theoretical base, researchers may elucidate the role of individuals' self-esteem in organizations. True, the results sometimes may be more complicated than those that were anticipated. But, that should only serve to whet scholars' appetites for further, clarifying research.

Delineating a Theory of Self-esteem. The preceding sections provide several examples of how organizational researchers may study the role of self-esteem more profitably by working from a theoretical base. In each instance it was suggested that self-esteem may be related to factors central to some already existing theory of human behavior within the organizational context. Certainly, the guiding conceptual force in such analyses is the already existing theory. Thus, according to expectancy theory, self-esteem should influence motivation through the mediating role of expectancies; according to this theory, any factor that affects expectancies should have an impact on motivation. Or, self-esteem could moderate reactions to positive inequity because of the potential relationship of the former to processes such as dissonance, for example. Once again, any factor related to dissonance arousal may moderate workers' reactions to positive inequity.

Still another theoretical approach to studying self-esteem would attach to it a more central conceptual focus. Rather than starting with some pre-existing theory and then determining the role of self-esteem within that theory, it may be useful to begin with a theoretical analysis of the nature of self-esteem. Given this starting point, it then may be possible to discuss the implications of this theoretical stance for a wide variety of behaviors and attitudes within work organizations.

Just such an effort was made in the late 1960s by Korman (1966, 1970) in his consistency theory of self-esteem. More specifically, Korman posited that individuals are motivated to think, feel, and act in ways that enable them to maintain their preexisting level of self-esteem. Within this theoretical position, Korman claimed that it was possible to explain the relationship of self-esteem to a wide variety of work attitudes and behaviors including occupational choice and task performance. For example, some studies have shown that high SEs outperform their low self-esteem counterparts. According to consistency theory, such behavior is motivated (at least in part) by the workers' desire to maintain a consistent view of themselves.

Korman's consistency theory simply fails to account for the results of many studies (see chapter 2). The major point, however, is that Korman should be applauded for his efforts to provide a theoretical account of self-esteem, the validity of which can then be subjected to empirical test. In part because of the failure of the theory to account for many empirical findings, an alternative conceptual analysis of the nature of self-esteem will be offered (see chapter 3). Of course, the merit of this theory must be evaluated in light of past and future research findings. In any event, the constant evaluation of theory in light of empirical evidence should clarify the role of self-esteem within organizations to a greater extent than has hitherto occurred.

This chapter began with the assertion that employees' self-esteem is a fundamental cause (or at least predictor) of their work behaviors and attitudes; numerous examples were provided in which self-esteem was related to workers' behaviors before, during, and after their entry into organizations. In sharp contrast to this assertion and supportive examples, much empirical research has demonstrated that personality in general (Mischel 1973); personality within work organizations (Mitchell 1979); self-esteem in general (Wylie 1979); and self-esteem within work organizations (Tharenou 1979) are unrelated to the dependent variables within their respective domains. Indeed, the actual yield of most previous investigations of self-esteem has been rather disappointing. Most studies have attempted to correlate personality with behavior in a direct or "main effect" sense. The consistently unimpressive results—most correlations fail to exceed the .30 limit, if they are that high at all—are similar to those obtained in most research in personality psychology (Mischel 1968).

This book is not about the actual yield of previous research on personality (including self-esteem) within work organizations; rather the book considers the potential insights about human behavior in organizations that may be uncovered through more systematic research on self-esteem processes. The handful of examples referred to at the beginning of the chapter, as well as recent theoretical arguments (for example, Weiss & Adler 1984), suggest strongly that past research may not reflect adequately the true role of self-esteem within work organizations. To realize that potential, however, organizational scholars must provide careful theoretical reasoning about the relevance of self-esteem before doing their studies.

This chapter briefly touched upon several different kinds of theory-driven strategies for studying self-esteem within work organizations: self-esteem considered within the context of existing theory, self-esteem viewed as a way to evaluate the relative accuracy of competing theoretical positions, and self-esteem assigned a central focus, around which a theoretical statement is developed, replete with implications for employees' behaviors and attitudes. Although the strategies differ somewhat from one another, they all imply that it may be more profitable to consider the conditions under which self-esteem is related to work behaviors and attitudes, rather than to explore self-esteem as a main effect predictor of employees' actions and feelings. It is worth noting that a similar movement toward person-situation interactionism is afoot in personality psychology. In response to the empirically-stimulated crisis in personality, many scholars (Magnusson & Endler 1977; Mischel 1973; Sarason, Smith & Diener 1975) have argued that to the extent that personality influences human behavior, it is likely to do so in interaction with situational variables. By employing the theory-driven strategies described already, those who study self-esteem at work simultaneously will be heeding another important theoretical calling in personality psychology: person-situation interactionism.

Overview of Subsequent Chapters

Central to the discussion thus far is that employees' self-esteem may have important consequences for their work attitudes and behaviors. Chapters 2 through 4 will review relevant research and consider its theoretical and practical implications. More specifically, chapter 2 discusses the relationship between self-esteem and occupational choice, job searching strategies, task performance, satisfaction, and the relationship between performance and satisfaction. In the task performance domain, some studies have uncovered a positive relationship between self-esteem and work performance. Many others, however, have obtained no relationship, and a handful (for example, Weiss & Knight 1980) even have exhibited an inverse relationship between self-esteem and performance. Accordingly, the close of chapter 2 calls for a contingency model to help us understand the conditions under which high SEs will perform better, no differently from, or even worse than low SEs.

Chapter 3 presents the elements of one possible contingency model: the plasticity hypothesis. The crux of this reasoning—that low SEs are more prone to external influence than are high SEs—is hardly novel. However, the implications of this prospect are far-reaching for a variety of organizational issues discussed in greater detail in chapter 4; these include the effects of layoffs on survivors, the effects of peer-group interaction on performance and commitment, the effects of early socialization experiences and observational learning on role taking, and the effects of negative feedback on subsequent performance and communication. Chapter 5 discusses some of the intriguing practical and theoretical issues that emerge from the many studies showing low SEs to be more susceptible to influence than their high self-esteem counterparts. Chapter 6 discusses the antecedents of employee self-esteem. A review of empirical research on the work and nonwork factors affecting self-esteem is presented; the managerial implications of this theory and research is offered.

To this point self-esteem has been treated as an independent (chapters 2 through 5) or dependent (chapter 6) variable. Chapter 7 analyzes self-esteem as a motivational process. The need to save face, it is argued, is an extremely important drive affecting workers' thoughts, feelings, and actions. The implications of this social psychological fact of life will be considered.

The eighth and concluding chapter provides a future research agenda, including discussions of methodological improvements in the assessment of self-esteem, the impact of employees' self-esteem on their work environments, and the notion of collective (rather than individual) self-esteem. In addition, a matter of considerable practical significance will be analyzed in detail: how to diagnose employees' self-esteem level. More specifically, many studies have found that high and low SEs respond differently to identical organizational stimuli. As a result, the practitioner who wishes to effect change in employee behavior often must take into account the self-esteem level of the employees whose behavior is the target of influence; what works for the low SEs may not for the high SEs, and vice versa. Of course, the implication of this fact is that the influencing agents (for example, the manager, consultant) must be able to make accurate judgments of the workers' self-esteem. The interested reader may wish to turn to that section in chapter 8 at any time. Chapters 2 through 5 suggest that employees' self-esteem and workplace factors jointly and interactively affect their work behaviors and attitudes. Therefore, in order to make accurate inferences about workers' self-esteem one must observe their behavior as well as the organizational context in which their behavior occurs. The specific substance of what is meant by "organizational context" is described in detail in earlier chapters of the book; for that reason I suggest that such material be read prior to the section in chapter 8 on judging employees' self-esteem. More generally, the fact that it is important to make accurate inferences of employees' self-esteem reflects a central goal of this book: to highlight the reciprocal relationships between empirical research, theory, and managerial practice.

2
Self-esteem:
Some Correlates and Consequences

lthough psychologists have offered a variety of definitions of self-esteem, most agree that it is a trait referring to individuals' degree of liking or disliking for themselves. Thus, the essence of self-esteem is the favorability of individuals' characteristic self-evaluations. Certain people show a generalized tendency to evaluate themselves (that is, their identities, behaviors, cognitions) positively whereas others do not. Individuals' self-esteem varies across situation and times; that is, people have both global and situation-specific self-esteem. For example, university professors probably have more favorable opinions of themselves when engaged in intellectual than athletic activities, whereas for the professional athlete just the opposite is likely to be true. Given the simultaneous existence of global and specific self-esteem it may be worth discussing: how the two are related, and why this book focuses primarily (but certainly not exclusively) on the former rather than the latter.

Global and Specific Self-esteem

On both logical and empirical grounds, global and specific self-esteem are related to one another. The logical basis rests on the fact that "wholes" (for example, global self-esteem) inevitably must be connected somehow to their component "parts" (for example, specific self-esteem). The empirical basis is that many studies show significant associations between measures of global and specific self-esteem (Rosenberg 1979). However, the relationship between global and specific self-esteem actually is quite complex; this complexity also may be illustrated on conceptual and empirical grounds. For example, several factors have been shown to moderate the relationship between global and specific self-esteem. To the extent that specific self-esteem refers to an aspect that is important or central to individuals' self-concept, it should be more strongly related to their global self-esteem. Summarizing research on the relationship between perceived social class or status (a form of specific self-esteem) and global self-esteem, Rosenberg (1979) has found a much stronger correlation among adults than children. One explanation is that social class is a much more important component of adults' than childrens' self-definition.

It is not only the centrality of particular types of specific self-esteem, but also their internal consistency that could affect the linkage between specific and global self-esteem. For example, suppose that a person rated his self-esteem very favorably (9 or 10 on a 10-point scale) on several specific dimensions known to be central to his self-esteem, but very poorly (1 or 2) on two other specific central dimensions. If global self-esteem were computed as the average of specific self-esteem—a questionable procedure about which more will be said shortly—the person would have a rating of 5–6, even though none of his specific self-esteem ratings were close to that point. Would it be appropriate to say that this person has medium global self-esteem? Perhaps. Or, perhaps it makes little sense to talk about global self-esteem in such an instance. In either case, it is likely that the phenomenological nature of this person's global self-esteem is very different from that of someone who rated himself with a 5 or 6 on each of the four specific self-esteem dimensions. To the extent that individuals' specific self-esteem (along dimensions central to their self-concept) is internally consistent, there is bound to be a stronger relationship between their specific and global self-esteem.

It has been suggested that the relationship between specific and global self-esteem is complex, by demonstrating that several variables (centrality, consistency) moderate the relationship between the two. Rosenberg (1979) elaborates further on the complexity of this part-whole relationship:

> Since any totality is in some sense made up of the parts that constitute it, many researchers proceed by acquiring information about the individual's attitude toward his specific characteristics and adding up the responses in order to arrive at a global self-esteem. The initial drawback to this procedure is that it overlooks the extent to which the self-concept is a structure whose elements are arranged in a complex hierarchical order. Hence, simply to add up the parts in order to assess the whole is to ignore the fact that the global attitude is the product of an enormously *complex synthesis* of elements which goes on in the individual's phenomenal field. It is not simply the elements per se but their relationship, weighting, and combination that is responsible for the final outcome. The subject himself may be as ignorant as the investigators about how this complex synthesis of elements has been achieved (p. 21).

It is our lack of understanding of how specific domains of self-esteem are synthesized into global self-esteem that may make specific and global self-esteem appear independent of one another. Moreover, Rosenberg's commentary calls attention to the possibility that the measurement of global self-esteem may not fully capture its conceptual complexity. As Rosenberg implied, researchers usually ask participants to evaluate their self-esteem across a variety of situations; the operational definition of global self-esteem typically is an average score, sometimes weighted for item importance, but more often not. This procedure makes the assumption that the whole (global self-esteem) is the additive sum of its parts (specific self-esteem), which may grossly oversimplify the nature of the relationship between the whole and its parts. Given that the precise way(s) in which the parts sum to form the whole are unknown, the averaging procedure—which makes the least complex assumptions—is appropriate; however, the operational definition of global self-esteem (computed rather simply) should not blind us to the fact that there are probably quite complex processes through which specific self-esteem dimensions are formed into global self-esteem.

The decision to focus the book primarily on global rather than specific self-esteem was based on conceptual as well as pragmatic considerations. Conceptually, global self-esteem seems relevant across a wide variety of situations, whereas specific self-esteem (by definition) is not. This is not to say that global self-esteem is a more important determinant or predictor of employee behavior than specific self-esteem in all situations; in certain situations, specific self-esteem may be more important than global self-esteem (for example, see Shrauger 1972). However, we would expect the relevance of specific self-esteem to be limited to certain conditions, whereas global self-esteem might have a more general influence across situations.

The pragmatic consideration is that most researchers have employed measures of global self-esteem; far less often have they assessed specific self-esteem, either alone or in conjunction with global self-esteem. Given that this book largely is research driven, it seems appropriate to focus on global rather than specific self-esteem. Specific self-esteem will not be ignored entirely; chapter 6, which discusses the antecedents of self-esteem, considers both types of self-esteem.

Related Constructs

The construct of self-esteem often is used synonymously with a variety of related constructs. For example, Rosenberg (1979) has defined the self-concept as "the totality of the individual's thoughts and feelings that have reference to himself as an object" (p. 7). Strictly speaking, the term *self-concept* is not an evaluative one; it includes self-relevant thoughts and feelings that are not inherently positive or negative (for example, "I am an employee at Organization X"). However, self-concept is identical to self-esteem if the former pertains to its evaluative aspect. Other synonyms include "self-acceptance," "self-worth," "self-confidence," "self-assurance," and "self-efficacy." All of these constructs are highly related to self-esteem. However, in all instances there are slight differences between the construct and self-esteem. For example, self-acceptance refers to individuals' attitudes toward their self-esteem. In theory, it is possible for people not to like themselves, but vary in the extent to which they are accepting of that self-evaluation. Self-worth refers to individuals' perceptions of their value in their own and/or others' eyes. Once again, it is possible for people to have low self-esteem but still value themselves to a certain degree.

The terms *self-confidence* and *self-assurance* seem identical to the construct of "self-efficacy" (Bandura 1977), which refers to individuals' beliefs that they can execute successfully the behavior(s) required to produce (presumably desired) outcomes in a given situation. Self-efficacy describes individuals' beliefs about their ability and/or motivation, and whether such attributes will enable them to perform necessary behaviors. In general, high self-esteem individuals have more favorable efficacy beliefs than do their low self-esteem counterparts. Nevertheless, for a number of reasons it is entirely possible for an individual to be high in self-efficacy but not in self-esteem. All of us probably are familiar with individuals whose self-esteem is much lower than it should be; such persons may be exceedingly competent in behavioral domains that are central to their self-esteem. Moreover, they even may be quite aware of, and believe in, their competence. Still, such persons may not like themselves. Moreover, as Rosenberg (1979) has pointed out, the distinction between self-esteem and self-confidence may help reconcile apparently conflicting results in studies exploring gender differences in self-evaluation. One might predict sexist discrimination and socialization into feminine sex roles to engender lower self-esteem among women than men. In fact, some studies support this assertion, whereas others do not. In a comprehensive review of the literature, Maccoby and Jacklin (1974) suggested that females may not have lower self-esteem but do have lower self-confidence than males.

A second distinction between self-esteem and self-efficacy stems from the specificity of the constructs. Self-efficacy is situation specific. Some researchers (for example, Shrauger 1972) have studied task-specific self-esteem by assessing individuals' confidence about succeeding at a given task; this operational definition of task-specific self-esteem appears to be synonymous with self-efficacy. Self-esteem typically refers to a global construct that taps individuals' self-evaluations (and not merely their confidence judgments) across a wide variety of situations.

The differences between self-esteem, on the one hand, and self-worth and self-efficacy, on the other, may be examples of the distinction between evaluation and belief that often is discussed by attitude theorists (for example, Bagozzi & Burnkrant 1979). Thus, individuals' evaluations of themselves (that is, their self-esteem) sometimes are different from their beliefs about themselves (for example, their perceptions of their self-worth, or their self-efficacy expectations). Terms and constructs such as self-concept, self-acceptance, self-worth, self-assurance, self-confidence, and self-efficacy are highly related to self-esteem. Indeed, in the discussion of empirical research in this book, self-esteem may have been operationalized by the use of one of its correlates. The preceding discussion has focused not on the similarities between self-esteem and its related constructs, but rather on some of their (sometimes quite subtle) dissimilarities (Brief & Aldag 1981).

Having defined self-esteem, and having distinguished it from related concepts, I now will discuss some of the research questions that organizational scholars traditionally have raised in their studies of self-esteem.

In general, the mainstream literature on self-esteem in organizations is fraught with null and/or inconsistent findings. Still, it is useful to present this information for several reasons. First, in several instances (most notably the studies investigating the relationship between self-esteem and occupational choice), the findings are relatively consistent, and thus deepen our knowledge considerably. Second, and more generally, this brief review will serve to familiarize readers with ongoing topics of concern among researchers interested in the role of self-esteem within organizations.

As stated in chapter 1, employees' self-esteem may affect (or at least predict) their behaviors and beliefs before, during, and after their entry into work organizations. The review of the existing literature is similarly organized along this temporal dimension. We will consider how individuals' self-esteem is related to preentry behaviors, in particular, their occupational or career choice, and the process and outcome of their job searching. Just as important, organizational scholars and practitioners have hypothesized that employees' postentry work behaviors and attitudes can be predicted from their self-esteem. In particular, there have been many studies exploring the relationship between workers' self-esteem and job performance, job satisfaction, and the correlation between their performance and satisfaction. These questions are among those about employee self-esteem that have been researched (Tharenou 1979).

Self-esteem and Occupational Choice

Imagine the buzz of confusion that surrounds us as we contemplate what we would like to do for a living—or, as it has come to be known, what we are going to do "when we grow up." For many, if not most of us, choosing a career or an occupation is a very trying task. What am I good at? What am I interested in? What occupation or career has an ample number of openings? What occupation or career will provide me with at least an adequate amount of pay? These are merely some of the myriad of questions that flow through our minds as we wrestle with this difficult decision.

Given the personal significance of this decision, it seems important to understand the factors that affect individuals' occupational choices. At first blush, it may seem that such factors are obvious; after all, it could be argued, people will choose the career for which they are personally well suited. More specifically, they will choose the jobs that are congruent with: their needs and wants, whether they be intrinsic (for example, high job variety) or extrinsic (for example, high pay) to the job itself; and their abilities to perform the activities associated with the particular vocation. But wait—the factors affecting occupational choice must not be all that obvious; many individuals have chosen careers for which they probably are not especially well suited. Therefore, it becomes important to identify additional factors that may affect occupational choice.

To be sure, individuals' needs and abilities do influence their career choice. However, many other situational or external variables also could affect such decisions. Thus, market conditions may force them to choose a vocation that is at least somewhat incongruent with their needs and abilities. For example, certain persons may be well suited for a career in acting. However, the difficulties associated with finding full-time employment in such a career are great. Or, social pressures from family members, friends, or society at large may channel individuals into careers that are personally alien to them. For instance, some individuals may choose to work in their families' businesses, not because doing so is near and dear to their hearts, but rather because they will be able to avoid the sanctions that family members might impose on them for not working in the business.

The preceding analysis suggests that a multitude of factors—both internal and external to individuals—may affect their vocational choice. The results of empirical research have shown that individuals' self-esteem may moderate the extent to which internal versus external factors influence such decisions. More specifically, Korman (1966) sampled a group of undergraduate business students who were leaning toward careers in either accounting or sales. All participants completed measures of self-esteem and "interaction orientation." The latter measure refers to the extent to which individuals desire jobs that require social interaction. Clearly, a career in sales requires more interpersonal dealings than one in accounting. Not surprisingly, those headed toward sales rated themselves as higher in interaction orientation than those leaning toward accounting. Of greater importance (see table 2–1), this was especially true for the high rather than the low self-esteem participants. The low SEs' interaction orientation ratings were only slightly higher if they were leaning toward sales rather than accounting.

In another study, Korman (1967) explored whether students' self-esteem was related to the extent to which they chose vocations for which they believed that they possessed the needed abilities. Student subjects once again had claimed to have made a fairly clear occupational choice. They were asked to indicate the extent to which they possessed two abilities that were highly required for occupational success, and two abilities that were not highly required for occupational success. It was shown that high SEs rated themselves much more favorably on the ability dimensions that were highly required (but not on those that were not highly required) than the low SEs.

Table 2–1
Students' Interaction Orientation as a Function of Their Self-esteem and Occupational Choice

	Occupational Choice	
Self-esteem	Accounting	Sales
High	19.9	24.7
Low	21.8	22.7

Source: Korman 1966, p. 482.
Note: Higher scores reflect a stronger interaction orientation.

Lest the reader wonder whether Korman's findings are still true today and generalizable to a wider variety of aspiring professionals than salespersons and accountants, it should be mentioned that I regularly attempt conceptual replications of Korman's results. The subjects in these studies have been drawn from a variety of college campuses (Tufts University, University of Arizona, Columbia University); moreover, both undergraduate and MBA students have been sampled. All are asked to describe briefly their future career plans. They also indicate what they would most desire from their chosen career; the extent to which their chosen career is likely to fulfill those desires; an ability that would be important for them to have in order to be successful in their chosen career; the extent to which they believe that they do, in fact, have that ability; an ability that would be of lesser importance in order for them to be successful; the extent to which they believe that they have the less important ability; and their self-esteem.

Invariably, the following findings emerge:

1. High SEs believe that their chosen career is likely to satisfy their desires to a greater extent than do low SEs.

2. High SEs believe that they possess more of the ability that is important for them to have in order to succeed.

3. There is a weaker, though typically still significant relationship between self-esteem and perceived possession of the ability of lesser importance.

Note that all three findings are consistent with those obtained in the late 1960s by Korman. Moreover, the present findings are far more general than Korman's, in that participants had embarked upon a wide variety of career paths; furthermore, we allowed the students to define their relevant needs and abilities, and then asked them to rate themselves along those dimensions. By contrast, in Korman's investigations, the researcher defined the relevant needs (that is, interaction orientation). The fact that such consistent results emerged over time and across procedures is, therefore, all the more impressive.

Based on the findings of Korman and myself, we can say that individuals' self-esteem is positively related to the extent to which they see their chosen careers as need-fulfilling, and themselves as possessing the ability needed to succeed. However, the meaning or implications of these positive relationships are highly dependent upon the causal relationship between the related variables.

Most studies that incorporate self-esteem as an independent variable (indeed, most studies that incorporate personality more generally as an independent variable) are correlational in nature. As in any correlational study, there are at least three possible causal explanations of the significant association between variables. For example, it is possible that individuals' self-esteem caused them to rate themselves as more or less well-suited for their chosen vocations. There are at least two possible ways in which this could have occurred. First, their self-esteem may have affected their actual choice of vocations. Second, their self-esteem may have influenced the extent to which they perceived themselves as well-suited for their chosen vocation. Note that these two possibilities have very different practical implications. If the former were more accurate, then it suggests that low SEs may require vocational counseling in order to increase the likelihood that they will choose careers congruent with their needs and abilities. If the latter were more accurate, then vocational counseling for low SEs would be relatively ineffective. The implication in the latter case is that low SEs would rate themselves as less well suited for whatever career choice they had made.

A recent study of reemployment attempts by a sample of highly educated, unemployed workers lends support to the former hypothesis (Shamir 1986). In this study it was found that low SEs were more willing than high SEs to consider job offers that compromised their needs about two important features of the job: level of pay and professional content. In essence, low SEs were more willing than high SEs to choose jobs that did not suit them. Of course, the generalizability of low SEs' greater tendency to choose jobs for which they were not well-suited is questionable; Shamir's results were obtained in the context of previously employed but currently unemployed workers who were seeking to become reemployed. Whether low SEs are more willing than high SEs to choose less suitable jobs in other situations—for example, initial entrants to the labor market—is a matter to be resolved through further research.

Of course, there are other explanations for the positive relationship between self-esteem and perceived suitability of career choice. It is possible that perceived suitability influenced self-esteem; subjects may have come to evaluate themselves more or less favorably depending on the extent to which they rated themselves as well-suited for their chosen vocation. Yet another possibility is that a third variable was causally predominant over self-esteem and suitability of vocational choice. For instance, it is possible that other personality variables, such as intelligence, influence individuals' self-esteem and perceived career suitability, and is thus responsible for a spurious correlation between the latter two variables.

In explaining the relationship between individuals' self-esteem and the suitability of their vocational choice, Korman (1970) clearly favored the causal predominance of the former over the latter variable. More specifically, Korman suggested that individuals act and think in ways that reinforce, or are consistent with, their existing level of self-esteem. Presumably, the greater tendency of high SEs than low SEs to choose careers for which they are well-suited enables both groups to maintain their prior level of self-esteem. It may be misleading, however, to hypothesize that self-esteem causally affected occupational choice; moreover, even if Korman's preferred way of describing the causal relationship between self-esteem and occupational choice is correct, it is far less than certain that his consistency theory offers the most appropriate explanation of that causal relationship (also see chapter 3).

Self-esteem and the Search for Jobs

Having decided upon their particular vocations, individuals next must embark on the (sometimes just as arduous) task of locating a job within their chosen vocation. How might people job-hunt most effectively? What information sources should they seek? Should they talk to an employment agency? Should they read the want ads in their local newspapers? Or, should they pursue more informal strategies, such as personal contacts or word-of-mouth sources?

In addition to these normative or prescriptive questions, it is instructive to learn how individuals actually search for jobs, and how they fare at their job interviews. Of particular relevance is whether their self-esteem relates to the process and/or outcome of their job search. A study by Ellis and Taylor in 1983 addressed several relationships between self-esteem and job-search process and outcome. Participants were undergraduate and MBA business students who completed a self-esteem measure four months prior to graduation. The process and outcome of their job hunting were assessed over the next several months. Compared to their low self-esteem counterparts, high SEs were less apt to rely on formal sources—that is, employment agencies and newspaper ads—to acquire information. Contrary to prediction, there was no relationship between self-esteem and use of informal information sources such as friends and relatives and direct application to the prospective employers.

A more recent study by Shamir in 1986 lends considerable generality to the findings of Ellis and Taylor (1983), as well as support for their predictions. Ellis and Taylor studied primarily new entrants to the labor market; Shamir explored the job-searching behaviors of considerably older, unemployed workers who were seeking reemployment. For those individuals who did find jobs, there was a relationship between their self-esteem and the way in which they found the job. Those who found their jobs through the government's labor exchange—the study was performed in Israel; the *labor exchange* is the government's employment service—had a "lower level of self-esteem than those who had found their jobs through more 'individualistic' methods such as using personal contacts or direct applications to prospective employers" (Shamir 1986; p. 70). It is noteworthy that both Ellis and Taylor (1983) and Shamir (1986) found low SEs to be more reliant than high SEs on formal sources for gaining employment, in that such sources are less likely than are informal ones to lead individuals to job attainment (Rosenfeld 1975).

Finally, it is worth mentioning several other findings on the self-esteem/ job search relationship discovered by Ellis and Taylor (1983). Specifically, high SEs were more likely than low SEs to file the number of applications that they stated previously they would file, make a favorable impression at their job interviews, and actually receive job offers (see also Kanfer & Hulin 1985).

Self-esteem and Work Attitudes and Behavior

The research on occupational choice and job searching suggests that individuals' self-esteem is a significant predictor of their behaviors in the process of gaining entry into work organizations. Just as important, self-esteem might relate to employees' work behaviors and attitudes on the job; the remainder of this chapter focuses on this issue. Many studies have failed to document a relationship between self-esteem and work attitudes and behaviors; however, this should not be taken to mean that self-esteem is not an important determinant or predictor of work attitudes and behavior. Rather, investigators typically have explored self-esteem in the organizational context in ways that may have masked its potential influence.

Many organizational scholars have sought to delineate the antecedents of job performance and job satisfaction; accordingly, the relationship between self-esteem and both of these dimensions is considered here. In addition, the moderating impact of self-esteem on the relationship between performance and satisfaction will be analyzed.

Self-esteem and Performance

Does individuals' self-esteem relate to their work performance? A common belief is that self-esteem is positively and causally related to performance. After all, this reasoning goes, self-esteem is directly related to self-efficacy or expectations for success; since such expectations often are directly correlated with motivation, and since motivation is one determinant of performance, it follows that high SEs will outperform their low self-esteem counterparts. Indeed, several field and laboratory studies have obtained a positive relationship between self-esteem and performance (for example, Korman 1970). However, the vast majority of studies have shown no significant self-esteem/performance relationships (Brockner 1983; Tharenou 1979) In fact, inverse relationships between self-esteem and performance even have been obtained under certain conditions (Brockner & Guare 1983; Brockner & Hulton 1978); Weiss & Knight 1980).

In reviewing such findings, Tharenou (1979) remarked that "the evidence in relation to the self-esteem-performance relationship has raised more questions than it has answered. Until more . . . appropriate research designs are employed with self-esteem as a moderator variable, as the outcome of contintingency design, or as involved in interaction effects, the questions will remain unanswered" (p. 335).

Tharenou is suggesting that attempts to explore the sole impact of self-esteem on performance are not likely to be light-shedding. However, the joint and interactive effects of self-esteem and other theoretically-derived variables on performance are likely to produce results of far greater (statistical and psychological) significance. For example, although self-esteem is highly correlated with success expectations or self-efficacy beliefs, it is true that such expectations are only one determinant of motivation. According to expectancy theory, individuals must value as well as expect to succeed in order for their motivation level to be high; also, motivation is only one determinant of performance. For individuals to perform capably, they must be willing and able to do so. This reasoning suggests that self-esteem will be most positively correlated with performance for individuals who are high in ability and who value the importance of performing well (see Hollenbeck et al. 1987). Note that the findings of Hollenbeck et al. are perfectly consistent with Tharenou's (1979) call for the need to explore the interactive effects of self-esteem and other variables on performance.

Self-esteem and Job Attitudes

Many studies reflect researchers' interest in employees' work attitudes, most notably job satisfaction. Job satisfaction has been shown to be significantly associated with numerous important work behaviors. (Work performance, by the way, often turns out not to be one of those behaviors. Contrary to the intuitive notion that the happy or satisfied worker is the productive worker, many studies have shown this to be true only under relatively delimited conditions, for example, Bhagat 1982). For example, satisfied employees, compared to their less satisfied counterparts are less likely to turnover, less likely to be absent from work, less likely to desire unionization, and more likely to live longer (Feldman & Arnold 1983).

Given the significance of the correlates of job satisfaction, it is important to identify the causes (or at least correlates) of job satisfaction. Self-esteem is one such variable; many studies have demonstrated that high SEs are more job satisfied than low SEs (Tharenou 1979).

Although self-esteem and job satisfaction are statistically related, it is difficult to interpret the meaning of such findings. It could be that self-esteem causes job satisfaction and/or that job satisfaction causes self-esteem. A third possibility is that some third variable is correlated with both self-esteem and job satisfaction and thereby causes the (spurious) relationship between the two. As an example of this last possibility, individuals have been shown to differ in *negative affectivity,* the disposition to experience aversive emotional states (Watson & Clark 1984). Those high in negative affectivity have a generalized tendency to evaluate themselves (for example, their traits, attitudes, and moods) more unfavorably). Thus, it could be that negative affectivity is the third variable that causes individuals to rate their self-esteem and job satisfaction similarly. Brief et al. (in press) make a similar point about studies exploring the relationship between job stress and job satisfaction. They present data to suggest that the typical inverse relationship between job stress and job satisfaction is due, at least in part, to the fact both constructs are highly correlated with individuals' negative affectivity; more specifically, upon controlling for negative affectivity, Brief et al. found that the relationship between stress and satisfaction was not significant.

Self-esteem and the
Performance-Satisfaction Relationship

It is commonly believed—sometimes even in the face of contradictory evidence—that job performance and satisfaction are highly related. Presumably, at least two explanations could be offered. First, as hypothesized earlier, satisfied workers are thought to be more productive than dissatisfied employees. Second, higher levels of performance should elicit greater satisfaction than lower levels of performance. Relevant research, however, simply has failed to substantiate either hypothesis on a consistent basis (Iaffaldano & Muchinsky 1985).

Given these disappointing results, it has since become fashionable to identify factors that might moderate the performance-satisfaction (or satisfaction-performance) relationship. Several researchers (for example, Korman 1970) have suggested that self-esteem is one such moderator variable. Indeed, several studies have confirmed Korman's hypothesis that high SEs are more apt to exhibit a positive performance-satisfaction relationship than are low SEs (for example, Jacobs & Solomon 1977; Lopez & Greenhaus 1978). However, the vast majority of studies have shown either mixed results (for example, Dipboye et al. 1979) or that chronic self-esteem level is not a consistent moderator of relationships involving satisfaction (Tharenou 1979; Tharenou & Harker 1984).

It may be useful to speculate about the reasons for the inconsistent results in studies exploring the moderating role of self-esteem in the relationship between performance and satisfaction. It is unclear in such studies whether self-esteem is moderating the extent to which satisfaction is causally influencing performance, or the extent to which performance is causally affecting satisfaction. Most studies simply lump both relationships into the same statistical analysis. This could lead to nonsignificant effects if the moderating impact of self-esteem differed between the two causal relationships. More specifically, Korman's (1970) consistency theory implies that self-esteem will moderate the extent to which performance causally influences satisfaction. In particular, high SEs should be more apt than low SEs to derive satisfaction when performance is relatively high and dissatisfaction when performance is low. But, what if the causal impact of satisfaction on performance is greater among low SEs than high SEs? Most empirical studies would combine these two possibilities into a single analysis. Given such impure hypothesis testing, it is little wonder that previous findings have proven inconclusive. In order to give a fairer test to Korman's (1970) hypothesis that self-esteem moderates the causal impact of performance on satisfaction, it is necessary to employ a methodology that allows a clear assessment of the causal effect of performance on satisfaction. For example, longitudinal designs (such as cross-lagged panel correlations), or well-controlled procedures in which participants are randomly assigned to different performance conditions, should enable the investigator to test the extent to which performance determines (subsequent) satisfaction. Self-esteem then could be explored as a moderator variable within the context of such methodologies. If Korman is correct, then high SEs should show a stronger performance-satisfaction relationship than their low self-esteem counterparts.

To complicate matters further, even within the performance-leads-to-satisfaction domain there are conflicting predictions concerning the moderating impact of self-esteem. On the one hand, and contrary to the Korman consistency hypothesis, low SEs' degree of work satisfaction may be more dependent on their work performance than will high SEs'. The rationale is that low SEs are in greater need of self-esteem than are high SEs (Jones 1973). Thus, positive work experience will be particularly satisfying and negative work experiences especially frustrating to the great need for esteem possessed by low SEs.

On the other hand, high SEs' job satisfaction may be more influenced by their task performance than low SEs'. Several rationales underlie this prediction. First, as Korman (1970) has suggested, individuals will "find most satisfying those job and task characteristics which are consistent with their self-cognitions" (p. 32). Said differently, positive work performance is consistent with high SEs' self-cognitions whereas negative work performance is inconsistent. Both statements are less true for low SEs. Accordingly, the positive performance-satisfaction relationship should be stronger for the high SEs than the low SEs. Second, and possibly related to the first, low SEs may have more difficulty feeling satisfied following a positive work performance because relative to high SEs they are less apt to perceive (or fully appreciate) their success. Several studies have shown that in the face of identical and objectively positive feedback, low SEs believe that they have been less successful than their high self-esteem counterparts (Diener & Dweck 1980; Shrauger 1975). Somewhat paradoxically, then, low SEs may have a great desire for positive feedback, such as successful work performance, but their perceptual style may make it difficult to perceive or assimilate self-relevant positive feedback (for example, Maracek & Mettee 1972). The net effect of the low SEs' conflicting esteem and consistency needs may be to cancel one another, and thereby render non-significant the moderating impact of self-esteem on the performance-satisfaction relationship.

This reasoning does more than provide an account of the inconsistent results in past research exploring the moderating impact of self-esteem on the performance-satisfaction relationship; it also may help identify some of the conditions under which self-esteem will moderate the relationship between performance and satisfaction. More specifically, assuming that the performance-satisfaction relationship under discussion is the one in which the former causally affects the latter, it is proposed that low SEs will exhibit a stronger performance-satisfaction relationship than high SEs provided that performance quality is unambiguous. Indirectly supportive evidence stems from a review of research on the effects of self-esteem on attitudes toward others (Jones 1973). In these experiments, subjects of varying levels of self-esteem are asked to indicate their attraction toward others, after receiving positive or negative evaluations about themselves from the others. In a sense, subjects in these studies receive unambiguous feedback about their "performance" at a social task, and then rate their "satisfaction" with the provider of that feedback. Results consistently demonstrate that low SEs' liking for the other is more sharply influenced by the others' evaluation: whereas all participants like positive evaluators more than negative evaluators, this is especially true among the low, rather than the high self-esteem participants.

Past research has yielded few conclusions about the moderating impact of self-esteem on the work performance-job satisfaction relationship. This is not to say, however, that self-esteem is not a relevant moderator variable. As discussed, methodological problems in many previous studies may have made it impossible to disentangle the nature of the causal relationship between performance and satisfaction. Yet another possibility, suggested by the results of several studies (London & Klimoski 1975; Lopez 1982), is that the moderating impact of self-esteem is, in turn, moderated by additional factors. Clearly, further research is needed to evaluate these hypotheses.

Summary

Focusing on previous mainstream research on the role of self-esteem in organizations, I have tried to demonstrate how individuals' global self-esteem may be related to their behaviors and attitudes both prior to and after they have entered the work organization. Empirically, the self-esteem variable appears to have some promise. Self-esteem is consistently related to vocational choice decisions, job-searching process and outcome, and job satisfaction.

Theoretically, the results of past research are far less conclusive. Most studies exhibiting significant results have employed correlational designs, making it extremely difficult to draw causal inferences. Even more problematic is the lack of a unifying theoretical framework to account for the myriad of significant results. The consistency theory proposed by Korman (1970) simply has not stood the test of time (compare Dipboye 1977a). According to that theory, high SEs should choose vocations that are better suited to their needs and abilities to a greater extent than low SEs, consistently outperform their low self-esteem counterparts, and exhibit a more significant positive relationship between performance and satisfaction than low SEs. While the results of past research generally are supportive of the first proposition, the bulk of the available evidence does not support the latter two. In chapter 3 I attempt to provide a theoretical analysis of self-esteem, which should enable theorists and researchers to appreciate better its potential role in elucidating human behavior in organizations.

3
Self-esteem and Behavioral Plasticity

B
ehavioral plasticity refers to the extent to which individuals' actions are susceptible to influence by external and, particularly, social cues. To explain the construct's relationship to self-esteem, three examples are presented in which the target person's behavior could be influenced by a range of organizational events. Of greatest importance is whether the target persons' level of self-esteem affects (or moderates) the actual impact of the organizational events on their work behaviors.

1. Person A is a midlevel manager. One day a subordinate makes a useful recommendation for some procedural change. Because the suggestion seems quite reasonable, Person A suggests to her supervisor that the change be implemented; Person A's boss approves of the change and helps to facilitate its introduction. Unfortunately, and contrary to the expectations of all concerned—Person A, her subordinate, and her supervisor—the change in procedure produces dismal results. Several weeks later, a second subordinate approaches Person A and makes another suggestion for procedural change (on a different subject matter). On the surface at least, this suggestion also seems meritorious. Given Person A's previous negative experience in recommending suggestions for change up the organizational hierarchy, how willing would Person A be to recommend this new suggestion? More succinctly, would Person A's self-esteem affect her willingness to do so?

2. Person B is a member of a work group whose members must coordinate its activities with one another in order to accomplish their tasks. Recently, some sharp differences of opinion have occurred between Person B and fellow workers about the most effective method of performing his tasks. To what extent will Person B change his opinion about effective task accomplishment so as to conform to that of fellow group members? More specifically will Person B's level of self-esteem affect the extent to which he changes his opinions to coincide with the group's?

3. Person C, a research and development scientist, has been working on a project for some time. Some days are filled with positive feedback; that is, Person C appears to be making progress on the project, causing his peers and

superiors to heap lavish praise upon him. Unfortunately, some other days are fraught with negative feedback; Person C cannot seem to make any headway on the project. Furthermore, Person C senses the disapproval from peers and superiors. Would the feedback Person C receives during a particular day (or week) affect the quality of his performance on the immediately subsequent day (or week)? Even more germane, would Person C's self-esteem influence the impact of the feedback on subsequent performance?

In each of these examples workers in the organizational setting could emit, at least in theory, a variety of responses. For instance, Person A may or may not be more reluctant to recommend the new suggestion to the superior; Person B may or may not change his opinion about how to perform his task; Person C's work performance may or may not be affected by the prior feedback. Given the potential variety of responses, it becomes crucial—on theoretical as well as practical grounds—to understand better the factors that might affect workers' actual responses.

One such variable is the workers' level of global or chronic self-esteem. This is not to say that workers' self-esteem is the only individual difference moderator of their workplace reactions; nor is self-esteem necessarily the single most important moderating variable. However, there are theoretical bases and much empirical evidence suggesting that employees' self-esteem moderates the impact of events in the workplace on their behaviors and attitudes. More specifically, a central theme in this chapter is the plasticity hypothesis, which posits that low SEs (often, though not always) are more susceptible to influence by organizational events than their high self-esteem counterparts (Brockner 1983). To explain the moderating impact of employees' self-esteem in the examples given already and other instances, it is first necessary to consider the psychological bases of low SEs' greater tendency toward behavioral plasticity.

Psychological Bases of Plasticity

Social psychological theory and research identify the processes underlying the inverse relationship between self-esteem and behavioral plasticity. McGuire (1972) has discussed the various mechanisms by which external (social) cues affect behavior. In his information-processing analysis McGuire argues that individuals' attitudes and behaviors will be influenced by external cues to the extent that individuals attend to external cues, comprehend the meaning of those cues, and yield to the cues. In other words, for cues to influence behavior they must clear a series of psychological hurdles. If the cues fail to clear any one (or more) of these hurdles then they will have minimal impact on behavior or attitude.

According to this analysis, then, low SEs may be more plastic for any or all of the following reasons: they may be more attentive to external cues; they may extract greater understanding of the cues' meanings; and they may be more yielding. I know of no evidence to support the second proposition; nor is it clear that low SEs literally attend more to external or social cues than their high self-esteem counterparts. However, several social psychological theories offer compelling reasons to expect low SEs to be more yielding to external cues than high SEs.

Social Comparison

Festinger (1954) suggested that in the absence of objective reality individuals rely on social cues to govern their thoughts, feelings, and actions. Moreover, the social comparison process is instigated by individuals' uncertainty concerning the appropriateness of their beliefs and behaviors. Thus, factors affecting individuals' level of uncertainty should influence the extent to which they engage in the social comparison process. Self-esteem is one variable that is (inversely) related to uncertainty concerning the correctness of one's beliefs and behaviors. Thus, low SEs may be more plastic than high SEs because of the former group's greater tendency to engage in uncertainty-produced social comparison processes.

Need for Approval and Self-presentation

Social psychologists (for example, Baumeister 1982; Goffman 1959; Snyder 1981) have written extensively about self-presentation processes in social interaction. In essence, they argue that individuals often go to great lengths to portray particular images of themselves in the minds of significant others. One such impression that individuals try to foster is that of being an attractive, likable person. Moreover, one self-presentation strategy that individuals use to make themselves appear likable is conforming to the behaviors and attitudes of the significant others (Jones 1964).

According to this reasoning, individuals' need to gain the approval of others should influence the extent to which they engage in the self-presentation strategy of conformity, that is, going along with (or being influenced by) the behaviors and attitudes of others. By definition, low SEs would seem to have a greater need for others' approval than their high self-esteem counterparts. Not liking themselves, low SEs may be especially dependent upon others to provide them with positive evaluations. This analysis thus provides an additional explanation of the inverse relationship between self-esteem and behavioral plasticity: low SEs may conform with (that is, be influenced by) social cues in order to win favor in the eyes of real or imagined others.

Self-diagnosticity

The third basis of plasticity primarily focuses on low SEs' greater susceptibility to influence by negative feedback. More specifically, one factor that moderates the effect of negative feedback is the extent to which individuals perceive such feedback to be revealing (to themselves and/or significant others) of other aspects of their self-concept. Typically, when individuals receive negative feedback about themselves, it is limited in scope. For example, individuals may be told that they performed poorly on a job interview, or an exam, or certain job dimensions. Far rarer are those instances in which they are given all-encompassing negative evaluations (for example, "You are a totally worthless person.").

Although negative feedback typically is limited in scope objectively, people undoubtedly vary in the extent to which they generalize such feedback to other domains of themselves. For example, if a first term MBA student leaning toward a career in management consulting performed poorly on the first exam in an organizational behavior course, he or she could make any or all of the following self-diagnostic inferences from the negative feedback: I am a poor student in organizational behavior; I am a poor student in qualitative (that is, nonmathematical) MBA courses; I am a poor MBA student; and I am not well suited for a career in management consulting. Moreover, this individual may even consider the negative feedback to be diagnostic of aspects of his or her self-concept that are unrelated to his or her identity as a student and aspiring professional. For example, the poor test performance may lead to the inferences that one is a lousy tennis player, undesirable romantic partner, and incompetent cook. In short, negative feedback is perceived to be self-diagnostic to the extent that the perceiver goes beyond the information given by the feedback.

It seems reasonably straightforward that the impact of negative feedback on individuals' subsequent beliefs and behaviors will be heightened to the extent that the feedback is perceived to be more, rather than less, self-diagnostic. Moreover, factors affecting feedback self-diagnosticity should also moderate the influencing power of the feedback. Clinical psychological theorists (for example, Kohut 1971) have implied that self-esteem is one such factor. Relative to high SEs, low SEs are more likely to view negative feedback as self-diagnostic. Said differently, low SEs, because of their feelings of personal insecurity, are probably more apt to ask themselves questions like, "What do my behaviors—especially those that shine negatively about me—say about me (as a person)?" The more self-assured attitude of high SEs, however, would be less likely to engender such concerns. To reiterate, the self-diagnosticity analysis provides another psychological basis of low SEs' greater plasticity, particularly in response to negative feedback.

Taken together, the three bases of plasticity may explain why low SEs often are more susceptible to influence by organizational events than their high self-esteem counterparts. In the context of the examples at the beginning of this chapter, one can expect: Person A to be less willing to communicate the new suggestion if she were low rather than high in self-esteem; Person B to be more likely to go along with the group's opinion if he were low rather than high in self-esteem; and Person C's performance to be more adversely affected by negative feedback if he were low rather than high in self-esteem. Although all three bases of low SEs' greater plasticity could account for these findings, it seems most likely that uncertainty-based social comparison is the primary explanation in the first example, need for approval and self-presentation is most appropriate in the second instance, and the tendency to view negative feedback as self-diagnostic is most relevant in the third. That is, if Person A were low in self-esteem, she would feel especially uncertain about the correct way to respond, and rely on the information from her immediate social environment, which implied that communicating information up the hierarchy did not yield the desired outcome. If Person B were low in self-esteem, he would feel especially concerned with winning the approval of his fellow workers, and might, therefore, conform to their opinions. If Person C were low in self-esteem, he would have the tendency to view the negative feedback as self-diagnostic, which is more likely to influence subsequent performance.

The notion that low SEs are more yielding to external and social influence is hardly novel, having been discussed in different contexts by clinical, personality, and social psychologists (for example, Berkowitz & Lundy 1957; Janis 1954; Rogers 1951). The implications of this notion, however, are considerable for numerous topics of contemporary interest in organizational behavior.

Self-esteem and Plasticity:
Implications for Employee Performance

Managers continually wrestle with ways to improve the job performance of their subordinates; toward that end they may introduce a variety of interventions (for example, technological changes, training programs). Nevertheless, it is not uncommon for them to find some subordinates to be very responsive to such interventions, whereas others are either slightly or not at all affected.

One—but, of course, not the only—explanation of such variation in responsivity may be embedded in the previous analysis of self-esteem and behavioral plasticity. An important implication of that discussion is that low SEs' cognitions often are more susceptible to influence by external cues than are high SEs'. That is, if low SEs are more uncertain about the correct way to think, feel, and act they will be more likely to rely on external and social cues to guide their thoughts and behaviors. The notion that low SEs' cognitions are more manipulable than high SEs' is noteworthy; the field of psychology in general and organizational psychology in particular has witnessed a resurgence of interest in the role of cognition. More to the point, many organizational scholars (for example, Mitchell 1982) believe that one of the most effective ways to affect employee productivity is by influencing those cognitions that mediate work performance.

Performance-relevant cognitions occur at three points in time: *prior to* the individuals' performance. For example, some employees enter the performance situation expecting to succeed, whereas others approach their work with far more negative expectations. Such expectations may have a powerful influence on performance, typically in a self-fulfilling fashion; *during* the actual task performance. For example, individuals may focus their attention on the task at hand, or they may become self-preoccupied during task performance. It seems reasonable that the former attentional set is more likely to facilitate performance than the latter. In addition, the extent to which individuals perform their task while thinking about trying to attain a specific, challenging goal has been shown to have a positive effect on performance (Locke 1968); and *subsequent to* their task performance. For instance, the attributions that workers make for their performance may sharply affect their subsequent work performance. Workers who blame themselves for a prior poor performance may have greater difficulty performing capably on a subsequent task.

Much prior research has shown that cognitive factors such as expectancies, attention, goals, and attributions may sharply affect employees' work performance. Furthermore, more recent research has shown that factors designed to affect such cognitions are more likely to influence the work performance of low rather than high SEs. Taken together, the research findings suggest that it is rather difficult to alter high SEs' performance through the manipulation of external cues (that presumably affect cognition). By contrast, low SEs' cognitions are much more easily manipulable, which may account for their greater behavioral plasticity. This reasoning may provide some insight into managers' inability to heighten the work performance of some of their subordinates; high SEs may be relatively difficult to influence, especially if the success of managers' interventions is mediated by the cognitive factors described above.

Most of the studies presented in this chapter have been conducted under controlled laboratory conditions, which raises the obvious question of the generalizability of the findings to the organizational context. Of course, the question of whether the results of laboratory studies generalize to organizational settings ultimately is an empirical one. Two facts give us reason to be at least somewhat optimistic about the external validity associated with the assertion that low SEs often are more behaviorally plastic than their high-esteem counterparts. First, and more generally, Locke (1986) recently has compiled a series of papers comparing the results of laboratory versus field studies across a variety of mainstream areas of inquiry in organizational psychology, including performance appraisal, goal setting, participation in decision making, and the relationship between job performance and job satisfaction. The basic finding is that across areas of inquiry, the same results were obtained in the field as in the laboratory.

Second, and more specifically, much of the research discussed in chapter 4 has explored the relationship between self-esteem and behavioral plasticity in field settings. Like many of the studies to be described momentarily, the results lend strong support to the plasticity hypothesis. Of course, many of the laboratory studies to follow should be buttressed with analogous field experimentation. Pending the outcomes of such research, however, it is tentatively proposed that the conceptual underpinnings of the laboratory research may be quite externally valid, and, therefore, of considerable theoretical and practical significance.

In all of the laboratory studies, subjects of varying levels of self-esteem are required to perform some cognitive task. Furthermore, each study includes at least one experimental manipulation designed to affect some performance-relevant cognition. The cognition could be relevant to performance at any or all of three points in time: before, during, or after the individual is working at the task.

Cognition Prior to Performance

Perhaps the single most performance-relevant cognition that individuals bring to their work is their expectation for success. Many studies have shown that expectations for performance are correlated with individuals' actual performance (for example, Vroom 1964), and that low SEs have lower expectations for their performance in evaluative situations than do high SEs (for example, Coopersmith 1967). The plasticity hypothesis, furthermore, posits that low SEs' expectations are more easily influenced than are high SEs' expectations. The results of several studies are consistent with this assertion. In one such study (DePaulo et al. 1981), subjects were asked to work on two tasks, one described to be easy and the other depicted as difficult. It seems likely that participants' performance expectations were more favorable prior to working on the easy than the difficult task. If so, then performance should have been better in the former than in the latter case. In fact, workers did perform better on the easy than the difficult task, but only if they were low (rather than high) in self-esteem. Conceptually analogous findings also have been reported by Dipboye, Phillips, and Shahani (1985), Hollenbeck and Brief (1987), Raben and Klimoski (1973), and Sigall and Gould (1977).

Cognition During Performance

The workers' attentional focus during task performance can have a pronounced impact on their performance. More specifically, to the extent that individuals are self-preoccupied—that is, worrying about their ability to perform adequately—rather than task-focused, their performance is bound to suffer. A handful of studies have shown that low SEs' attentional focus, and hence task performance, is far more susceptible to influence by external cues than it is for high SEs. Shrauger (1972) had subjects of varying levels of self-esteem perform a task under one of two conditions: half were tested in the presence of an onlooking audience whereas others were not. (Research has shown that the presence of an observing audience may increase self-focused attention; Carver & Scheier 1978.) The task performance of high SEs was unaffected by the audience variable. However, low SEs' performance was significantly different in the two conditions; they performed far worse in the presence of the audience—presumably the condition associated with heightened self-focused attention—than in its absence.

Several studies have replicated and extended these results (for example, Brockner & Hulton 1978). In one study (Brockner 1979a), it was reasoned that if low SEs' attentional focus was more easily manipulable than that of high SEs, then the former group also should be more influenced by attentional manipulations designed to facilitate rather than interfere with performance. In this experiment, subjects of low and high self-esteem worked on a task under one of four conditions:

1. Self-focus: This condition was analogous to the audience condition in the Shrauger (1972) study.

2. Task-focus: In this condition workers received prior instructions emphasizing the importance of their concentrating on the task at hand.

3. Combined Self-focus and Task-focus: Subjects in this condition were exposed to both elements described in 1 and 2.

4. No Focus: control condition. Participants in the no focus condition were exposed to neither element described in 1 and 2.

The performance of low, but not high, SEs was influenced by both attentional focus cues (see table 3–1). Replicating the results of Shrauger (1972), low SEs performed worse when self-focus was high rather than low. Extending Shrauger (1972), and in a more optimistic vein, low SEs performed better when task-focus was high rather than low. More recently, Strack et al. (1985) also have found that task-focus inductions have a more facilitative effect on the task performance of individuals with negative, rather than positive, self-evaluations.

Goal Setting

Goals—the standard of performance that the worker is consciously trying to achieve—are an additional cognition that may be highly relevant during task performance. Locke et al. (1981) have demonstrated that the "goal-setting effect" is one of the most widely replicated findings in industrial and organizational psychology: across a wide variety of participants, settings, and tasks it has been shown that workers who are focused on specific, difficult goals

Table 3–1
Errors Committed as a Function of Self-esteem, Self-attention, and Task-attention

Self-esteem	Self-attention	Task-attention	
		Task-Focus	No Task-Focus
High	Self-focus	4.43	2.50
	No self-focus	3.00	4.18
Low	Self-focus	4.40	7.22
	No self-focus	1.75	3.60

Source: Brockner 1979a.
Note: Higher scores reflected poorer performance.

are more productive than those attentive to easy goals, nonspecific goals, or no goals at all.

The practical utility of such findings is considerable, and, in fact, goal-setting procedures have been fruitfully implemented in a number of organizational settings (see, Latham & Locke 1979). In their review article, Locke et al. (1981) point out that not all individuals are equally affected by goal setting. However, there has been a lack of theoretical progress in research exploring individual difference moderators of the relationship between goals and performance. As Locke et al. (1981) concluded, "the only consistent thing about the studies of individual differences in goal setting is their inconsistency" (p. 142). Several of the reasons cited by Locke et al. to account for such inconsistencies are identical to Weiss and Adler's (1984) explanations of the inconclusive findings of many studies exploring more generally the relationships between personality and work behavior. For example, many goal-setting studies have failed to provide a strong theoretical rationale for the moderating impact of the individual difference variables explored in the given study.

The greatest current concern, of course, is the role of employees' self-esteem in their response(s) to goal setting. Several studies have shown that self-esteem interacts with the presence or absence of specific, difficult goals to affect performance; however, the results of these studies are mixed. For example, in one study (Brockner 1986), subjects high and low in self-esteem performed a task; half were assigned a specific difficult goal, whereas half were not. Overall, productivity was greater in the presence than the absence of the specific, difficult goal—but primarily among the low rather than the high SEs. Similarly, Korman (1970) had subjects of varying levels of self-esteem set their own goals prior to task performance. Some subjects set relatively hard goals, whereas others set fairly easy goals. Task performance was then assessed as a joint function of self-esteem and goals. Once again, subjects overall tended to perform better if they had set hard rather than easy goals, but only if they were low rather than high in self-esteem. Both findings, of course, are consistent with the behavioral plasticity hypothesis.

On the other hand, other goal-setting results not at all consistent with the plasticity hypothesis were reported by Carroll and Tosi (1970). In that study, managers high in self-esteem worked harder in response to difficult goals, whereas those low in self-esteem actually worked less hard. Similar results were obtained in the "assigned goal" condition in a recent laboratory experiment by Hollenbeck and Brief (1987). Other results in the Hollenbeck and Brief study—in which goal difficulty and goal origin were manipulated orthogonally—supported a more complicated version of the plasticity hypothesis. Some subjects had more difficult goals than others; furthermore, some subjects set their own goals, whereas others had those same goals assigned to them. Overall, there was a significant goal difficulty × goal origin interaction: the typically positive relationship between goal difficulty and performance was greater in the self-set than assigned condition. Furthermore, this interaction was moderated, in turn, by participants' self-esteem. Consistent with the plasticity hypothesis, the difficulty × origin interaction described already was exhibited to a much greater extent by the low SEs than the high SEs.

To summarize, these studies all have demonstrated that self-esteem interacts with goals in some way to affect performance. However, the precise nature of the interactive relationship between self-esteem and goals varies considerably across studies. A closer analysis of the goal-setting literature may clarify such inconsistent results, and in so doing help identify the conditions under which low versus high SEs will exhibit greater productivity as a function of goal setting. Goal-setting theorists generally agree that it is the acceptance, and not the mere setting, of the goal that mediates heightened productivity (Erez & Kanfer 1983). The crucial theoretical task, then, is to delineate the factors that affect individuals' goal acceptance. Furthermore, we need to consider how self-esteem may relate to the factors affecting goal acceptance.

From expectancy theory (for example, Steers 1984), it seems likely that three broad categories of factors will have an impact on goal acceptance: individuals' beliefs about their abilities to perform the behaviors necessary for goal attainment (that is, their self-efficacy beliefs, Bandura 1977); individuals' goal instrumentality beliefs, defined by Yukl and Latham (1978) as "the extent to which . . . outcomes are perceived to be contingent upon goal attainment" (p. 309); and the extent to which the outcomes of goal attainment are valued (for example, job security, pay, promotion). Workers' goal acceptance should be greater when they believe that they are capable of performing the behaviors necessary for goal attainment, when perceived goal instrumentality is high, and when the outcomes of goal attainment are valued.

It seems highly likely that self-esteem is positively correlated with individuals' self-efficacy beliefs, that is, their perceived ability to perform the behaviors necessary for goal attainment, and especially if goal attainment is believed to be difficult. Similarly, it seems reasonable that self-esteem is positively related to goal instrumentality beliefs. Research has shown that high SEs are more likely than low SEs to perceive contingency between their behaviors and the outcomes of their behaviors. This is true, regardless of whether such beliefs are general, as measured by the Rotter (1966) Locus of Control Scale, or more specific to goal setting, as measured by Yukl and Latham's (1978) goal instrumentality scale.

The proposed positive relationships between self-esteem and both self-efficacy and goal instrumentality may explain the results of those studies (for example, Carroll & Tosi 1970) in which high SEs responded more productively than low SEs to specific, difficult goals. However, with the three-factor model of goal acceptance, it is possible to envision circumstances in which low SEs may be more responsive than high SEs to specific, difficult goals, as was found in the study by Korman (1970). That is, low SEs may value the positive outcomes associated with goal attainment to a greater extent than high SEs under certain conditions; for example, when the "valued outcome" consists of winning favor in the eyes of others, such as the individual(s) who assigned the goal to the worker, then low SEs may work harder than high SEs.

Or, if the setting of the goal serves to focus the workers' attention on the task at hand, rather than their felt inadequacy in being able to attain the goal, then low SEs may be more responsive. For example, the presence of the goal may keep the worker focused on the need to attain the goal, or may encourage strategy formulation for attaining one's goals. In essence, goal setting may serve as a task-focus manipulation (Hollenbeck & Brief 1987), which has been shown to facilitate the performance of low SEs moreso than high SEs (Brockner 1979a; Brockner & Hulton 1978).

This analysis suggests that the moderating effect of self-esteem on the goal-setting and performance relationship will, in turn, be moderated by additional factors. Factors that make salient workers' self-efficacy and/or goal instrumentality beliefs are likely to lead high SEs to exhibit greater productivity in response to goals than their low self-esteem counterparts. For example, if goal attainment is believed to be very difficult, or if the evaluative aspects of the performance setting is emphasized, then self-efficacy beliefs are apt to be elicited. Under such conditions, high and low SEs' differential feelings of self-efficacy are apt to be salient, and thus the former group should outperform the latter (for example, Hollenbeck & Brief 1987).

Alternatively, factors that make salient the task-focusing qualities of the goal-setting treatment, or social approval that one stands to gain by goal attainment are likely to elicit greater goal-induced productivity among low than high SEs. For example, if the goal or the path to successful goal attainment is attention-getting, then task-focused attention is apt to be high (and, correspondingly, perhaps self-focused attention will be low). These are precisely the circumstances under which goal setting should elicit a greater boost in productivity among low rather than high SEs.

Whether the typical inverse relationship between self-esteem and behavioral plasticity will be obtained in the goal-setting context is no simple matter. To complicate the issue even further, there is even some evidence that the factors affecting goal acceptance not only are correlated with self-esteem, but also may interact with self-esteem to affect task performance. Specifically, Yukl and Latham (1978) reported a positive correlation between self-esteem and goal instrumentality. Given the modesty of this correlation, however, $(r = .35)$, there were still a reasonable number of people who were low in self-esteem and high in instrumentality, or high in self-esteem and low in instrumentality. The productivity of these two groups, as well as those who were both low in self-esteem and instrumentality, and those high on both dimensions were then compared. The self-esteem and instrumentality variables combined interactively to predict productivity (see figure 3–1). High SEs were equally productive regardless of their level of instrumentality; low SEs were much more productive when their instrumentality was high rather than low. Note that this pattern is wholly consistent with the plasticity hypothesis.

In sum, there is some empirical evidence that self-esteem moderates the impact of goal setting on performance. A more detailed conceptual analysis suggests, however, that additional factors must be considered prior to predicting whether it is the low or the high SEs whose work performance will be more facilitated by goal setting. The conceptual analysis has received indirect support, that is, many of the component parts have empirical backing. However, to date there have been few direct tests of the model. An important future research agenda, then, is to test the propositions set forth here. Doing so will serve two purposes. First, at the theoretical level of analysis, the proposed research may identify some boundary conditions of the general tendency for low SEs to be more susceptible to influence; the reasoning described already suggests that under certain conditions high SEs will be more influenced (by goals) than their low self-esteem counterparts. Second, and at a more practical level, the results may have implications for managers who use, or are contemplating the use of, goal-setting programs to heighten their subordinates' work performance. It seems likely that the success of the goal-setting program chosen by managers will depend on the workers' self-esteem, in conjunction with a host of other variables; ultimately, the key to success will be to tailor the goal-setting procedure to the subordinates' self-esteem, in the context of the relevant factors cited already.

Cognition After Performance

Thus far I have suggested that the determinants of performance-relevant cognitions (for example, expectancies, attentional focus, goal instrumentality) generally have greater impact on the performance of low than high SEs. The cognitions discussed to this point were believed to be salient either prior to performance (for example, expectancies) or during the actual performance

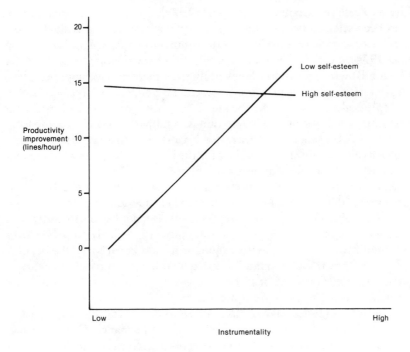

Source: Yukl & Latham 1978, p. 320.

Figure 3–1. Interactive Effect of Self-esteem and Instrumentality on Productivity

(for instance, attentional focus). It seems equally plausible, however, that workers' posttask cognitions will have important implications for their subsequent performance.

Typically, following task performance, workers receive feedback of some sort. At least three types of feedback are possible: positive, negative, and ambiguous. Moreover, several cognitions may mediate their reactions to the feedback, such as what they attend to and remember about their performance and its associated feedback, or the type of attribution that they make for their performance. Given the different types of feedback and the different kinds of cognitions potentially associated with each, in theory there are a large number of possibilities to consider.

This section focuses on the impact of workers' attributions for negative feedback on their subsequent performance. Why choose postfailure attributions in particular? Two reasons. First, much research has shown that low and high SEs are more apt to differ in their response to negative, rather than positive feedback (for example, Zuckerman 1979). Second, the attribution process has been selected because the causal explanations that individuals make for their (work) performance is a key determinant of subsequent functioning (Weiner 1974). Consider the following examples of two individuals (Person A and Person B) who are anxiously awaiting their performance appraisal. Person A is a bit on edge, because he suspects that his superiors have been somewhat displeased with his work. During the appraisal meeting he is told that his performance for the period in question was subpar. In pondering the feedback, Person A becomes quite distressed because he attributes his poor performance to his "innate" lack of ability for the job. As a result, his subsequent performance and morale plummet even further.

Like Person A, Person B suspects that her superiors have been somewhat disappointed with her work. Her meeting with her superiors confirm this suspicion. On her train ride home, however, Person B does not feel overly distressed. Rather, she believes that her poor performance is not likely to persist over time; with a little bit of extra effort, and/or a little bit of luck, she believes that she can "turn things around." Consequently, she approaches her work with renewed vigor over the next few months, and, just as she expected, her performance begins to improve dramatically.

These two examples suggest that failure feedback can have negative or positive effects on individuals' subsequent work performance. One of the factors that affects whether failure feedback serves to increase or decrease subsequent performance may be the workers' attributions for the prior failure. Such attributions differ along three dimensions (Abramson, Seligman & Teasdale 1978).

1. Locus of control. The cause of the poor performance may be due to factors internal to the individual (for example, lack of ability) or external to that person (for example, a very difficult task at which most persons would fail).

2. Stability. The cause of the poor performance may be due to factors that are likely to remain stable (for example, lack of ability) or unstable (for example, lack of effort) over time.

3. Globality. The cause of the poor performance may be due to factors that are likely to generalize across situations (for example, general lack of intelligence) or not (for example, lack of intelligence in a specific subject area).

Seligman and his colleagues (1979) have developed an individual difference measure of "attributional style." Those having an "optimistic" style attribute negative outcomes to external, unstable, and specific causes, whereas those having the "pessimistic" style attribute such outcomes to internal, stable, and global factors. Much research (see Peterson & Seligman 1984) has shown that the optimistic style leads to renewed vigor following negative feedback (as in the case of Person B), whereas the pessimistic style leads individuals to exhibit helplessness (that is, passivity, withdrawal, or poor motivation) subsequent to failure (as in the case of Person A). For example, in one study (Seligman & Schulman 1986) the attributional style of life insurance agents was used to predict job performance (as measured by their sales commissions). The rationale for studying insurance agents is that the task of selling insurance is one fraught with failure and rejection from prospective customers. (This aspect of the job may account for the high turnover rate among life insurance agents; as Seligman and Schulman reported, studies by the Life Insurance Marketing Research Association have shown that 78 percent of the agents hired in the United States quit within three years of service.) Consequently, the agents' attributional style may predict (if not determine) their job performance, provided that they possess the necessary level of ability. Seligman and Schulman discovered in their cross-sectional study of experienced agents that those having an optimistic attributional style were significantly more productive than the agents who had a pessimistic attributional style.

In a second study, one that was prospective rather than cross-sectional, the authors not only replicated the relationship between attributional style and sales performance, but also discovered that the optimistic style was associated with a much lower turnover rate than the pessimistic style. More specifically, 71 percent of the pessimists but only 46 percent of the optimists had quit within their first year on the job.

The practical implications of these findings are considerable; they suggest that organizations can reduce the costs of poor performance and turnover by ensuring that jobs fraught with negative feedback are filled by persons having an optimistic rather than pessimistic attributional style. Even when Seligman and Schulman (1986) controlled for the more traditionally used predictor of performance among insurance agents—the Aptitude Index Battery—attributional style predicted their performance and turnover. Or, if certain individuals or groups are known to have a pessimistic attributional style, then management may try to encourage them to adopt a more optimistic one, especially subsequent to negative feedback.

More recently, Seligman (as reported in Trotter 1987) has employed content analysis of individuals' explanations for past events in order to predict their subsequent functioning. For some provocative examples, he has discovered that women's attributional style (measured in 1943) predicted their psychological health forty years later. In addition, Hall of Fame baseball players who performed between 1900–1950 were shown to exhibit a strong association between attributional style and longevity; those with an optimistic style (such as "Nothing but the breaks beat me in that game.") tended to live longer than those having a pessimistic style (for example, "I know that I haven't got the stuff that I used to.").

It may be possible to content analyze the attributional style of individuals in order to predict whether they will respond to negative outcomes with renewed vigor (like Person B) or helplessness (like Person A). A particularly vivid example of how two individuals responded very differently to the same negative outcome appeared on the front page of *The New York Times* on January 28, 1987, one year after the Challenger disaster that claimed the lives of seven U.S. astronauts. Two rocket engineers, Allan McDonald and Roger Boisjoly, were employees at Morton Thiokol, Inc., the manufacturer of the rocket whose faulty design was alleged to be responsible for the disaster. In their testimony before the Presidential commission investigating the Challenger disaster, McDonald and Boisjoly revealed that they had opposed the launching, but that they had been overruled in their judgment by their superiors. The article then described the reactions of these two men during the past year to this very negative event:

> Mr. McDonald, his authority restored after the Presidential commission expressed outrage that he was stripped of his responsibilities for telling the truth, has emerged as the spokesman for Thiokol and its newly designed rocket boosters. . . . He has channeled all his energy into the nitty-gritty of getting the shuttle flying again, not allowing himself to dwell on the past.
> Mr. Boisjoly . . . has told friends that he could never work on the shuttle again. Since the summer he has been on an extended sick leave from Thiokol. . . . At times he wonders aloud whether there was anything more he could have done to stop the launching.

It is tempting to speculate that the engineers' attributional style is responsible for their reactions to having their decisions overruled, which culminated in the Challenger disaster. If Seligman's reasoning is correct, then the records should show that McDonald's attributional style is far more optimistic than is Boisjoly's; indeed, future research may content analyze the public testimony of these two men in order to test this hypothesis.

Although there is a growing array of evidence linking individuals' attributional style to their reactions to negative feedback, left unspecified thus far is the role of self-esteem. There are at least two ways in which employees' self-esteem may be relevant to our discussion of attributional style. First, there is considerable evidence that low SEs have a more pessimistic attributional style than their high self-esteem counterparts (Fitch 1970; Tennen & Herzberger 1987). Indeed, this difference in attributional style may explain (at least in part) the often-found tendency for failure feedback to have a more negative effect on the subsequent performance of low than high SEs (Brockner 1979b; Shrauger & Sorman 1977).

Second, and perhaps of greater relevance to our self-esteem and behavioral plasticity discussion, it may be that low SEs' failure attributions are more easily manipulable by external cues than are those of high SEs. Support for this hypothesis would do more than buttress the theoretical link between self-esteem and behavioral plasticity; it may have considerable practical value to managers who have the task of providing feedback to employees in ways that heighten (or, at least, do not dampen) their subsequent work performance. Presumably, by encouraging subordinates (and especially low SEs) to attribute negative outcomes to more external, unstable, and specific causes, the subordinates' subsequent level of motivation should be higher.

The results of several studies suggest that low SEs' postfailure attributions are more malleable (Brockner & Guare 1983; Klein, Fencil-Morse & Seligman 1976). In these studies, subjects of varying levels of self-esteem worked at a task and were provided negative feedback about their performance. Some were led to believe that the cause of their poor performance was internal, others were led to believe that the cause was external, while still others were given no information at all. Performance at a subsequent, supposedly unrelated task was then assessed. Consistent with the plasticity hypothesis, low SEs' performance was dramatically affected by the attribution variable, such that they performed much better in the external condition than in all others. The performance of high SEs, in sharp contrast, was virtually identical across the different conditions.

The presentation of studies supportive of the self-esteem and behavioral plasticity position has fractionated performance-relevant cognitions into different periods during which they were thought to be most salient: before, during, and after task performance. This compartmentalization process, while useful for categorical purposes, overlooks the possibility that the cognitions themselves may be highly interrelated. For example, favorable prior expectations may cause workers to be relatively task-focused (rather than self-focused) during the actual performance of the work. Similarly, individuals who approach a task with favorable expectations but then perform poorly are quite likely to make nonself (that is, external) attributions for their poor performance. Basic attribution research has shown that outcomes that disconfirm prior expectations are more likely to be attributed to external causes (Harvey, Ickes & Kidd 1976). In a more pessimistic vein, it is possible that low SEs' preperformance cognitions (that is, negative expectancies) may influence their thoughts during (that is, self-focused attention) and after work performance (that is, internal failure attributions).

To illustrate how the cognitions may interrelate and provide further evidence on the plasticity hypothesis, consider the effect of success versus failure feedback on the subsequent performance of low and high SEs. Several studies (for example, Shrauger & Rosenberg 1970) have shown that individuals generally perform better following success than failure. Why might this be so, and especially for low SEs?

1. Expectancies. The effect of the success-failure variable may be to alter workers' expectations for their performance at a subsequent task, such that they approach it far more optimistically following success than failure.

2. Attentional Focus. It is possible that failure induces self-focused attention (whereas success may elicit task-focused attention). Thus, following failure, workers may be more self-focused than subsequent to success, accounting for the better performance in the latter than the former condition.

3. Goal Setting. Related to attentional focus above, it is possible that

success causes individuals to focus on the task in ways that facilitate performance. For example, prior success may "psychologically free up" the worker
to think about strategies for effective performance, which is believed to be
one of the mediators of goal-setting effects (Locke et al. 1981). Said differently, failure and its resultant self-focused attention probably interferes with
workers' abilities to set goals or contemplate strategies to achieve goals.

4.   Attribution. It may not merely be the outcome, but rather the attribution for that outcome that influences subsequent performance. Thus, failure
coupled with pessimistic attributions for the failure may cause workers to
perform worse than following success.

Any or all of these cognitive mechanisms could mediate the impact of feedback on subsequent performance. Moreover, the plasticity hypothesis posits
that such performance-relevant cognitions are more manipulable among low
than high SEs, suggesting that success versus failure feedback may have a
greater effect on the subsequent performance of the former than the latter
group.

Precisely such results have been obtained in both laboratory experiments
and field studies. In the laboratory experiments (Brockner 1979b; Shrauger
& Sorman 1977), workers of varying degrees of self-esteem were randomly
assigned to receive positive (success condition) or negative (failure condition)
feedback about their performance at a prior task; all participants' performance
at a subsequent task was then assessed. Low SEs performed better in the success than failure condition, whereas no discernible difference existed for the
high SEs. Further analyses revealed that the two groups did not differ in their
performance in the success condition. However, following failure, low SEs
performed far worse than high SEs.

In a more recent laboratory experiment, Campbell and Fairey (1985)
demonstrated that it may not even be necessary for individuals to experience
success-failure feedback directly in order for self-esteem differences in subsequent performance to emerge. In this study, subjects of varying levels of self-
esteem merely were asked to explain the hypothetical reasons for their performance at the upcoming anagrams task. At random, half were required to
explain the cause of a hypothetical success, whereas half were asked to attribute the cause of a hypothetical failure. Consistent with the plasticity hypothesis, high SEs' actual performance was influenced to a far lesser extent than
was low SEs' by this rather unusual manipulation of performance-relevant
cognitions. More specifically, low SEs performed much better in the "explain
success" than in the "explain failure" condition, whereas high SEs performed
equally well in the two conditions. Such findings, of course, are perfectly compatible with the results of studies investigating the effects of actual success-
failure feedback on the task performance of low and high SEs.

A field study by Brockner, Derr, and Laing (1987) explored the effect of
self-esteem and success-failure feedback on task performance in the following

manner: management students' self-esteem was assessed on the first day of class. Five weeks later, they took the first midterm exam, which, in short essay format, required them to apply theory and research covered in the lectures and/or assigned readings to the solution of a managerial problem. One week later, the students were given feedback about their performance; those earning a grade of B or better (45 percent of the entire class) were considered to have received relatively positive feedback, whereas those earning a grade of C or poorer (55 percent of the class) were assumed to have received negative feedback. Students then took their second midterm exam five weeks later.

The results showed that there was no relationship between self-esteem and performance on the initial exam. That is, equal proportions of high and low SEs received positive versus negative feedback concerning their initial exam performance. Of greatest relevance was the students' performance on the second exam as a function of their self-esteem and feedback from the initial exam. The results supported the plasticity hypothesis (see table 3–2): low SEs' performance on the second exam varied considerably as a function of the feedback they received concerning their initial performance; this was less true for the high SEs. Moreover, in the studies showing success-failure feedback to have a greater impact on the subsequent performance of low than high SEs, the results usually are attributable to the failure conditions. Indeed, both groups performed equally well following success feedback, but low SEs performed much worse than high SEs subsequent to failure feedback (see table 3–2).

Taken together, the laboratory and field studies exploring the joint effects of self-esteem and feedback on subsequent performance provide strong support for the plasticity hypothesis. It is worth mentioning that the consistency in results occurred in spite of vast methodological differences between the laboratory and field studies. In the lab studies, the effect produced by the feedback variable had a high degree of internal validity, in that workers had been randomly assigned to the different feedback conditions. Thus, within each self-esteem group we are in a position to draw causal inferences concerning the impact of feedback on performance.

Table 3–2
Performance on Second Exam as a Function of Self-esteem and Feedback from Initial Exam

	Feedback from Initial Exam	
Self-esteem	*Positive*	*Negative*
High	84.73	76.16
Low	83.38	63.05

Source: Brockner, Derr & Laing 1987, p. 322.
Note: Higher scores reflect better performance; maximum score = 100.

One major difficulty of the results of laboratory studies, of course, is their external validity. To what extent, one might wonder, do the results of the laboratory studies generalize to "real-world" performance settings? The results presented in table 3–2 suggest that such self-esteem effects are generalizable, at least within the context of management students' exam performance. Of course, the internal validity of the field study is questionable in that students had not been randomly assigned to receive positive or negative feedback about their initial exam performance. In short, the two different empirical approaches complement one another; the strength of one is the weakness of the other. The fact that similar results emerged in spite of the methodological differences is, therefore, all the more compelling.

Concluding Comments

This chapter has proposed a way for organizational scholars and practitioners to think about the impact of individuals' self-esteem on their work attitudes and behavior. The basic notion is that the cognitions, and ultimately the performance of low SEs, are more easily influenced than are those of high SEs. The psychological bases of plasticity were considered. Theoretically, low SEs may be more plastic than their high self-esteem counterparts for any or all of the following reasons. *Social comparison.* Lacking self-confidence or certainty in their own beliefs and behaviors, low SEs are prone to regard external or social cues as guides for appropriate thought and action. *Need for approval and self-presentation.* Not liking themselves, low SEs are especially dependent on the receipt of positive evaluations from others. One way to receive such positive evaluations, they might reason, is to conform to (that is, be influenced by) the beliefs and behaviors of significant others. *Self-diagnosticity.* Having a shaky sense of self-identity, low SEs may be especially prone to perceive negative feedback as reflective or revealing of other important self-aspects.

Based on a cognitive framework of employee motivation and performance, the results of numerous studies were presented suggesting that low SEs' performance-relevant cognitions—before, during, and after their actual task performance—were more plastic than were those of high SEs. As a result, low SEs were shown to perform either relatively better or worse across a wide variety of situations, whereas the performance of the high SEs was much more consistent across situations.

It should be emphasized that the results of other studies presented in chapters 1 and 2, even those sometimes interpreted within a different theoretical framework, also are consistent with the plasticity hypothesis. Recall, for example, the discussion in chapter 2 on the relationship between self-esteem and occupational choice. It was suggested that occupational choice may be determined by factors internal or external to the individual. Internal factors include individuals' needs for job fulfillment and their abilities to do the job well. External factors include social pressures, such as those exerted by friends or family members, and broader societal factors (for example, market conditions). Korman (1966, 1969) and I repeatedly have found that high SEs are more likely than are low SEs to choose vocations that are need-fulfilling and for which they possess the necessary ability; in essence, high SEs exhibit a greater tendency to base their vocational choice on internal factors. Of course, such findings are consistent with the possibility that low SEs' vocational choice decisions are more plastic, that is, prone to influence by external factors. (Such an inference is based on the premise that internal and external determinants of behavior are inversely related, which may or may not be the case.) Further evidence, also indirectly supportive of the notion that low SEs' vocational choices are influenced by external factors, stems from research by Korman (1968) of industrial foremen. In that study it was found that foremen lower in self-esteem were more likely to report that their parents supervised their jobs and tasks than were the foremen higher in self-esteem. It seems entirely possible that the external (parental) influence also may have had a greater impact on the vocational choice of the low than the high self-esteem foremen.

The results of a study by Weiss and Knight (1980) also are consistent with the plasticity hypothesis. In that study subjects performed a problem-solving task in which prior information search was functional for successful task performance. As predicted, low SEs searched for more information and, as a result, actually performed significantly better than the high self-esteem participants. One of the psychological bases of plasticity is social comparison, motivated by individuals' uncertainty concerning their beliefs and behaviors. It was suggested previously that low SEs, because of their chronically greater levels of uncertainty, may be more apt to engage in the social comparison process, and thus exhibit plasticity. Similarly, Weiss and Knight explain the tendency of low SEs to engage in greater information search and consequently perform better than high SEs as due to the former group's greater uncertainty.

In conclusion, this chapter has defined plasticity, explained the psychological bases of plasticity, and presented evidence supportive of the plasticity hypothesis. Moreover, the results of several self-esteem studies in the organizational behavior literature (Korman 1966; Weiss & Knight 1980) are perfectly consistent with the plasticity hypothesis, even though such studies were not intended to be critical tests of the hypothesis. The notion that low SEs are more behaviorally plastic than high SEs is not novel. However, the implications of this prospect are far-reaching, both for theoretical and practical issues related to individuals' behavior within organizations.

4
Self-esteem, Behavioral Plasticity, and Employee Behavior

The central thesis of this chapter is that employees' self-esteem influences their reactions to a range of organizational events. Across a variety of contexts, it will be shown that the work behaviors and attitudes of low SEs are more susceptible to influence than are those of their high self-esteem counterparts. The moderating effect of self-esteem will be considered in discussions of the effects of peer group interaction on workers' performance and attitudes, performance appraisal feedback on workers' subsequent performance, feedback on communication processes, socialization on role taking, modeling on leadership, and organizational stress on work behaviors and attitudes.

These topics were chosen for a host of reasons. First, they encompass a variety of organizational independent variables (peer group interaction, performance appraisal feedback, modeling, and stress). Second, they constitute a range of worker dependent variables in organizations (motivation, performance, communication, leadership, and work attitudes). Third, they demonstrate the role of employees' self-esteem during and after their entry into organizations; the discussion of self-esteem and each of occupational choice and job searching (see chapter 2) demonstrated the relevance of this personality trait prior to their entry into organizations. Fourth, empirical research has been performed on each of these topics, the results of which lend support to the claims made. As will soon become apparent, there is considerable backing for the plasticity hypothesis, a conclusion most compelling in light of the fact that researchers have investigated very different questions and have used a variety of methodologies to do so.

Peer-group Interaction, Self-esteem, Performance, and Attitudes

The plasticity hypothesis states that low SEs' work behaviors and attitudes are affected by their social environment to a greater extent than are high SEs' behaviors and attitudes. One of the most salient aspects of employees' social environment is their work group. Group theorists have delineated the wide range of social influence processes that occur in the group context (for example, Hackman 1986). More specifically, within their groups, employees may be required to work interdependently with others in order to accomplish the group's tasks. In the process of working with others, they are apt to be exposed to cues for appropriate behavior (for example, ways to optimize performance, norms and values concerning the conduct of the work). Moreover, the group process itself can vary a great deal on dimensions such as cooperativeness, cohesiveness, and supportiveness.

In addition to the fact that interactions with one's work group expose employees to a myriad of social influence processes, it is likely that such processes have great impact on their work behaviors and attitudes. Many studies (Mowday, Porter & Steers 1982) have shown that employees exhibit greater job satisfaction and commitment to the work group to the extent that the group is characterized by high cohesiveness, cooperation, and esprit de corps. The effect of such group properties on productivity is a bit more complicated; if the work group values productivity, then cohesiveness tends to heighten productivity. On the other hand, if the group has established the norm to be non-productive, then cohesiveness should lessen productivity even further (Schachter et al. 1951; Stogdill 1972). The synthesizing principle that can account for the consequences of cohesiveness is that group members are more influenced by the interaction processes within groups that are high rather than low in cohesion; perhaps this is because individuals value their group membership more in the former than the latter case.

Cohesive groups that have developed norms to be productive—for example, in which members cooperate in sharing performance-relevant information, and provide more intangible sources of social support for goal attainment—thus promote positive attitudes and heightened performance. The plasticity hypothesis, furthermore, suggests that group members who are low rather than high in self-esteem are more apt to be the beneficiaries of such a supportive group atmosphere. Low SEs' performance may be especially facilitated because of their tendency to respond to cues for effective performance provided in their work group; the performance of high SEs, who lack the uncertainty that prompts low SEs to be more susceptible to external influence, may be less likely to be facilitated by such a supportive group atmosphere. Moreover, low SEs' satisfaction may be particularly heightened by a supportive work group; not liking themselves, low SEs may be especially dependent on the social approval and support that they receive from their fellow work group members in order to feel good about their jobs. Of course, the plasticity hypothesis also predicts that groups lacking such esprit de corps will have a more negative impact on the work behaviors and attitudes of low rather than high self-esteem group members.

The moderating impact of self-esteem on the relationship between work group processes and each of performance and work attitudes was explored in a field study by Mossholder, Bedeian, and Armenakis (1982). The participants were nursing employees who completed measures of self-esteem and peer-group interaction (PGI). As the authors report, PGI "can be thought of as incorporating activities such as encouraging team effort and group goal attainment, developing and exchanging job related information, and contributing to mutually satisfying relationships through attentive/supportive interpersonal behaviors" (p. 577). Items from this scale include: How much do persons in your work group encourage each other to work as a team?; To what extent do persons in your work group help you find ways to do a better job?; and When you talk with persons in your work group, to what extent do they pay attention to what you're saying?

Measures of the nurses' work attitudes included items tapping propensity to leave (for example, If I were completely free to choose, I would prefer to continue working in this hospital) and job tension (for example, How much do you feel that you have to do things on the job that are against your better judgment?). Work performance was measured by supervisor ratings.

On all three dependent variables—propensity to leave, job tension, and work performance—self-esteem moderated the impact of PGI; more specifically, the tendency for greater PGI supportiveness to reduce both propensity to leave and job tension was significantly more pronounced among low SEs than high SEs. Furthermore, low SEs performed much better when PGI was high rather than low, whereas the work performance of high SEs was uninfluenced by the PGI variable.

Such results have a host of theoretical and practical implications. Theoretically, they support the plasticity hypothesis, and extend its applicability more directly into the organizational context. At the practical level, managers wishing to influence employee performance through work group dynamics need to attend to the effects of individual differences among group members. Work group settings in which there is apt to be a highly supportive PGI may have the most beneficial impact on low SEs. In a more pessimistic vein, work group settings characterized by a nonsupportive PGI may be most detrimental to the performance and attitudes of low SEs. Thus, in assigning individuals to already-formed work groups, managers would be well advised to place low SEs in a high PGI-supportive group, and avoid placing low SEs in low PGI-supportive groups; in fact, Mossholder, Bedeian, and Armenakis's (1982) results showed that high SEs are more apt (than low SEs) to prosper in a low PGI-supportive group.

A second managerial implication concerns the extent to which managers devote their efforts to foster a supportive PGI among their subordinates' work groups. Group dynamics literatures generally stress the need for work groups to develop an atmosphere in which members are mutually supportive of their attempts to attain group goals. If the group manager has little knowledge of the group members' self-esteem, then it probably makes sense to cultivate a supportive PGI; after all, such an atmosphere should help low SEs and not harm the high SEs. However, if the group members generally are known to have high self-esteem, then it may not be prudent or cost effective for managers to devote as much time facilitating a supportive PGI. The managerial effort needed to foster a supportive PGI may be considerable. The results of the Mossholder, Bedeian, and Armenakis's 1982) study suggest that managers' attempts to promote a supportive PGI may not produce enough desirable behavioral and attitudinal outcomes among high SEs to justify the managers' expense. Thus, rather than prescribing that managers always go to great lengths to cultivate a supportive PGI among group members, Mossholder, Bedeian, and Armenakis's (1982) study implies that it is worthwhile for managers to foster a supportive PGI to a greater extent in groups in which at least some of the members are low in self-esteem (than if all members are high in self-esteem). The relative nature of the preceding statement bears repetition. I am not suggesting that managers should not try to foster a supportive PGI in groups in which members are high in self-esteem. Rather, it is simply being suggested that the payoff for managers—in terms of enhancing group members' work attitudes and/or performance—is likely to be greater among members who are low rather than high in self-esteem.

Performance Appraisal, Self-esteem, and Subsequent Performance

Throughout individuals' tenure in their work organization they receive evaluative feedback concerning their performance. This feedback may be transmitted through informal mechanisms (for example, peers and/or coworkers may take them aside during lunch break to inform that they are performing well or poorly); in addition, most organizations have a formal performance-appraisal system through which workers are provided with feedback.

One purpose of the appraisal process—whether informal or formal—is to counsel the recipient of the feedback. Thus, if employees are positively reinforced through feedback for a job well done, they should remain motivated to perform well. Moreover, receiving negative feedback should motivate workers to take corrective action, especially if the means to do so are made clear. The counseling function of the performance appraisal process thus is of great significance to individuals and/or organizations. Most workers perform poorly in some way to varying degrees; the far more severe problem occurs when they fail to take corrective action. Clearly, there are a number of reasons why workers may not take corrective action (for example, their inherent lack of ability, or a reward system that does not encourage improvement). One of those reasons, however, is the inadequacy of the feedback-giving process itself.

Performance-appraisal scholars (Beer 1986) have identified several pitfalls in the performance appraisal process. For one, the evaluator may be prone to a wide variety of errors and biases. Consequently, the evaluative feedback that the worker receives may not be valid. Second, the feedback may be valid, but transmitted in such an insensitive manner that it literally falls on deaf ears. Note the unfortunate "opportunity cost" that the organization incurs in this instance; employees have the chance to receive accurate feedback which, if properly assimilated, may serve to improve their subsequent performance. If the evaluative feedback is delivered inappropriately, then they will fail to capitalize on this opportunity.

A third problem, highly related to the second, is that the evaluator fails to tailor the feedback to the employee. All individuals do not respond identically to the same evaluation; feedback that is motivating for one person may have no effect on, or actually have a negative effect on another. The discussion in chapter 3 on the effects of feedback on subsequent performance suggests that self-esteem may moderate workers' reactions to performance appraisal feedback.

The results of laboratory (Shrauger & Sorman 1977) and field (Brockner, Derr & Laing 1987) studies have shown that negative feedback has a more adverse effect on the subsequent performance of low than high SEs. The fact that low SEs' subsequent performance is affected more negatively by failure feedback than is high SEs' performance has important implications for the performance appraisal process. More specifically, managers somehow must convey negative feedback to low SEs so as to heighten, or at least not dampen, their subsequent performance. Furthermore, negative feedback that adversely affects low SEs may be perfectly appropriate for high SEs. To reiterate, managers must convey feedback—especially negative feedback—in ways that fit the individual being appraised.

How might managers convey negative feedback to low SEs to facilitate (or at least not inhibit) their subsequent performance? To address this practical question, consider a theoretical account of the effects of failure or negative feedback on subsequent performance. Wortman and Brehm (1975) have proposed that negative feedback can facilitate or interfere with subsequent performance. More specifically, individuals initially exhibit increased motivation in response to failure, perhaps as a way to "make up for" the prior setback. If such increased strivings are met with continued failure, however, the individual stops trying; this type of withdrawal response inevitably will lead to poor performance. Furthermore, according to Wortman and Brehm, the importance of the failure feedback moderates both the heightened motivation and withdrawal responses. Failure feedback of greater importance heightens the magnitude of the increase in effort early on, and the withdrawal response later on, in the temporal sequence (see figure 4–1).

The results of several laboratory experiments (Brockner & Elkind 1985; Brockner et al. 1983; Dyck, Vallentyne & Breen 1979; Tennen & Eller 1977) have lent support to the Wortman-Brehm (1975) model. In these studies

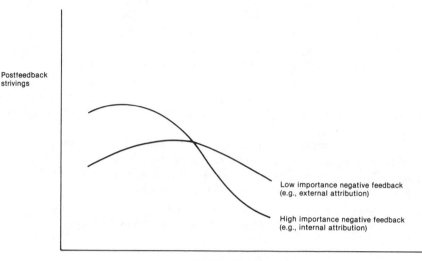

Source: Wortman & Brehm 1975.

Figure 4–1. Wortman and Brehm's Hypothetical Model of Invigoration and Withdrawal

participants were pretreated with negative feedback: all of them performed poorly at a task. For some the duration of their poor performance was relatively short; for others the duration of their failure was more extended. Furthermore, half of the participants were led to attribute their poor performance to internal causes. (These subjects had been informed that most of the previous participants had performed quite well; thus, upon encountering failure, these subjects should be more apt to make an internal attribution.) The remaining half of the participants were led to attribute their poor performance to external causes. (This group was informed that most of the previous participants had performed rather poorly; thus, upon encountering failure, this group should be likely to attribute it to the difficulty of the task.) It seems reasonable that the attribution variable relates to the perceived importance of the failure feedback. Negative feedback attributed to internal causes should be more ego-involving or significant than negative feedback due to external factors.

Consistent with the Wortman-Brehm (1975) model depicted in figure 4–1, it has been shown that subsequent to a failure of a short duration, participants perform better if the attribution for that failure is internal (high importance) rather than external (low importance). In addition, subsequent to a longer duration failure, participants perform worse if the attribution is internal rather than external.

What about self-esteem? If low SEs generally are more behaviorally plastic, and if they are more susceptible to the influence of failure in particular, then it stands to reason that they would be more affected by the characteristics of the failure. If the duration of, and attribution for, failure interactively affect individuals' subsequent work performance, then these factors should have an even stronger impact on those low rather than high in self-esteem. In fact, this is precisely what has been found (see table 4–1). The Wortman and Brehm (1975) model suggests that workers' tendency to perform better following a short-duration rather than a long-duration failure should be more true in the high importance (internal attribution) than low importance (external attribution) condition. Such a tendency was exhibited to a far greater extent by the low than high SEs (see table 4–1).

Although the data in table 4–1 make an important theoretical point, there are at least four difficulties associated with trying to extrapolate from such results to the issue of how managers may convey negative feedback to their subordinates. First, the external validity of the results from these laboratory studies should be established before we can more definitely offer managerial prescriptions for performance appraisal. Second, on the assumption that the results of the laboratory studies are replicated in more ecologically valid settings, managers still will have to distinguish between failure of short versus long duration. This distinction is crucial given that perceived importance seems to interact with failure duration in affecting subsequent performance. Third, and related to the second, managers will need to be able to identify their low versus high self-esteem subordinates. As mentioned previously in this chapter, performance appraisals may be ineffective because the feedback provided was not tailored to the recipient. Appraisal-related factors that have a dramatic impact on low SEs may have little or no effect on the high SEs. Fourth, and finally, we must consider the validity of the performance appraisal itself. In table 4–1 it was shown that low SEs performed relatively well in the small-failure/internal and large-failure/external attribution conditions. In the latter

Table 4–1
Number of Anagrams Solved as a Function of Self-esteem, Attribution for Failure, and Duration of Failure

Self-esteem	Attribution for Failure	Duration of Failure	
		Short	Long
High	Internal	15.26	16.40
	External	14.60	15.58
Low	Internal	17.06	14.00
	External	13.80	16.58

Source: Brockner & Elkind 1985, p. 358.
Note: Higher scores reflect better performance; maximum = 20.

case, the attribution feedback was veridical; the reason why subjects performed poorly on the previous task was in fact due to the difficulty of the task. In the former case, however, the attributional information was false; subjects were merely led to believe that the reason for their failure was internal rather than external. The following managerial dilemma is thus implied: should managers ever convey false feedback to subordinates, if that feedback is expected to heighten the subordinates' subsequent performance? Given that the function of management is one of task accomplishment through other people, then it could be argued, on the one hand, that managers have license to distort reality, if in so doing they will elicit greater subordinate productivity.

On the other hand, however, it may be costly—both intrapersonally and interpersonally—for the manager to act in such deceptive ways. For one, the manager may experience considerable role conflict (between performing his managerial duties and acting in an ethically appropriate fashion). Moreover, acting deceptively, even if for the "betterment" of the organization, may set a dangerous precedent for performing other, perhaps even more unethical behaviors.

At the interpersonal level, the subordinate may suffer some negative consequences. Upon being given false information, they may fail to take certain corrective measures that may ultimately bolster their longer term performance. For example, what if workers were inappropriately informed that the cause of their poor performance was external (rather than internal)? The external attribution may facilitate subsequent performance in the short run; however, an internal attribution may have motivated the employees to take part in a training and development course intended to remedy their deficiencies. Having done so, their longer term productivity prognosis may be enhanced to an even greater degree. In addition, managers who convey false evaluative feedback run the risk of losing credibility—perhaps irreparably—if they are caught in their deceptive acts.

Employees' self-esteem may dictate the impact of evaluative (and especially negative) feedback on their subsequent behavior. This assertion has a host of theoretical and practical implications, and for that reason I encourage further research exploring the moderating effect of self-esteem in response to evaluative feedback. Moreover, it is important for such future research efforts to be well-grounded in theory. The underlying framework utilized here (Wortman & Brehm 1975) is a structural model; it focuses on the factors that affect the impact of negative feedback on individuals' subsequent motivation.

Yet another way for future researchers to consider the moderating impact of self-esteem in response to evaluative feedback is to adopt a process model of feedback, such as the one proposed by Ilgen, Fisher, and Taylor (1979). According to the process model of Ilgen, Fisher, and Taylor, the effect of feedback on subsequent behavior can be fractionated into a series of psychological events in which individuals perceive the feedback, evaluate its validity or accuracy, determine whether they are personally responsible for the outcome of the behavior(s) being evaluated, assess whether they wish to improve their subsequent behavior, translate such desires for improvement into specific goals, and, finally, act on their goals for improvement. Future research may proceed by considering the role of self-esteem at each step in the feedback process. For instance, Dipboye (1987) recently has employed this process model to explain why feedback often does not have its intended corrective effects on employee behavior. His basic thesis is that employees often exhibit defensive or otherwise self-serving reactions at each step in the process, so that potentially useful evaluative feedback falls on deaf ears.

Moreover, one of the factors that Dipboye suggests may moderate the degree of the self-serving reactions to feedback at each step in the process is employees' level of self-esteem. For example, high SEs tend to hold more favorable perceptions of their performance than low SEs, even if there is no objective performance difference between the two groups (Brockner & Lloyd 1986; King & Manaster 1977; Shrauger 1972). In addition, there is some evidence that high SEs make more internal (external) attributions for positive (negative) feedback than their low self-esteem counterparts (for example, Adler 1980; Fitch 1970). Moreover, Dipboye suggests that self-esteem may relate to other steps in the process model, including individuals' desire to succeed on subsequent tasks and their future goal setting. The point is that the postfeedback behavior is actually the culmination of a series of psychological events that preceded it; in order to understand and predict the way in which self-esteem moderates the impact of feedback on subsequent behavior, it is necessary to delineate the relationship between self-esteem and each of the psychological events that are believed to occur within the process model.

Future research also needs to explore the role of self-esteem in individuals' feedback-seeking tendencies. As Ashford and Cummings (1983) point out, the existing feedback literature offers an overly reactive view of individuals' role in the feedback process. According to most analyses, the organization provides feedback to employees (in various forms) and the employees respond to the feedback (as in the model offered by Ilgen, Fisher & Taylor 1979). Ashford and Cummings suggest that it is more accurate to say that individuals seek feedback on a proactive basis. Such feedback-seeking strategies include monitoring (that is, observing the information environment and in particular the behavior of other actors for useful feedback cues), and inquiry (that is, directly asking others for feedback). The Ashford and Cummings analysis suggests that prior to the processes individuals exhibit in reacting to feedback, they may engage in a variety of feedback-seeking behaviors; moreover, it is possible that their self-esteem will relate to the amount and/or specific nature of feedback-seeking behaviors.

For example, it has been shown that poor performers tend to avoid self-diagnostic information (Zuckerman et al. 1979) presumably in order to ward off the blow to their self-esteem associated with receiving negative feedback. It is possible that low SEs, who at least tend to think that they are poor performers, will be more likely to avoid self-diagnostic feedback than their high self-esteem counterparts (Ashford 1986; Brockner & Wallnau 1981). Moreover, much research has shown that individuals process information in ways consistent with their existing level of self-esteem (see Shrauger 1975; for a review). If so, then low SEs may draw different conclusions than high SEs about the meaning of the feedback that they have sought; for example, low SEs may interpret evaluative feedback much more negatively than high SEs, even if there is no objective difference in the nature of the feedback. In addition, whether low and high SEs differ in their tendencies to use the monitoring versus inquiry strategy of feedback-seeking is worth exploring.

Previous research has demonstrated support for the plasticity hypothesis, particularly in the context of how negative feedback affects subsequent performance (for example, Brockner, Derr & Laing 1987; Brockner & Elkind 1985; Shrauger & Sorman 1977). Still, one cannot help but believe that past research only has scratched the surface in its quest to uncover the role of self-esteem in the feedback process. Future research might proceed by exploring the relationship between self-esteem and the various processes associated with the receipt of feedback, as in the model offered by Ilgen, Fisher, and Taylor (1979); and/or the various aspects of employees' proactive feedback-seeking behavior, as analyzed by Ashford and Cummings (1983).

Feedback, Self-esteem, and Interpersonal Communication

The preceding section suggests that negative feedback will elicit very different reactions from high and low SEs, such that the latter group's performance is dampened to a greater extent than the former's. The differential influence of negative feedback on low versus high SEs has been confined thus far to the domain of job performance. However, it seems likely that negative feedback differentially influences other work behaviors of low and high SEs.

Interpersonal communication is such an example. Scholars and practitioners alike are acutely aware of the role of communication processes as determinants of organizational effectiveness. Sometimes inappropriate information is communicated; in other instances information is communicated when it should not have been, and as the aftermath of the Challenger disaster has implied, information may be withheld when it should not have been.

Consider the following example of a communication dilemma, originally introduced at the outset of chapter 3. An employee (Party A) recommends a change in some workplace procedure to his or her superior (Party B). This recommendation sounds reasonable, causing Party B to suggest to his or her superior (Party C) that it be implemented. Suppose further that Party C approves the implementation, but that contrary to the expectations of all concerned the new procedure produces negative outcomes for the organization. Would the negative feedback associated with the prior suggestion make individuals more unwilling to communicate other plausible suggestions for organizational improvement? Will Party A be unwilling to offer other suggestions? Moreover, if Party A does communicate other ideas, will Party B be willing to recommend the implementation of those ideas to Party C? Of greatest current concern, how might the self-esteem level of Party A and/or Party B influence the impact of the negative feedback on their subsequent willingness to communicate?

The latter question—that is, the moderating impact of Party B's self-esteem—was addressed in a study by Brockner, Derr, and Laing in 1987. Undergraduate students of varying self-esteem levels were instructed to play the role of a manager in a hypothetical organization. They read the following scenario:

> You are a supervisor in a manufacturing company. You have been with the company for five years. You have been praised by your manager on several occasions for your excellent work record. The company has a suggestions-award program, which encourages employees to submit suggestions to improve workplace procedures. Recently, one of your employees submitted a suggestion to you which recommended that days of stockage of parts on hand be reduced in your section. He told you that he had checked with suppliers and that they had assured him that they could supply parts on a seventy-two-hour turnaround from the date of ordering. Of course, you were interested because this would enable you to cut down on the cost of maintaining inventory. You also checked things out and found your employee's information to be substantially correct. So, you endorsed your employee's suggestion upward to your boss. Shortly, management approved the suggestion and your boss directed you to implement the new parts ordering procedure in your section (pp. 325–326).

Three feedback conditions were created. Two groups of subjects were informed that the new procedure yielded negative outcomes ("after you implemented the new procedure there was a time when the entire assembly line was in danger of being shut down because your section was not able to provide the subassemblies for which your section is responsible"). Moreover, one of these two groups received information designed to heighten the degree of threat associated with this negative feedback. In this threatening-failure condition, subjects were told that they were severely criticized by their boss and that any repetition of this kind would probably result in their censure in the company. The other group of negative feedback participants—that is, those in the failure condition—were not given the latter information. Finally, a third group of participants were not provided with any feedback about the outcome of the new procedure (control condition).

All participants were then given an opportunity to recommend to their superior another subordinate's suggestion for procedural change. Specifically, subjects were told:

> This morning, while you were drinking coffee in the supervisor's break room, another of your employees brought a suggestion to you. Your employee suggests a change in assembly line procedure which would tie together three steps of the current procedure into one and thereby increase efficiency and increase the amount of output from your section. On the surface, your employee's suggestion seems to have merit (p. 326).

All participants then indicated the extent to which they would be willing to recommend the subordinate's suggestion to their immediate superior; of greatest interest was the relationship between participants' self-esteem and their willingness to communicate.

The plasticity hypothesis suggests that the feedback variable will have greater impact on low SEs' (than on high SEs') willingness to communicate. In particular, low SEs should be less willing to communicate if they have received negative feedback than if they have not, especially if the degree of threat associated with the feedback has been heightened. This prediction of the low SEs' behavior seems to follow directly from the psychological bases of plasticity.

1. Uncertainty. Lacking certainty in their own reactions to the subordinates' new suggestion, low SEs may have been especially susceptible to influence by cues from their environment concerning appropriate behavior. Their environment had just jolted them with negative feedback, especially in the threatening-failure condition. As a consequence, low SEs may have inferred that being unwilling to communicate the new suggestion was the more prudent course of action.

2. Need for approval/self-presentational. Not liking themselves, low SEs may have been particularly dependent upon receiving a positive evaluation from their superior. Low SEs thus may have inferred that by repeating a behavior that had just elicited negative feedback they would be unlikely to receive the sought-after positive evaluation; moreover, the motivation to receive positive feedback should be heightened even further in the threatening-failure condition.

3. Self-diagnosticity. The negative feedback may have a greater effect on low SEs because this group is prone to interpret evaluative feedback—especially that which is negative—as self-diagnostic. Said differently, the negative feedback may have led low SEs to infer, "I can't do anything right. Therefore, I better keep my mouth shut this time."

Table 4–2
Willingness to Recommend New Suggestion as a Function of Self-esteem and Feedback

	Feedback		
Self-esteem	*Threatening Failure*	*Failure*	*Control*
High	5.35	5.09	5.32
Low	3.58	4.14	5.56

Source: Brockner, Derr & Laing 1987, p. 327.
Note: Scores could range from 1–7, with higher scores reflecting greater willingness.

The results confirmed predictions (see table 4–2). High SEs' willingness to communicate was relatively high in all three instances, and unaffected by the experimental treatment. Low SEs, in sharp contrast, were highly willing to communicate in the control condition; however, they were far less willing to do so if they had just received negative feedback. Their reluctance to communicate was heightened even further by the threat associated with the negative feedback.

Such findings are perfectly consistent with the plasticity hypothesis. Furthermore, they extend the range of dependent variables, which show high and low SEs' differential susceptibility to influence. Further research should explore whether other employee behaviors are jointly affected by prior feedback and self-esteem. For example, does the self-esteem level of bank loan officers moderate the effect of negative feedback concerning an initial loan on their willingness to make additional loans (to the same client, or even different clients)? Does the self-esteem level of entrepreneurs moderate the effect of negative feedback concerning an initial venture on their tendency to engage in other entrepreneurial behaviors? Pending further research, it tentatively can be suggested that individuals' self-esteem may moderate the impact of evaluative, and especially negative, feedback on a host of their behaviors within the organizational setting. This "syndrome" of behavioral responses to feedback, furthermore, may stem from the same underlying psychological processes: the very bases of behavioral plasticity.

Two other aspects of the results in table 4–2 are worthy of mention. First, the findings were based on a role-playing methodology in which college students were asked to respond as managers. Whether similar findings would emerge in actual organizations, in which managers rather than college students serve as participants, is an empirical question.

Second, it is clear that the negative feedback—especially in the threatening-failure condition—caused low SEs to be much less willing to communicate the new suggestion than their higher self-esteem counterparts. Far less certain, however, is whether it was the high or low SEs who responded more adaptively to the negative feedback. On the one hand, it could be argued that the high SEs responded more appropriately. After all, the new suggestion should be evaluated on its own merits. If it seems to be an idea whose implementation will benefit the individual and/or the organization, then it may well be prudent to communicate that information to one's superior. On the other hand, it could have been the low SEs who acted smarter. Perhaps this group learned to look before they leaped. Previous research (Weiss & Knight 1980) has shown that low SEs tend to engage in greater information search than high SEs prior to solving a problem. As a result, low SEs may solve problems more effectively than high SEs in those instances in which information search is positively related to problem-solving efficacy. Low SEs thus may have been reluctant to communicate the new suggestion due to their desire to seek additional information. Given the immediately prior negative consequence of acting without a thorough information search, they may have been unwilling to act so hastily again. More generally, this reasoning raises another important theoretical and practical issue: the adaptive value of behavioral plasticity (see chapter 5).

Socialization, Self-esteem, and Role-taking Tendencies

Scholars and practitioners alike have long been interested in the socialization processes through which individuals learn information that is relevant to their lives as members of the organization. When employees initially enter organizations, their experiences are bound to be filled with uncertainty. How can I most efficiently perform my work? How should I relate to my coworkers? What kinds of behaviors are inappropriate in my interactions with my boss? How can I climb the career ladder in this organization? How should I dress? These may be some of the dozens of issues that confront new employees. Their degree of success as organization members will depend, to a large extent, on their ability to learn the answers to these and other questions.

Just as new employees have lots of questions (that is, uncertainty) about appropriate work behaviors and attitudes, organizations, for their part, attempt to socialize the new employees so that they adopt the work roles and values that the organization prescribes. Moreover, the socialization practices that organizations use can vary dramatically. Certain organizations have concrete, institutionalized ways of socializing its new recruits, in which the organization goes to great lengths to inculcate its desired norms and values in the new hires. Other organizations adopt more of a laissez-faire approach to socialization; the strategy in the latter instance is more one of letting the new employees figure things out for themselves.

Building on the work of Van Maanen and Schein (1979), Jones (1986) recently has described a host of dimensions of organizations' socialization styles that seem related to the institutional versus laissez-faire distinction drawn here, including collectivism, formality, predictability, and social support. *Collectivism* refers to the extent to which "new recruits go through common learning experiences designed to produce standardized responses to situations" (Jones 1986, p. 264). *Formality* refers to the extent to which new employees are separated from other organizational members while they learn their work responsibilities (for example, through an offsite orientation program). *Predictability* pertains to newcomers being given information about the sequence of activities and experiences they will encounter in their tenure in the organization (for example, the career ladder), including the timetable associated with the sequence of activities and experiences. Social support refers to the extent to which the socialization process includes mentoring behavior by more experienced colleagues, as well as supportive reactions from coworkers and supervisors alike. Institutional socialization practices are high in collectivism, formality, predictability, and social support, whereas laissez-faire ones are not.

It is not being suggested that the institutional socialization style is unilaterally more favorable than the laissez-faire style (for the employees and/or the organization). On the one hand, the institutional style reduces members' uncertainty about appropriate work behaviors and attitudes, and thereby encourages them to adopt the organization's perspective. On the other hand, the laissez-faire style requires employees to shift for themselves, and in so doing, might facilitate a more innovative problem-solving style.

Jones (1986) explored the relationship between an organization's socialization style and employees' role-taking tendencies; that is, the dependent variable was whether the new recruits adopted a "custodial" or "innovative" role. The former refers to accepting the status quo (as defined by the organization) and passively accepting the basic requirements of tasks or roles; the latter refers to newcomers deciding "to change the methods for performing their roles or even their missions" (Jones 1986, p. 264).

The comparison between institutional and laissez-faire socialization styles is meant to suggest that self-esteem may moderate the relationship between organizations' socialization style and employees' role-taking tendencies. Given that the entry period is filled with uncertainty, it stands to reason that low SEs—who are generally more uncertain about the correctness of their own ways of thinking and acting—will be more susceptible to influence by the external agent (that is, the organizations' socialization style). In particular, low SEs should be more apt than high SEs to adopt a custodial role orientation in response to an institutional style of socialization.

In his study on the relationship between organizations' socialization style and employees' role-taking tendencies, Jones (1986) also explored the moderating impact of self-efficacy (Bandura 1977), an individual difference variable closely related to self-esteem (see chapter 2). As predicted, institutional socialization was associated with more custodial (less innovative) role adoption on the part of the new employees. In addition, and in support of the plasticity hypothesis, the relationship described here was considerably more pronounced among the employees who were low rather than high in self-efficacy.

The fact that employees' self-efficacy moderated the socialization/role-adoption relationship has considerable implications for organizational socialization processes. To cite merely one, it offers one explanation of the failure of certain socialization styles to have their intended effects; it just may be that employees who are high in self-esteem—confident of their own definition of the work situation—will be less prone to influence by an institutional socialization style.

More generally, the Jones (1986) study not only supports the plasticity hypothesis, but also suggests that researchers interested in the socialization process may wish to consider whether employees' self-esteem is a relevant (moderator) variable in their theoretical and empirical efforts. For example, is it the case that low self-esteem renders employees susceptible to influence by all sorts of socialization styles? The results of the Jones (1986) study merely enabled us to conclude that low SEs were more likely than high SEs to adopt a custodial role orientation in response to an institutional (rather than laissez-faire) socialization style; the study did not necessarily demonstrate that low SEs were more apt than high SEs to adopt an innovative role orientation as a function of a laissez-faire style. Based on the discussion of the nature of low self-esteem, it seems likely that low SEs can be more easily influenced than high SEs into a custodial role orientation (by an institutional style of socialization); however, this does not necessarily mean that low SEs can be more easily manipulated (than high SEs) to become more innovative (in the face of a laissez-faire style). The custodial role orientation seems more similar to low SEs' customary style than does the innovative one. Thus, an important task for future researchers interested in the moderating impact of self-esteem in organizations' socialization styles is to determine which styles are most likely to yield support for the plasticity hypothesis. As discussed in greater detail in chapter 5, low SEs are not always more prone to influence by external cues than their high self-esteem counterparts.

Modeling, Self-esteem, and Leadership Behavior

Although employees' rate of learning about appropriate work behaviors and attitudes probably is at its greatest during their early tenure in the organization, the acquisition of job-related information is an ongoing process. Much of the learning that takes place in organizations is based on direct reinforcement. Indeed, there is a growing awareness in organizations that principles of behavior modification may be fruitfully applied to enhance employees' learning of their necessary duties (Luthans & Kreitner 1975). Just as clearly, however, reinforcement does not seem to be necessary for learning to occur. A number of organizational scholars (Manz & Sims 1981; Weiss 1977) have noted that employees acquire vast amounts of information vicariously, by observing the behaviors of relevant models.

Much of the early research on modeling processes consisted of laboratory experiments intended to delineate the effects of various model characteristics on the observers' degree of imitative behavior (Bandura 1971). Some of the factors shown to have a positive effect on imitative behavior include the model's similarity to the observer, likability, and successfulness. There has been far less research on the impact of observer characteristics and of the interaction between model and observer characteristics on the extent to which observers match the model's behavior.

The plasticity analysis suggests that the observer's self-esteem may be an important determinant of imitative behavior. On the assumption that the model is an appropriate source of information—that is, the model is reasonably successful, competent, and/or similar to the observer—there are several reasons to expect low SEs to exhibit greater imitative behavior than their high self-esteem counterparts. First, appropriate models convey information about how one should think, feel, and act. Of course, individuals should be more reliant on models' cues to the extent that they are uncertain of the appropriateness of their own beliefs and behaviors. As discussed in the section on socialization, low SEs tend to be less certain than high SEs about many self-aspects, including the correctness of their beliefs and behaviors.

Second, low SEs may be more likely to imitate models to the extent that their relationship with the model includes some degree of dependency; that is, if the observer is dependent upon the model to dole out some reward, then the observer may imitate the model as an act of ingratiation (Jones 1964). Presumably, by making himself seem similar to the model, the observer attempts to win favor in the model's eyes, and thereby increase the chance that the model will respond favorably to the observer. Given low SEs' greater (than high SEs') need for approval, the former group may be more likely to make themselves appear similar to the model.

The role of self-esteem on modeling processes was tested in a study by Weiss (1977). In this field study, first level supervisors and their direct superiors independently described their own leadership behaviors. The amount of modeling—that is, the degree of similarity in these ratings—was assessed as a function of three attributes of the model (that is, the superior) and the self-esteem of the observer (that is, the first level supervisor). Attributes of the model included his or her success in the organization, competence, and reward power over the observer. The latter measure referred to the observers' beliefs about the model's control over valued resources (for example, "How much does your supervisor's opinion determine whether or not you receive a raise in salary?").

Consistent with previous research on the effects of the model's attributes per se, there was a significant tendency for subordinates to imitate the model to the extent that the model was seen as successful or competent. Contrary to predictions, there was no relationship between the model's perceived reward power and the observers' imitation of the model. Of greater importance was the moderating impact of the observers' self-esteem in the relationships described. The results were highly consistent with the plasticity hypothesis (see table 4–3). For low SEs, there were significant positive relationships between each of the model's success, competence, and reward power and the extent to which the superior and subordinates' leadership behaviors were similar. High SEs, in sharp contrast, did not imitate their superior as a function of the model's attributes.

It is worth mentioning that different bases of plasticity could have accounted for the results in table 4–3. More specifically, the significant effect of the model's success and competence on low (but not high) SEs' imitative behavior may have been mediated by the former group's greater uncertainty concerning the correctness of their leadership behaviors. When in a state of uncertainty, observers should be especially attentive to the information conveyed by high credibility models: those deemed to be successful and/or competent.

The significant impact of the model's reward power on low (but not high) SEs' degree of modeling may have been due to low SEs' greater need for approval. In other words, low SEs may have mimicked models of relatively high reward power in order to ingratiate themselves. If their attempts at ingratiation were successful, then low SEs might gain the benefits of their superior's high reward power.

Weiss (1977) has demonstrated that the plasticity hyphthesis is applicable to the modeling of leadership behaviors. Furthermore, there is reason to think that the plasticity hypothesis is germane to a wide variety of modeling processes in organizations. Peers may provide cues concerning appropriate problem-solving strategies, modes of social interaction, styles of dress, and work values (Weiss 1978), to name a few. Mentors (Kram 1983) may model not only leadership behaviors, but also cues for appropriate career management and methods of efficient work performance. In short, vicarious experience may be a pervasive process by which individuals learn the ropes in their work organizations. Further research is needed to determine whether, as we suspect, low self-esteem employees are more susceptible to a model's influence across a variety of organizational contexts (Brockner, O'Malley, Hite & Davies 1987). Moreover, future research should identify the delimiting conditions of the inverse relationship between self-esteem and modeling. It may be that employees, especially those low rather than high in self-esteem, are most prone to the influence of a model during their initial period of job tenure (as in the study by Jones 1986). During this stage of socialization, workers' uncertainty

Table 4–3
Correlations Between Subordinates' and Supervisors' Behaviors as a Function
of Subordinates' Self-esteem

	Attribute of Supervisor		
Subordinates' Self-esteem	Success	Competence	Reward Power
High	–.16 (*p* < .10)	–.10	–.02
Low	.16 (*p* < .10)	.36 (*p* < .01)	.48 (*p* < .01)

Source: Weiss 1977, p. 98.
Note: More positive correlations reflect greater similarity between subordinates' and supervisors' behaviors.

levels may be considerable (and heightened even further among low SEs), enabling the model to have a high degree of impact.

Stress, Self-esteem, Performance, and Satisfaction

Employees often are exposed to stressors in their work organizations, such as conflictual relationships with their coworkers, emotionally draining (for example, repetitive) work, a noxious physical environment, and competitive external market conditions. Some stressors are chronic, others acute. In any event, stress is no trivial matter in work organizations; excessive levels may cause workers to perform suboptimally, to feel dissatisfied, to want to leave the organization, and to develop painful physical and/or psychological symptoms. Indeed, many organizations are searching for innovative ways to help control employees' stress (Mitchell 1982; Steers 1984). Witness, for example, the growing popularity of programs in stress management.

One major source of organizational stress stems from employees' role perceptions. For a variety of reasons, individuals often perform multiple duties that are in direct conflict with one another. For example, in matrix organizations individuals have at least two formal superiors. If these superiors place demands on the subordinate that are in direct opposition to one another then the subordinate is likely to experience role conflict. Other types of role strain include role overload and role ambiguity. In role overload, employees' jobs require them to perform duties associated with too many roles. For example, managers often report that one of the more stressful aspects of their jobs is that they have to play too many roles: administrator, technical expert, psychologist, politician. Role ambiguity refers to instances in which the individuals' formal responsibilities are not clear. As a result, the employee is constantly in a state of uncertainty concerning his exact job duties.

In general, the stress associated with various role perceptions can be considerable. However, there is reason to expect such stressors to have greater adverse impact on low SEs than high SEs, a notion perfectly compatible with the plasticity hypothesis. Why? Low SEs are more uncertain about the appropriateness of their work behaviors and attitudes. Consequently, they are more likely to be influenced by work-related environmental cues. In theory, the formal duties associated with one's work role should provide much information concerning appropriate modes of behavior. What would happen, however, if the cues stemming from one's role include the various sources of role strain? All else being equal, it should be the individuals who are most reliant on role-related information—for example, low SEs—who should be most influenced by such sources of role strain.

There is an additional reason to posit that low SEs will be more (adversely) affected by the stress of role strain than their high self-esteem counterparts. By their very nature, stressors test individuals' coping abilities. High SEs' greater self-confidence may enable them to ward off the impact of the stress to a greater extent than low SEs. Not only, then, are low SEs more likely to experience the stress of role strain (due to their greater reliance on external cues), but also low SEs may be more apt to exhibit the negative consequences of role strain (due to their lower perceived abilities to cope with the stress).

A study by Mossholder, Bedeian, and Armenakis (1981) explored the effects of various role strains and self-esteem on work performance and attitudes. Participants were nursing employees at a large hospital in the Southeast. They completed measures of role conflict (for example, "I work under incompatible policies and guidelines"), role ambiguity (for example, "I know what my responsibilities are"), self-esteem, and job satisfaction. Employee performance was determined by supervisory ratings. The results of this study are presented in table 4–4. Consistent with the plasticity hypothesis, only the job performance and satisfaction of low SEs was significantly (and negatively) affected by the various role strains. Role ambiguity led to decreased satisfaction and role conflict produced poorer performance—but only among low SEs.

While the data in table 4–4 support the plasticity hypothesis, several limitations of those findings should be mentioned. First, they were obtained only for those employees at lower organizational levels (licensed practical nurses and nurse assistants). For those employees at a higher level (registered nurses and nurse practitioners), there were significant (negative) correlations between role strain and satisfaction, but self-esteem did not play a moderating role. Moreover, at the higher level there was no overall correlation between role strain and performance, and self-esteem did not play a moderating role. In essence, such findings suggest that the moderating impact of self-esteem in stress reactions is, in turn, moderated by other factors. Perhaps the employees at the higher levels generally were high in self-esteem, making subgroup analyses (as in table 4–4) impossible or incapable of detecting any moderating effect of self-esteem.

Table 4–4

Correlations Between Role Ambiguity and Satisfaction, and Between Role Conflict and Performance as a Function of Self-esteem

Self-esteem	Role Ambiguity/Satisfaction	Role Conflict/Performance
High	$-.19 \ (p < .10)$	.14
Low	$-.48 \ (p < .001)$	$-.30 \ (p < .05)$

Source: Mossholder, Bedeian & Armenakis 1981.

Second, the results in table 4–4 merely demonstrate that for low SEs certain types of role strain are associated with particular outcomes; however, they do not explain why role ambiguity led to decreased satisfaction (but not performance), whereas role conflict led to decreased performance (but not satisfaction). Mossholder, Bedeian, and Armenakis (1981) speculate that this pattern of results may have been a function of the setting in which the study was conducted.

> It is plausible that role ambiguity would generally not affect performance in a hospital setting since in such environments professional ethics and performance standards are fixed by accrediting and professional bodies. . . . Employees working in the nursing field could rely on external guidelines to provide clarity in the face of role ambiguity. In contrast, conflict itself may be institutionalized in settings like hospitals where role conflict stems largely from the dual authority system (administrative and professional) commonly present in such structures. Given this condition it is reasonable to assume that the performance of . . . (high self-esteem individuals) who are generally less affected by negative or conflicting environmental stimuli should be better than the performance of . . . (low self-esteem individuals) who are more susceptible to such stimuli (p. 232).

In addition to raising issues of theoretical significance, the findings of Mossholder, Bedeian, and Armenakis (1981) are replete with practical implications. A basic tenet of managerial psychology is that subordinates must be well suited for their jobs in order to enhance individual and organizational outcomes. That general dictum can be applied to this specific situation. If subordinates are low in self-esteem, then it would seem especially important for managers to minimize the various sources of role strain that subordinates might encounter in their jobs. For example, managers may do a careful role analysis to ensure that it does not expose the role occupant to excessively conflicting and/or ambiguous demands. If the role analysis suggests such sources of role strain are present, then managers may attempt to reduce or eliminate the role strain (for example, by providing the occupant with more explicit job descriptions to reduce ambiguity). Note that such managerial efforts may be less necessary if the subordinate is high rather than low in self-esteem.

Of course, the inherent nature of some jobs is such that it must expose the incumbent to considerable levels of role strain (for example, individuals who occupy boundary-spanning positions). At least two options are open to the manager in such instances. First, they can exert influence during the selection process to ensure that the "right" individuals are matched to particular jobs. If the job is believed to be associated with little role strain, then it probably matters little whether the occupant is of low or high self-esteem. On the other hand, if the job is known to induce a good deal of role strain, then it may be more necessary for the occupant to be high rather than low in self-esteem.

Second, if a job must (inevitably) encompass considerable role strain, and if a low self-esteem person must (inevitably) occupy that job, then it is important for managers to create a work environment that either attempts to enhance the individual's self-esteem or, at the very least, does not activate the individual's low self-esteem. As implied by previous sections in this chapter, fostering a supportive peer group interaction or delivering performance appraisals in a nonthreatening way are two managerial actions that should have beneficial impact on low SEs; such managerial behaviors may go a long way toward buffering the effects of role-related stress on the work behaviors and attitudes of low SEs.

Layoffs, Self-esteem, and Survivor Reactions

Employees may be exposed to the impact of more acute stressful stimuli in addition to chronic sources of stress, such as the discomfort of role strain. Acute stressors refer to those temporary, albeit sometimes quite dramatic events that tax employees' coping abilities. An extreme example of acute stress occurred at Arrow Electronics in 1980. While attending a convention in Westchester County in New York, many of the key executives perished in a hotel fire. Needless to say, this event had a highly stressful impact on the remaining employees, and threatened Arrow's very existence.

Less extreme than the Arrow example, but still quite significant, is the stress produced by work layoffs. It is quite evident that work layoffs are extremely stressful for those individuals who are laid off. Indeed, much research has explored the psychological and sociological effects of becoming unemployed (for example, Eisenberg & Lazarsfeld, 1938; Kaufman 1982; Warr 1983). An intriguing possibility that has received far less attention is that work layoffs also may be quite stressful for those individuals who are not laid off: the so-called survivors in the organization.

Elsewhere I have described in detail an organizing framework with which to study the effects of layoffs on survivors (Brockner 1988). The framework consists of three components. First, layoffs have the potential to elicit a variety of stressful psychological states in survivors, including job insecurity (for example, if the layoff is expected to be followed by additional cutbacks); positive inequity or guilt (Adams 1965); for example, if survivors perceive that they, rather than their dismissed coworkers, could have been laid off); and anger (for example, if the layoff is perceived to be unnecessary or illegitimate).

Second, the psychological states have the potential to affect a variety of survivors' work behaviors (performance, turnover) and attitudes (commitment, satisfaction). For example, job insecurity may affect performance in an "inverted-U" fashion, as a special case of the relationship between anxiety and performance (Yerkes & Dodson 1908); very low or high levels of job insecurity might interfere with performance (though for different reasons), whereas moderate levels of insecurity might actually facilitate performance. Positive inequity or survivor guilt may heighten survivors' work motivation, and thus lead to an increase in performance. Anger might cause survivors to act out their feelings in the form of reduced performance.

The third component of the organizing framework considers the factors that moderate the actual impact of layoffs on survivors' work behaviors and attitudes. The moderator variables are relevant at two points in the organizing framework: the effect of the layoff on the survivors' psychological states, and the influence of the psychological states on work behaviors and attitudes. The moderator variables are drawn from five categories of factors including the nature of the work, the formal organization, the informal organization, external (to the organization) affairs, and, of greatest current relevance, individual differences between survivors.

An example from each of the first four categories is presented here.

1. The nature of the work. Layoff survivors are apt to feel more insecure and/or positive inequity to the extent that they were task-interdependent rather than independent with their dismissed coworker.

2. The formal organization. Layoff survivors may feel more insecure and angry if the organization fails to provide compensatory services to the laid-off workers (for example, outplacement, severance pay).

3. The informal organization. Historically, the normative behavior in some organizations (for example, Kodak) is not to lay off workers in times of hardship. As a result, employees in such organizations come to expect job security. What would happen, however, if these organizations violated their historical standards and workers' expectations by implementing layoffs (as Kodak has done recently, in a reversal of form)? It seems likely that norm-violating layoffs are more anger-arousing because of their questionable legitimacy—both in the eyes of those laid off and those remaining—than are those which are not unexpected.

4. External factors. If workers who are laid off are unable to find reason-

ably comparable work elsewhere, then the survivors are likely to feel heightened sources of emotional upset. This could occur, for example, if the layoffs are implemented by an organization that is the predominant employer in the geographic region.

What about self-esteem? It is quite possible that this individual difference variable will influence the impact of such situational factors as the nature of the work, the informal and formal organization, and external considerations. More specifically, the plasticity hypothesis posits that such factors will have a greater effect on survivors who are low rather than high in self-esteem. For example, let us assume that the layoff is one that evokes job-insecurity-produced anxiety. Survivors may be worried about their ability to retain their jobs, especially if they believe that the likelihood of their own retention is dependent upon their postlayoff performance. (Interestingly enough, there is anecdotal evidence that survivors do, in fact, believe that the basis of future layoff decisions is on the merit of their work motivation and performance, even when such a basis does not enter into the thinking of top management who makes such decisions.) Possessing greater self-confidence in their abilities, high SEs probably will feel less job-insecurity-produced anxiety than low self-esteem survivors. Whether such self-efficacy beliefs are realistic is another matter. It is simply being suggested that high SEs believe that they can perform better than low SEs; such beliefs on the part of high SEs may reduce their job-insecurity-produced anxiety.

It is also possible that survivors low in self-esteem will be more reactive then high SEs to the extent that the layoff arouses positive inequity or "survivor guilt" instead of, or in addition to, job insecurity. There is some anecdotal evidence that layoffs can cause guilt among those who were not laid off. To cite an extreme example, survivors of Nazi concentration camps in World War II reputedly felt guilty about not being killed when so many of their brethren had suffered that fate. Closer to the organizational context, an article appearing several years ago in *The Wall Street Journal* (January 20, 1984, Vol. CX, No. 14, p. 12) described employees' reactions to compulsory overtime in the automobile industry (in which many of their coworkers had been laid off). Among the sources of psychological distress mentioned was the discomfort associated with receiving such high wages when many fellow employees had yet to be recalled for work. The article described the attitude of one employee as follows: "She is grateful to be working when unemployment is still high. But she feels guilty about how much she is working—nine or ten hours a day, sometimes six days a week." This employee's own words were: "It makes you feel bad that you're working overtime and others are desperate. I wish that (other) people could come in and work my overtime hours. If they could work a few hours a day, they could save their homes."

It is not intuitively obvious why survivors may feel guilty about the dismissal of their coworkers. Equity theory (Adams 1965), however, offers one possible explanation. According to this perspective, employees are very concerned with being treated fairly in the workplace. Perceived fairness is determined by assessing the relationship of one's work inputs (for example, work performance, expertise) and outcomes (for example, pay, status) to some standard (typically the outcome-to-input relationship of coworkers). If the outcome-to-input relationship between the self and others is comparable, then the employee is in a state of equity. If, however, the outcome-to-input relationship is unequal, then the employee experiences inequity. Note that it is possible for workers to experience two types of inequity. Negative inequity refers to instances in which the individual's outcome-to-input relationship is perceived to be less than that of relevant others; positive inequity refers to the perception that one's outcome-to-input relationship is greater than that of relevant others.

Equity theory further posits that inequity, whether negative or positive, is psychologically distressing, motivating individuals to change their behaviors and beliefs in order to reduce the distress. The precise nature of the distress caused by negative and positive inequity differs. Negative inequity arouses frustration and/or anger; positive inequity engenders guilt.

Let's relate equity theory to the layoff situation. It is possible that layoff survivors feel guilty because they perceive that they are in a state of positive inequity. This is most apt to occur if the survivors believe that they, rather than their coworkers, could have been laid off just as easily. Said in the terminology of equity theory, survivors may experience positive inequity to the extent that the perceived inputs of the survivors and laid-off workers are believed to be equal. Their respective outcomes—surviving versus being laid off—are clearly unequal, thus resulting in the perception of positive inequity among survivors.

Layoffs may engender guilt in survivors through the process of eliciting positive inequity. Moreover, the survivors' self-esteem may moderate the degree of, and/or reaction to, guilt arousal. In accordance with the plasticity hypothesis, low self-esteem survivors should experience a greater sense of positive-inequity-produced guilt than their higher self-esteem counterparts, for at least two related reasons. First, lacking confidence in their own judgments of the worth of their inputs and outcomes, low SEs may be more likely to engage in the process of comparing their inputs and outcomes to those of their coworkers. Second, what are low SEs likely to experience upon comparing their inputs and outcomes to others? Low SEs' perceptions of their inputs (or worth) are likely to be lower than high SEs. The net effect of these two tendencies is to make low SEs more likely to react to layoffs with the experience of positive-inequity-produced guilt.

In summary, layoffs have the potential to evoke a range of stressful psychological states among survivors, including job insecurity, positive inequity (guilt) and anger; the psychological states have the potential to affect survivors' work behaviors and attitudes. The extent to which layoffs actually arouse such psychological states, and/or the extent to which such psychological states are expressed in survivors' work behaviors and attitudes depends on situational factors, such as the nature of the work, the formal and informal organization, and extraorganizational factors. The effects of these situational factors may be moderated, in turn, by the self-esteem level of the survivors.

Survivors may exhibit their reactions to the stress of their coworkers' dismissal in a number of ways. To the extent that the layoff arouses job-insecurity-produced anxiety, survivors may work harder in order to increase their subsequent job security. In addition, they may exhibit other predictable responses to heightened levels of job insecurity (Greenhalgh 1983; Staw, Sandelands & Dutton 1981), such as greater job tension and health problems. If the layoff engenders positive inequity or guilt, then survivors may work harder, not to assure their job security but rather to redress the positive inequity. Several studies (for example, Adams & Rosenbaum 1962) have shown that workers respond to positive inequity by increasing their motivation (at least in the short run), presumably in order to restore equity to the situation.

Clearly, then, layoffs may produce a myriad of effects on survivors. The plasticity hypothesis further posits that such effects will be exhibited more by low rather than high self-esteem survivors, with one reservation: the degree of support for the plasticity hypothesis may depend upon the predominant psychological state evoked by the layoff. If the salient response is job insecurity and/or guilt, then there should be strong support for the plasticity hypothesis. If the prepotent response is anger, it is less clear whether low or high SEs will be more reactive. Moreover, it is possible that layoffs can instill other affective states, perhaps even of a nonstressful nature (for example, relief about not being laid off). Whether low or high SEs are more influenced by such types of layoffs also is a conceptual and empirical question.

My students, colleagues, and I have been conducting a series of studies on survivors' reactions to layoffs; the moderating impact of survivors' self-esteem figures prominently in this research. Several laboratory experiments already have been performed. In the first study (Brockner, Davy & Carter 1985), subjects of varying degrees of self-esteem were asked to perform two proofreading tasks as part of a "test validation" experiment. They were led to believe that another subject (who was really an accomplice of the experimenter) was proofreading a similar passage. After performing the first proofreading task, the subject and accomplice—who had been hitherto performing their tasks in separate rooms—were brought together "in order to take a break." Half of the participants were then exposed to a "layoff." The experimenter mentioned that because of an unforeseen "room scheduling problem" it would not be possible for both people present to complete the experiment, that is, perform the second proofreading task. The "really bad news" in all of this, subjects and accomplice were told, was that the person who had to leave would receive no remuneration for having participated in the experiment thus far. (Subjects were taking part in the study in order to receive extra credit in a course in which they were enrolled.) On a seemingly inpromptu basis, the experimenter then mentioned that it would be necessary to "draw lots" to determine which of the two "participants" would be able to remain. This lottery drawing always was rigged so that the accomplice was laid off while the true subject survived.

The remaining half of the participants witnessed no such layoff. Instead, they were brought together with the accomplice to take a break. All participants were then required to perform the second proofreading task. The primary measure was the quantity of subjects' performance on the two proofreading tasks.

The increase in performance from the first to the second task is revealed in table 4–5. Of greatest relevance to the plasticity hypothesis, low SEs were most apt to increase their work performance in the layoff relative to the no-layoff condition. Similar (albeit weaker) results have been obtained by Brockner et al. (1986).

The results in table 4–5 clearly demonstrate that the work performance of low SEs was more affected by the presence or absence of the layoff. Less clear is why such results were obtained. Recall that layoffs have the potential to arouse numerous psychological states in survivors (for example, job insecurity, guilt, anger). In order to delineate the factor affecting work performance in the Brockner, Davy, and Carter (1985) experiment, we deliberately structured the layoff so as not to cause survivors to worry about their own "job security." That is, there was no threat that they, like the accomplice before them, might have to leave the experiment without receiving credit. Job insecurity probably was not the predominant emotional state of survivors and, thus, was unlikely to mediate the findings presented in table 4–5.

Table 4–5
Increase in Number of Lines Proofread from First to Second Task as a Function of Self-esteem and Layoff

Self-esteem	Layoff	
	Yes	*No*
High	26.61	22.31
Medium	25.69	30.60
Low	52.10	17.07

Source: Brockner, Davy & Carter 1985, p. 236.
Note: Higher scores reflect greater increase in work performance. Each task consisted of 225 lines.

It is possible that such results were mediated by anger; perhaps survivors felt more angry in the layoff than the no-layoff condition due to the illegittimacy of the experimenter's dismissal of the accomplice. Several factors, however, render this intepretation less likely. First, layoffs are most apt to evoke anger in survivors to the extent that the layoff is seen as illegitimate. Much research (for example, Milgram 1974; Orne 1962) has shown that the researcher is perceived to have considerable legitimate power (French & Raven 1959) in the experimental setting. Second, and perhaps even more compelling, subjects reported feeling no more angry in the layoff than the no-layoff condition. In fact, questionnaire data from the studies performed by Brockner, Davy, and Carter (1985) and Brockner et al. (1986) strongly suggest that the layoff heightened survivors' guilt but not their job insecurity or anger.

Of course, in eliminating the possible anxiety and/or anger components from their layoff situation (in the service of heightened theoretical clarity), we may have stripped away important consequences of layoffs in actual organizational settings. To address this deficiency, we recently performed a study exploring the effects on participants' work performance of a layoff that either was or was not accompanied by job insecurity. In essence, this study (Brockner, O'Malley, Grover, Esaki, Glynn & Lazarides 1987) was a replication and extention of the initial experiment. Subjects of varying degrees of self-esteem either were exposed or not to the layoff described previously. The third independent variable was job insecurity. Half of the participants were led to believe that there was a moderate, though uncertain, chance that they would be laid off without receiving credit; moreover, whether they would "get the ax" would depend upon their performance on the upcoming task. The remaining half (as in the Brockner, Davy & Carter 1985, study) were given no such threat to their job security.

As in the initial study, participants exhibited a greater increase in work performance if they had just witnessed a layoff than if they had not. Of greater importance, as seen in table 4–6, the plasticity hypothesis once again received firm support. The work performance of low SEs was more sharply affected by the layoff variable than was that of the high SEs. Moreover, the self-esteem × layoff interaction described in table 4–6 was equally pronounced in the job-insecurity and no-job-insecurity condition. Does this mean that the job-insecurity variable had no effect on participants' work performance? Not necessarily. Questionnaire data suggested that the performance of low SEs was more influenced (than was high SEs' performance) by the layoff manipulation, but for very different reasons in the job-insecurity and no-job-insecurity conditions. In the former instance, low SEs reported greater levels of job insecurity, which could have spurred them on to work harder. In the latter case, low SEs did not report any greater level of job insecurity than high SEs, and yet the former group still outperformed the latter. Related findings suggested, however, that positive inequity (and not job insecurity) mediated participants'

Table 4–6
Increase in Number of Lines Proofread from First to Second Task,
as a Function of Self-esteem and Layoff

	Layoff	
Self-esteem	Yes	No
High	12.06	11.76
Low	22.14	9.74

Source: Brockner, O'Malley, Grover, Esaki, Glynn & Lazarides 1987.
Note: The results are collapsed across the job-insecurity variable, because the self-esteem × layoff interaction took the same form in both the insecure and secure conditions. Each task consisted of 164 lines.

performance in the no-job-insecurity condition. Thus, the plasticity hypothesis was supported in both the job-insecurity and no-job-insecurity conditions; low SEs worked harder than high SEs as a function of a layoff that was either accompanied by job insecurity or not, but for apparently different reasons in the two instances.

Layoffs and Survivors' Self-esteem: Some Speculations and Implications

The effects of layoffs—not only on those who are dismissed, but also on the survivors—are of considerable concern to practicing managers and scholars of organizations. The results of the initial studies on this topic suggest that survivors' reactions may well vary as a function of their self-esteem. Consistent with the plasticity hypothesis, the work performance of low SEs was more affected by the layoff than was that of their high self-esteem counterparts. I suggest that such self-esteem differences probably depend on the nature of the emotional state aroused by the layoff, which in turn is likely to be determined by task, organizational, and environmental factors. Low SEs seem to be more susceptible to influence by anxiety and/or guilt-arousing layoffs; whether this is true for anger-arousing layoffs, or layoffs that evoke other emotional states—not all of which need be negative—is an empirical question worthy of further pursuit.

A literal extrapolation of the results in tables 4–5 and 4–6 should not be made. Taken at face value, they seem to imply that in order to enhance survivors' motivation, layoffs should be conducted so as to arouse insecurity and/or guilt, discriminate against high SEs' chances of survival, and lower the self-esteem of the survivors.

It seems likely, however, that the survivors' job insecurity and/or guilt stimulated by layoffs may have other, more costly consequences. The vast literature on work-related stress suggests that many of the consequences of stress are dysfunctional to individuals and/or organizations. The stress of layoff survival, for example, could lead to reduced job satisfaction, lowered organizational commitment, and greater frequency of employee health problems. Future research should delineate the syndrome of symptoms elicited by layoff-produced stress (Greenhalgh 1983). If survivors' managers were to focus only on the heightened work performance possibly exhibited by (low self-esteem) survivors, then managers may conclude that the survivors were coping very well with the stress. In fact, it could be that the survivors also are manifesting other, perhaps more subtle, forms of dysfunctional behaviors.

Future research on survivor reactions to layoffs should be conducted in the actual organizational setting. The laboratory experiments were high in internal validity, but the external validity of these results was obviously questionable. A useful step in this direction was provided by Brockner, Grover, and Blonder (in press) who surveyed employees in a number of work organizations that had recently undergone layoffs. The layoffs were of varying degrees of severity (operationalized by the percentage of the work force that was dismissed); moreover, we assessed a host of factors thought to moderate survivors' reactions to layoffs, including the prior degree of role ambiguity in their job and their self-esteem. Dependent variables included organizational commitment, job commitment, and emotional upset. The severity variable was shown to relate to all three dependent measures; survivors reported feeling much less commitment to the organization and their jobs, and more emotionally upset in the severe than in mild layoff groups. In addition, and consistent with the plasticity hypothesis, employees' self-esteem moderated the joint effect of layoff severity and prior experience with role ambiguity on emotional upset. Low SEs who had little prior experience in their careers with role ambiguity reported feeling much greater upset in the severe than in the mild layoff condition (see table 4–7). Low SEs who had considerable experience with role ambiguity reported much more similar levels of upset in the severe and mild layoffs, and high SEs reported feeling relatively equally upset regardless of severity and role ambiguity. Perhaps prior experience served as a buffer against stress for low SEs in the severe condition. High SEs' dispositional nature may have been an ample buffer in the severe condition.

Not all of the results from this study were consistent with the plasticity hypothesis, however. Across conditions, there was a positive correlation between self-esteem and job commitment. At first blush, this finding appears to be directly counter to the results of the laboratory experiments (see tables 4–5 and 4–6), which revealed that the layoff caused a greater boost in the work performance of low SEs than their high self-esteem counterparts. However, there are many differences between the two studies that could explain the apparently discrepant results. Note that the field study (unlike the experi-

Table 4–7
Self-reported Emotional Upset as a Function of Self-esteem, Layoff Severity,
and Prior Experience with Role Ambiguity

| | | Prior Experience With Role Ambiguity | |
| | | High | Low |
Self-esteem	Layoff Severity		
High	Severe	1.80	1.11
	Mild	1.17	1.13
Low	Severe	1.52	2.06
	Mild	1.38	0.86

Source: Blonder 1976.
Note: Scores could range from 1–4; higher scores reflect greater emotional upset.

ments) was deficient in internal validity in two important respects: lack of a control group, and lack of a prelayoff measurement. It is thus quite possible that high SEs will report being more committed to their job than low SEs in both a layoff and no-layoff situation.

In addition, it is possible that very mild layoffs, such as the one concocted in the laboratory, have a more motivating effect on low SEs than on high SEs. However, more severe types of layoffs, in which real people are losing real jobs (as in the field study), may be a much more potent stressor, one with which high SEs cope better than low SEs. In any event, future studies of survivor reactions that possess internal and external validity are clearly warranted. Researchers should use methodologies that simulate laboratory conditions (experimental and control conditions, premeasurements and post-measurements) but do so in field settings. For example, my students and I are hoping to measure outcome variables (such as employees' motivation and satisfaction) in organizations in which there might be industry-wide cutbacks in manpower. Our plan is to obtain a baseline measure of the outcome variables prior to the onset of the layoffs, and, as much as possible, prior to employees' anticipation of the layoffs. It is likely that certain of these organizations will experience layoffs (experimental groups), whereas others will not (control groups). The outcome variables will then be assessed for a second time. In addition, factors that might moderate survivors' reactions, including their chronic self-esteem, will be measured.

There also are several areas of research closely related to the study of survivors' reactions in which workers' self-esteem may moderate their reactions to the organizational event. Much of the research on layoffs has explored the effects of layoffs on those who were laid off. Many of these studies have investigated how individuals' psychological well-being—including but not limited to their self-esteem—is affected by their employment status (for example,

Hartley 1980). Contrary to the conventional wisdom, those laid off do not always report an overall loss of self-esteem (Cobb & Kasl 1977) although they do report other sources of psychological distress such as depression and anxiety (Feather & Barber 1983; Kaufman 1982).

A study by Shamir (1986) also explored the relationship between unemployment, self-esteem, and well-being but did so in a way that tested the plasticity hypothesis. He investigated whether chronic self-esteem would moderate the relationship between employment status and psychological well-being, with low SEs' well-being more susceptible to influence by employment status than their high self-esteem counterparts. As stated in the discussion of role conflict, there are sound theoretical reasons to expect self-esteem to moderate workers' reactions to stressful events; becoming unemployed certainly is a significant stressor for many, if not most, individuals. Indeed, among a sample of highly educated Israeli adults, Shamir obtained strong support for the plasticity hypothesis: the lower the subjects' self-esteem, the more likely they were to feel more depressed if they were unemployed rather than employed. It, therefore, may be that employees' self-esteem moderates the effects of layoffs on those who survive as well as on those who are laid off (in ways consistent with the plasticity hypothesis).

Finally, it should be emphasized that layoffs are but one example of a number of exits that take place in organizations. Others—which have received far more empirical scrutiny—include turnover and absenteeism (Mowday, Porter & Steers 1982). The vast majority of research has explored the antecedents of organizational exits. Recently, however, scholars (Goodman & Atkin 1984; Mowday, Porter & Steers 1982; Staw 1980) also have begun to note that organizational exits such as turnover and absenteeism have numerous consequences, both negative and positive, at the individual, group, and organizational levels of analysis. Future research should explore the effects of individuals' self-esteem on their responses to the turnover and/or absenteeism of their fellow employees. To speculate, it may be that the absenteeism of coworkers may have a more negative impact on the work performance of low SEs than high SEs. This conjecture rests on two assumptions: coworkers facilitate performance in part by conveying cues for appropriate behaviors; and low SEs, less certain of themselves, are more apt to rely on cues provided by coworkers to guide their own behavior. Therefore, the absence of coworkers might have more disruptive effects on the task performance of low than high SEs.

Similarly, Brockner and Kim (1987) recently have studied the effects of coworker turnover on the work behaviors and attitudes of those who remain in the organization (that is, the stayers). The basic assumption is that after coworkers voluntarily leave to accept a job elsewhere, the stayers contemplate the meaning of the other's turnover for their own job situation. For example, the coworker's departure could stimulate a period of uncertainty in which the

stayers wonder whether they too should be "moving on." Any of a variety
of factors could affect the stayers' level of uncertainty, not the least of which
is whether the coworker left to accept a position that was better than, worse
than, or equivalent to his or her former position in the stayers' organization.
If the coworker left to take a better position, the stayers may be especially
prone to wonder, or feel worse, about the adequacy of their own position.
Indeed, across several different samples we have found that the stayers' self-
reported job satisfaction and intention to remain in the organization was
significantly lower when the coworker left for a better rather than a lateral
or worse position than the one he had occupied in the stayers' organization.
In addition, these studies provided some support for the plasticity hypothesis;
for example, low SEs felt more dissatisfied when the coworker had departed
for a better job and less dissatisfied when the coworker had left for a worse
job, relative to their high self-esteem counterparts.

Summary

This chapter explored some of the organizational and managerial implications
of the inverse relationship between self-esteem and behavioral plasticity. Taken
together, the research findings lend strong support to the plasticity hypothesis.
Across different research sites (field and laboratory), low SEs were shown to
be more affected by a variety of organizational stimuli (peer-group interaction,
evaluative feedback, socialization practices, leadership behaviors, role strains,
and work layoffs). Moreover, low SEs exhibited greater plasticity along
numerous dimensions (job performance, job commitment, hierarchical communication, role-taking tendencies, leadership style, job satisfaction, and work
motivation). See table 4–8 for a summary.

Granted, there are alternative explanations of the findings in some of the
studies. The field studies (Blonder 1976; Mossholder, Bedeian & Armenakis
1981; Mossholder, Bedeian & Armenakis 1982; Weiss 1977) are correlational
in nature; while they are high in external validity, they lack internal validity.
For example, Mossholder, Bedeian & Armenakis (1982) observed that low
SEs performed well with a supportive peer-group interaction but poorly with
a nonsupportive peer-group interaction. The performance of high SEs, by contrast, did not vary as a function of peer-group interaction. A plausible rival
explanation is that individuals' perceptions of the extent to which their performance depends on peer-group interaction has a negative effect on their self-
esteem. That is, workers who perceive that they need a supportive peer group
to perform well (and/or those who perceive that their performance suffers
in the face of a nonsupportive peer group) may have experienced reduced self-
esteem due to such dependency feelings. On the other hand, those who believe

Table 4-8
Summary of Studies Supportive of Plasticity Hypothesis

Authors	Independent Variables (Besides Self-esteem)	Dependent Variables	Subjects
1. Mossholder, Bedeian & Armenakis (1982)	Peer-group interaction	Desire to leave; Job tension; Performance	Nurses
2. Brockner & Elkind (1985)	Duration of failure Attribution for failure	Performance	College students
3. Brockner, Derr & Laing (1987)	Feedback	Willingness to communicate	College students
4. Jones (1986)	Socialization	Role taking	Employees in a variety of organizations
5. Weiss (1977) Weiss (1978)	Leaders' behaviors Leaders' values	Imitation Imitation	First level supervisors
6. Brockner, O'Malley, Hite & Davies (1987)	Reward allocation of partner	Imitation	College students
7. Mossholder, Bedeian & Armenakis (1981)	Role ambiguity Role conflict	Satisfaction Performance	Nurses
8. Brockner, Davy & Carter (1985); Brockner, O'Malley, Grover et al. (1987)	Layoffs	Performance of survivors	College students
9. Blonder (1976)	Layoffs Prior role ambiguity	Emotional upset of survivors	Engineers
10. Shamir (1986)	Employment status	Well-being	Highly educated Israeli adults
11. Brockner & Kim (1987)	Turnover	Job satisfaction of stayers	College students; employees in several organizations

Note: This list only includes studies described in chapter 4 for the first time; see chapter 3 for many other studies supportive of the plasticity hypothesis.

that their work behaviors and attitudes are less dependent on others may feel higher in self-esteem as a result.

There may be other explanations for the results obtained in the field studies. However, the plasticity hypothesis has the key virtue of parsimony over the rival hypotheses from the separate studies. All of the results presented in this chapter are consistent with the plasticity hypothesis. As a result, this notion rests on firmer ground than alternative explanations that may be idiosyncratic to each study.

At several points in this chapter, it was implied that low SEs are not always more susceptible to influence than high SEs. Much research supports the plasticity hypothesis; however, it does have delimiting conditions. Chapter 5 discusses this matter in some detail, as well as several other conceptual issues related to the plasticity hypothesis.

5
Self-esteem, Behavioral Plasticity, and Employee Behavior: Practical and Theoretical Considerations

I n laboratory and field settings and across a wide range of work behaviors and attitudes, research has shown that low SEs are more susceptible to influence by a variety of experimental or organizational stimuli. Three key issues of theoretical and practical significance will be discussed in this chapter.

1. The limiting conditions of the plasticity hypothesis. Is it always the case that low SEs are more susceptible to influence than their high self-esteem counterparts? Is the reverse ever true, and if so, what are the theoretical and managerial implications therein?

2. The adaptive value of behavioral plasticity. It is eminently clear that low SEs often are more plastic than high SEs. Far less certain is whether low SEs' greater plasticity is functional or dysfunctional—to the individual and/or the organization.

3. The relationship of behavioral plasticity to other theoretical analyses of employee self-esteem. Both Korman (1970) and Dipboye (1977a) have proposed comprehensive accounts of how workers' self-esteem may affect their job-related attitudes and behaviors. It may prove useful to compare and contrast these theoretical perspectives with that offered by plasticity.

These three issues form a (nonexhaustive) core of important questions, evoked by the material in chapters 3 and 4. As each issue is discussed, every attempt will be made to integrate theoretical implications with practical concerns.

Low Self-esteem and Behavioral Plasticity: Some Limiting Conditions

Although chapters 3 and 4 primarily were intended to provide evidence in support of the plasticity hypothesis, even in those chapters it was implied that low SEs are not always more susceptible to influence than their high self-esteem counterparts (for example, see the discussion of self-esteem, goal setting, and task performance in chapter 3). At this point it is appropriate to consider more fully some of the boundary conditions of the plasticity hypothesis. It should be emphasized that the ensuing discussion is not meant to suggest that the material in chapters 3 and 4 that supported the plasticity hypothesis is "wrong." Rather, my goal is to point out that even robust findings—such as those that support the plasticity hypothesis—have their limiting conditions. In this section three different outcome comparisons between high and low SEs are described that are contrary to the plasticity hypothesis; in addition, some of the organizational circumstances that give rise to such outcomes will be mentioned. The three outcome comparisons are no differences in the reactions of low and high SEs to environmental cues; the tendency for high SEs to be influenced more easily than low SEs; and the tendency for high and low SEs to differ in the direction, but not the magnitude, of their influence by external cues.

Limitation 1:
No Differences Between Low and High SEs

Under certain circumstances low and high SEs may respond equally to environmental cues. This could occur, for example, if the self-esteem variable simply was theoretically irrelevant to the matter at hand. Suppose, for instance, that an organization hired evaluation researchers to assess the impact of certain workplace innovations—bearing little conceptual relationship to self-esteem—on employee absenteeism. Suppose further that for "exploratory purposes," the researchers decide to evaluate whether self-esteem moderates the impact of such innovations on absenteeism. Lo and behold, the researchers discover that the absenteeism levels of low and high self-esteem employees do not differ as a function of the introduction of the innovation; should it be concluded that the plasticity hypothesis is "false" in this instance?

Perhaps more appropriately, the plasticity hypothesis should be viewed as irrelevant when there is little theoretical basis to expect self-esteem to interact with external factors to influence employee behavior. And yet, this is precisely one of the problems that has plagued organizational research on personality in general and self-esteem in particular, a point mentioned in chapter 1 (Weiss & Adler 1984). The fact that low and high SEs may not differ in their responsivity to external cues does not necessarily mean that the plasticity hypothesis is incorrect. Rather, it suggests that the plasticity hypothesis may be limited in scope to those conditions in which there are theoretical bases to expect individuals' self-esteem to affect their reactions to external cues. Again, this point seems almost tautological, but it is one that is all too frequently overlooked by those studying the role of personality variables in organizational behavior. The plasticity hypothesis, for example, specifies that one of the factors underlying low SEs' greater susceptibility to influence is their tendency to be uncertain about the correct way to think and/or act. In situations in which employees' level of uncertainty is not theoretically related to their work attitudes and behaviors, there is less reason to expect support for the plasticity hypothesis.

In other instances the self-esteem variable may be theoretically relevant, but rendered impotent by compelling situational factors. This notion relates to a basic question in person-situation interactionism (Mischel 1973): under what conditions do personality variables affect individuals' thoughts, feelings, and behaviors? As Mischel (1973), Weiss and Adler (1984), and others have pointed out, certain situations force virtually all individuals to think and behave in similar ways. For example, if a traffic light is red rather than green, virtually all drivers will stop their automobile. It probably matters little whether there are personality differences among drivers, even on dimensions related to driving behavior; almost all drivers can be expected to respond similarly. Said differently, the powerful situational cue (that is, the red traffic light) reduces all drivers' uncertainty about appropriate behavior. As a result, the drivers' personality should have little impact on their subsequent behavior.

This notion of situational strength can be related to the organizational example evaluating the impact of certain workplace innovations and self-esteem on absenteeism. It may well be that self-esteem is theoretically relevant to the nature of the innovation. However, the nature of the innovation may be so powerful that it leads all employees—regardless of their self-esteem—to think and act similarly. For example, suppose the innovation entails making employees more responsible for the way in which the work is performed. If the innovation is moderate in size and scope, then it is possible that low SEs— who may shun the added responsibility—will be more frequently absent than their high self-esteem counterparts. If, however, the innovation is very large in size and scope, then all employees—regardless of their self-esteem—may resent the burden of added responsibilities. In the latter case, the change was so powerful that it caused all individuals to respond the same way, regardless of their self-esteem. In the former case, the change was less dramatic, thereby enabling individual differences in self-esteem to influence behavior.

The managerial implications of the fact that low SEs may be no more susceptible to influence than high SEs are reasonably straightforward. If managers were to take the message in chapters 3 and 4 to an extreme—and conclude that it is always more easy to influence the work behaviors and attitudes of low than high SEs—then they may overestimate the ease of influencing low SEs. This could present problems if the situation were one in which it was especially important to influence the low rather than high self-esteem employees, or most of the employees were known to be, or at least suspected of being, low rather than high in self-esteem. For example, suppose that a group of subordinates were known to be poor performers and also low in self-esteem. If a manager took the plasticity hypothesis too literally, he or she may introduce certain interventions (for example, a training program) designed to improve the subordinates' performance, but have unduly high expectations about the subordinates' susceptibility to influence. Perhaps the training program does not tap into the factors that mediate low SEs' plasticity. Moreover, in overestimating low SEs' susceptibility to influence, change agents may not develop backup or contingency plans to influence the low SEs in the intended ways. In short, low SEs may not be relatively more responsive than high SEs to managerial and organizational factors to the extent that such factors either are conceptually unrelated to self-esteem or so constraining that they minimize the possible moderating role of individual differences.

Limitation 2:
The Tendency for High SEs to be More Influenced

The plasticity hypothesis implies that high SEs are not very easily influenced. However, there may be certain conditions in the work setting that affect high SEs more than their low self-esteem counterparts.

High self-esteem employees are used to thinking of themselves in positive, self-aggrandizing ways, whereas low SEs are not. Thus, external cues that threaten a positive self-image, somewhat paradoxically, may have a greater impact on individuals whose self-esteem is high rather than low. In other words, high SEs have more (self-esteem) to lose; given that individuals in general are motivated to preserve their self-esteem (see chapter 7), it may be the high (rather than the low) self-esteem employees who are more driven to act in ways that protect their self-esteem in response to external cues that threaten their self-image.

A similar argument was advanced by Aronson (1968, 1984), in his discussion of the nature of cognitive dissonance (Festinger 1957). According to this view, individuals experience dissonance not simply as a result of holding incongruous beliefs, but rather to the extent that they focus on their behaviors and/or beliefs that are inconsistent with their views as good, moral, competent, and likable persons. For example, in the classic forced-compliance dissonance study by Festinger and Carlsmith (1959), subjects performed an extremely boring task but told the next participant—who was actually an accomplice of the experimenter's—that the task was interesting. Aronson's (1968, 1984) analysis suggests that participants' dissonance is not caused by the inconsistency between the following cognitions: "I thought the task was boring," and "I told someone else that it was interesting." Rather, the dissonance is aroused by the incompatibility between these two cognitions: "I lied," and "Good people do not lie." Of course, the latter cognition is more likely to be maintained by high than low SEs. Therefore, if Aronson's self-esteem-based conceptualization of the nature of dissonance arousal is correct, then high SEs should be much more affected than low SEs by cues that threaten individuals' ability to maintain a positive self-image. Simply put, such cues are dissonance-arousing for high SEs because they are incompatible with the ways in which high SEs customarily think of themselves. Low SEs, by contrast, may experience less dissonance or no dissonance at all as a function of esteem-threatening stimuli because, quite literally, there is little inconsistency between the esteem-threatening stimuli and their typical self-views. Several studies in the experimental social psychology literature have shown high SEs to be more likely than low SEs to experience dissonance in response to esteem-threatening stimuli (Aronson & Mettee 1968; Crocker et al. 1987; Glass 1964).

Several more recent studies also illustrate that high SEs may be more affected than low SEs by esteem-threatening external cues. In a field study (Brockner, Derr & Laing 1987), students of management had performed relatively poorly on an initial course exam. Presumably, this poor performance was at least moderately esteem-threatening to the students, all of whom were majoring in business administration. Of interest here was the performance of these students on the next exam, as a function of their self-esteem. High SEs performed much better on the second exam than the first whereas low SEs showed no change (see table 5–1). Said differently, the poor performance on the first exam seemed to have had greater impact on the subsequent performance of the high SEs than the low SEs, results directly contrary to the plasticity hypothesis.

A second study (McFarlin 1985) suggests that following an esteem-threatening failure, high SEs may be more susceptible than low SEs to influence by performance-relevant cues. In this laboratory experiment, all participants experienced failure and then worked on a subsequent task, which consisted of a number of trials. One group of subjects was told that all of the trials were soluble (contingent condition), a second group was told that some of the trials were insoluble, although they were not told which ones were insoluble (non-contingent condition), whereas a third group was given no information at all (control condition). In reality, though unbeknownst to the participants, some of the trials actually were insoluble; of interest was the amount of time that subjects persisted on the insoluable trials. As indicated by the data in table

Table 5–1
Performance on Second Exam as a Function of Self-esteem and Negative Feedback Concerning Performance on the First Exam

	Examination	
Self-esteem	First Exam (%)	Second Exam (%)
High	67.50	76.16
Low	63.89	63.05

Source: Brockner, Derr & Laing 1987.
Note: All students had performed relatively poorly on the first exam.

Table 5–2
Mean Time Spent on Puzzles as a Function of Self-esteem and Contingency
Information

	Contingency Information		
Self-esteem	Noncontingent	Contingent	Control
High	13.02	25.06	16.55
Low	22.15	20.76	17.69

Source: McFarlin 1985, p. 160.
Note: Mean time is in seconds; higher scores reflect greater persistence.

5–2, high SEs were much more persistent in the contingent than noncontingent condition, whereas low SEs were not. Upon encountering the insoluble
trials in the noncontingent condition, high SEs may have decided that those
particular trials were the insoluble ones; as a result, it made little sense to persist. In sharp contrast, low SEs did not persist any less in the noncontingent
than contingent condition. One interpretation of the results in table 5–2 is
that the prior negative feedback differentially motivated high and low SEs to
attend to performance-relevant cues that would enable them to compensate
for the negative feedback.

A third series of studies (Crocker et al. 1987) explored participants' attitudes toward their own group and opposing groups as a function of their self-
esteem and the extent to which their self-esteem had been threatened. In one
study, for example, the researchers explored whether sorority members would
evaluate other sororities on campus more negatively if their own sorority was
low rather than high in status. Such a tendency could reflect individuals'
propensities to protect their self-esteem in the face of esteem-threatening
information (that is, that their own sorority was not prestigious). In fact,
members of low-status sororities did express more negative attitudes toward
the outgroups (that is, other sororities), but much more so if they were high
rather than low in self-esteem.

These three studies provide evidence that under certain conditions, high
SEs may be more susceptible than low SEs to influence by external cues. Moreover, they are consistent with prior theory (Aronson 1968, 1984) and research
(Aronson & Mettee 1968; Glass 1964), which has suggested that high SEs
are more responsive than low SEs to cues that threaten individuals' tendencies
to define themselves positively.

The prospect that esteem-threatening cues may have greater impact on
high SEs than low SEs has several practical implications. For example, suppose that high self-esteem employees have been performing rather poorly and
that their manager would like to communicate this information to heighten

the employees' subsequent performance. How might the manager deliver such feedback? At least within reasonable limits, it may be wise to lead high SEs to interpret the poor performance as esteem-threatening. By doing so, in essence, the manager is appealing to their high self-esteem; it may be too unpalatable or dissonance-arousing for them to contemplate their poor performance as reflective of their "true" selves. As a result, they may be energized to increase their effort for their own benefit and that of the manager and the organization.

Having decided that it is important to heighten the psychological significance that the high self-esteem employees attach to their poor performance, the manager then must decide exactly how to go about doing so. It may be possible to influence the perceived importance of the negative feedback through attributional processes. Thus, the employees may take the negative performance more seriously if they attribute it to internal factors, such as lack of ability or lack of effort, rather than external causes, such as task difficulty or luck. Or, if the employees can see how their negative performance elicits important, unfavorable consequences for other members of the organization and/or the organization as a whole, then they may attach greater importance to negative performance feedback.

The preceding discussion suggests that high SEs are more likely than low SEs to bounce back from, or compensate for, their own performance shortfalls. It is quite possible that high SEs also may be quite resilient in the face of the failures of other people. More specifically, imagine that incumbents of a particular job or role within an organization historically have performed poorly. The most recent incumbents had fared so poorly that they were forced to resign. When recruiting a new person to fill the slot, management may be wondering if they ever will be able to find someone who can stem or reverse this unfavorable historical tide. As the current crop of candidates is evaluated, it may be more important than ever to consider their levels of self-esteem. Indeed, it could be that high SEs may be able to respond to this difficult situation, to their and the organization's advantage. Because high SEs seem to thrive in the face of esteem-threatening situations, they actually may perform significantly better than if they had entered into a situation that was less psychologically loaded.

There is at least one alternative explanation of the McFarlin (1985) results (see table 5–2), which suggests another condition under which high SEs may be more responsive to external cues than low SEs. Perhaps the prior negative feedback that subjects encountered in that study was unrelated to the fact that high SEs were more influenced by the performance-relevant information than the low SEs. Rather, the explanation of high SEs' greater responsivity may stem from the nature of the performance-relevant information that individuals received prior to working on the task. More specifically, some performance cues directly prescribe a behavioral course of action; in essence, they tell the person what to do. Other performance cues, however, provide individuals with information that may be relevant to their upcoming task, but do not direct them to a particular course of action; such cues require individuals to decide for themselves upon a particular course of action.

It seems likely that high and low SEs are differentially responsive to these two types of performance cues. Low SEs may be more responsive to information that prescribes a particular course of action. Lacking confidence in their own judgment about the correct way to act, low SEs may be especially reliant upon, and even welcome, performance cues that prescribe a particular course of action. High SEs tend to be confident in their judgments of how they should behave; consequently, they may be especially responsive to external cues that provide them with relevant information, but then leave to them the task of deciding how to respond.

Subjects in the McFarlin (1985) study appeared to have received the latter type of performance-relevant information. They were told that some of the trials were insoluble, but they were not told which trials in particular were insoluble. Consequently, upon encountering a difficult trial, participants had to decide for themselves whether it was insoluble. If they believed it to be insoluble, then it made little sense for them to continue on the trial; instead, they should have moved on to the next one. High SEs were less persistent in the noncontingent condition than the low SEs (see table 5–2). Apparently, high SEs took it upon themselves to decide that the insoluble trials were, in fact, insoluble, causing them to spend less time at them.

More generally, high SEs may be more likely than low SEs to respond to external cues that require individuals' active involvement in deciding upon a particular course of action. What types of cues fit this description? It may be those that suggest that one course of action is more appropriate than others but also emphasize individuals' choice in the matter. In addition, certain cues provide more of a soft-sell; they offer individuals relevant information, but require them to draw their own conclusion about the appropriate way to respond.

A study from our laboratory (Sandelands, Brockner & Glynn 1987) measured subjects' persistence as a function of their self-esteem and information about the nature of the task. The information seemed to be of the sort that elicited participants' involvement in deciding whether, and how long, to persist. More specifically, half of the subjects were told that the nature of the task was such that the longer they persisted at the difficult trials, the more likely they were to solve them (continuous condition). The remaining half were told that the task was such that even if they persisted at the difficult trials, they may or may not be successful (discrete condition). This manipulation was designed to simulate a property of most tasks. For some (for example, cognitively simple but tedious tasks) performance is "effort-dependent," that is, the more individuals persist, the more likely they are to succeed. At other tasks (for example, those which require "sudden insight" into the correct solution) individuals may persist for a long time, without necessarily moving closer to their goal.

In addition, all subjects were instructed that their degree of persistence was entirely their own decision. In short, the nature of the task information manipulation seemed to require participants to become actively involved in deciding how long they wished to persist at the difficult trials. These are precisely the conditions under which high SEs should be more responsive to the performance-relevant information; Sandelands, Brockner, and Glynn (1987) discovered that high SEs were much more persistent in the continuous than the discrete condition, whereas low SEs were not.

Of course, much performance-relevant information that individuals receive prescribes behavioral courses of action more directly. Low SEs should be more influenced by such cues than their high self-esteem counterparts. For example, McFarlin, Baumeister, and Blascovich (1984) had subjects of varying levels of self-esteem work at difficult tasks after giving them concrete advice about whether to persist. Half were told to quit upon encountering a difficult trial (quit condition), whereas the other half were told to persist (persist condition). Not surprisingly, subjects were much more persistent in the latter than the former condition, and this was much more true for the low than the high SEs. In summary, then, whether low or high SEs are more influenced by cues that are relevant for task performance may depend on the extent to which such cues directly or indirectly prescribe a behavioral course of action. When the cues essentially tell people exactly what to do, low SEs seem to be more manipulable than high SEs. However, when the cues elicit individuals' involvement in deciding for themselves upon an appropriate course of action, then high SEs may be more influenced than low SEs.

These speculations—which include a clear departure from the plasticity hypothesis—can only be evaluated through further research. They are worth investigating for at least two reasons. First, future research may help to identify more definitively some of the boundary condition of the plasticity hypothesis. Second, research along these lines may elucidate the role of self-esteem in the organizational context, as a function of whether the work setting involves people in decision-making or not. As is discussed later in this chapter, it just may be that high SEs are more responsive than low SEs to cues in a work setting known to have a participatory culture, whereas just the opposite may be true in a nonparticipatory work context.

Limitation 3: Self-esteem Differences in the Direction but not Magnitude of Susceptibility to Influence

The preceding section discussed the fact that the plasticity hypothesis may be directly contradicted; under some conditions, for example, subsequent to an esteem-threatening failure, the behavior of high SEs may be affected more than that of low SEs. This section builds upon the previous one in two important respects. First, the range of esteem-threatening stimuli is expanded; in the preceding section threat of self-esteem was treated synonymously with prior negative feedback. However, organizational researchers have investigated the influence of individuals' global self-esteem in other situations that may threaten their self-esteem. Second, and perhaps more important, one may have inferred that esteem-threatening cues energize high SEs but have no effect on low SEs. As we shall soon see, the latter statement could not be farther from the truth. High and low SEs often respond to esteem-threatening situations in diametrically opposite ways; whereas high SEs often increase their resolve and "stick-to-it-tiveness," low SEs often react by withdrawing—either behaviorally or psychologically—from the task at hand. Thus, the concern here is no longer with whether low or high SEs are more easily influenced, rather, both may be susceptible to influence by the same cues, but in very different ways. Relevant research findings will be briefly summarized also. The moderating impact of self-esteem has been investigated in no fewer than five types of esteem-threatening situations. In each instance, high SEs responded with increased arousal, effort, and/or performance, whereas low SEs exhibited just the opposite responses.

Challenge. One type of threat to self-esteem occurs when individuals are posed with a difficult, challenging task. Challenging tasks are those that test the mettle of workers; they can be solved but not easily. Several experiments (DePaulo et al. 1981; Sigall & Gould 1977) have shown that tasks perceived to be difficult cause high SEs to strive harder than tasks not perceived as difficult; by contrast, low SEs tend to work less hard on tasks believed to be difficult rather than easy.

Overpayment. In one experiment (Brockner 1985) subjects performed a clerical task and either were paid an amount that was much more than the going rate (positive inquity condition) or equal to the going rate (equity condition). Higher SEs worked harder in the positive inequity than equity condition whereas just the opposite was true for the low SEs. One possible interpretation of these results is that the performance level implicitly demanded by the overpayment was viewed as highly challenging. High SEs, possessing the confidence needed to meet such a challenge, responded by redoubling their effort at the task; low SEs, who typically lack such confidence, appeared to have withdrawn their efforts from the task at hand.

Goal Setting. The classic goal-setting effect (Locke 1968; Locke et al. 1981) is that employees are more productive when working on a task while maintaining a specific, difficult goal in mind. Although scant, there is some suggestive evidence that high and low SEs may respond very differently to specific, difficult goals. In a field study of managers in an MBO (Management by Objectives) program, Carroll and Tosi (1970) found that for managers high in "self-assurance"—a trait that is presumably highly correlated with self-esteem—there was a positive correlation between goal difficulty and motivation. However, for managers low in self-assurance, there was an inverse relationship between goal difficulty and motivation. Such findings are perfectly compatible with those already presented in the challenge and overpayment discussions. That is, as the challenge (posed by goal difficulty) increased, the more likely it was for high SEs to increase motivation and low SEs to decrease motivation.

Reactance: The Case of Persuasive Communications. Psychological reactance has been invoked as an important theoretical process in two literatures in social psychology: attitude change and achievement motivation. Originally, Brehm (1966) hypothesized that individuals need to perceive freedom of choice in belief and/or behavior. Threats to perceived freedom instill the psychological state of reactance, which leads to belief and/or behavior change designed to restore the lost freedom. For example, if a persuasive communication is presented to individuals in a way that threatens their belief freedom (for example, "you have no choice but to agree"), then they may reestablish freedom by thinking or acting in a manner that is directly contrary to that espoused in the communication.

Brehm and Brehm (1981) speculated that freedom-threatening persuasive communications should arouse reactance only in those individuals who perceive that they are competent to exercise the freedom. This conjecture implies that high SEs should be more apt than low SEs to exhibit reactance in response to a freedom-threatening communication, because the former group is more likely than the latter to have relatively high self-assessments of their competence. This hypothesis was tested and confirmed in a study by Brockner and Elkind (1985). Subjects of varying degrees of self-esteem read a persuasive communication; a freedom-threatening message was attached to the communication half of the time (threat condition: "You have no choice but to agree with what you have just read"), whereas no such freedom threat appeared for the other half of the participants (no-threat condition). High SEs exhibited reactance, showing much greater resistance to the persuasive communication in the threat than the no-threat condition. Low SEs, in sharp contrast, were much less resistant to the persuasive communication in the threat than the no-threat condition.

Reactance: The Case of Achievement Motivation. As mentioned in chapter 4 (see figure 4–1), reactance also has been used to account for the effect of uncontrollable outcomes, such as failure, on individuals' achievement motivation. According to this logic (Wortman & Brehm 1975), when workers have performed poorly at a task in which it was important for them to do well, their initial response is reactance, through which they attempt to compensate for their poor performance. This reactance is expressed through increased motivation (and performance to the extent that effort and performance are positively correlated). Wortman and Brehm further suggested that if the reactance-inspired increase in motivation did not boost performance, then workers would exhibit "learned helplessness" (Seligman 1975), characterized most dramatically by a sharp drop in motivation. The results of one study— much like those found in the context of persuasive communications—have shown that high SEs respond to increasing amounts of failure with greater reactance, whereas low SEs do just the opposite, exhibiting learned helplessness (Brockner et al. 1983).

Reactance and Self-esteem: Implications for Participative Management. An issue with which organizations frequently wrestle is whether and to what extent they should allow employees to participate in workplace-related decisions (Vroom & Yetton 1973). This matter is stimulated by a host of concerns, not the least of which is that employees may be more satisfied and/or productive if they have had some input into the decisions that affect their daily work lives. Reactance theory may help explain the virtues of participative management. Simply put, organizations that do not favor participative management may interfere with employees' sense of freedom in the workplace. The ensuing sense of reduced freedom may form the essence of workers' resistance—manifested as lower satisfaction and/or motivation—to the achievement of organizational goals.

This is not to say that participative management always is an effective way to reduce employees' reactance (or resistance). Brehm (1966) pointed out that reactance in response to freedom-threatening cues only occurs when individuals have initial expectations of freedom. Thus, as Staw (1977) suggested, "in organizations with a tradition of hierarchical relations there should be little reactance aroused in employees who have come to expect a top-down approach. Reactance would be more of a problem in organizations with a history of participative management that attempt to institute hierarchical controls. Participation and freedom . . . are thus easier to expand than to contract" (p. 85).

In short, the expectation of being free to control one's destiny may be one of the factors that influences the impact of participative management on employee reactions. High SEs, whose past reinforcement history have led them to maintain relatively favorable control expectations, may respond more positively to participative management than their low self-esteem counterparts. At the very least, the empirical evidence suggests that threats to the freedom of high and low SEs—across the domains of attitude change and achievement motivation— are more apt to engender reactance in the former than the latter group. Thus, in contemplating whether to invoke participatory management in the service of overcoming reactance, managers should consider the host of factors that may directly or indirectly affect employees' prior expectations of freedom (for example, organizational traditions, workers' self-esteem). If this confluence of factors suggests that workers have come to expect freedom, then it may be prudent to employ a participatory style; alternatively, if such freedom expectations are low, then participatory management may be warranted to a lesser degree.

Limitation 3: Summary, Theoretical Integration, and Organizational Implications

A number of studies have shown that under certain conditions low and high SEs are equally influenced by external cues, but in opposite directions. In response to esteem-threatening situations, such as a challenging task, over-payment, difficult goals, and possible violations of attitudinal and behavioral freedom, high SEs seem to respond with increased vigor and assertion. In sharp contrast, low SEs respond to the very same situations by withdrawing behaviorally or psychologically from the task at hand.

Such findings seem internally consistent and may be explained by self-regulation theory (Carver & Scheier 1981), which describes how individuals go about bringing their actual behavior in line with their standards for ideal behavior. The portion of the theory that is most relevant to this discussion describes how individuals respond when progress toward self-regulation is interrupted. When behavioral self-regulation is interrupted, individuals often wonder whether they will be successful in their efforts. For example, consider the case of employees whose manager has set a specific, difficult goal for them to achieve. In the course of self-regulation, that is, trying to attain the goal, the workers undoubtedly will question whether they will be able to attain the goal. Or, imagine the plight of a junior executive who holds career aspirations of making it to the top. Given the difficulty of the task, this person is bound to contemplate at various points whether such lofty ambitions may be realized.

According to Carver and Scheier (1981), during this period of uncertainty people go through a process—whether consciously or not—of assessing the subjective probability of being able to perform the self-regulatory behaviors. If their outcome expectancy is positive, then they return to the process of self-regulation with renewed vigor and enthusiasm. If, however, their outcome expectancy is negative, then they tend to withdraw from the process of self-regulation and instead exhibit low motivation or passivity.

Note that the class of events that have been dubbed *esteem-threatening*, such as performing a challenging task, being overpaid for performing a task, trying to attain a specific, difficult goal, being exposed to freedom-threatening persuasive communications, and receiving failure feedback from a previous task, seem to be the very kinds of factors that interrupt behavioral self-regulation; according to Carver and Scheier (1981), such interruptions will cause individuals to assess outcome expectancies, which, in turn, set the stage for high and low SEs to respond in opposite ways. High SEs tend to be confident of their abilities to meet difficult challenges, leading them to return to the task of behavioral self-regulation with vigor. Low SEs, however, have far more pessimistic expectations for their attempts at self-regulation, thus causing them to disengage from the task at hand. Said differently, esteem-threatening circumstances for high SEs are precisely what the term *esteem-threatening* implies: situations, which, if not dealt with adequately, will lower the individuals' self-esteem. For low SEs, however, esteem-threatening circumstances not only threaten but also ultimately may lower or reinforce their existing self-esteem; that is, low SEs are not confident that they can deal with esteem-threatening situations, prompting them to act in ways (for example, withdrawing) that could solidify their low self-esteem.

The fact that low and high SEs may respond to external cues in directly opposite ways has practical as well as theoretical implications. One of the most important themes of this book is that organizations and practicing managers, in trying to influence the behavior of employees, often need to take into account the self-esteem level of those whom they wish to influence. This section highlights the opposite responses of low and high SEs and strongly emphasizes this theme. For example, suppose that managers wish to heighten the motivation level of their subordinates and have decided that the best way to do so is to challenge them. The operationalization of the challenge can take a number of forms (for example, posing them with a specific, difficult goal; or leading them to believe that very few employees are able to succeed at the task at hand). In any event, it is entirely possible that the high self-esteem workers will respond by redoubling their efforts at the task at hand, whereas the low self-esteem employees will react by withdrawing from it. In this particular example, the overall success of the managerial influence attempt should be proportional to the percentage of subordinates who are high, rather than low, in self-esteem.

Two different kinds of problems may arise, however, if the workers are not predominantly high in self-esteem. First, consider what would happen if the population to be influenced were relatively low in self-esteem. Overall, the influence attempt may backfire, producing results directly opposite to those that were intended. Second, and perhaps more typical, consider what would happen if there was variability in the self-esteem level of the to-be-influenced workers, such that they were fairly evenly distributed between high and low self-esteem. In theory, the reactions of the high and low SEs should "cancel" each other, making the net effect of the influence attempt appear to be minimal. Under such circumstances, the influencing agents are likely to conclude that their attempt to heighten the motivation level of subordinates "had no effect."

But, is such a conclusion warranted? I think not. If the overall lack of effect were due to the offsetting reactions of low and high SEs, then it is far more appropriate to conclude that the influence attempt did have a significant impact on subordinates, but that the precise nature of the impact depended on the subordinates' level of self-esteem. The danger is that the agents of the influence attempt may fail to perceive the true impact of the influence attempt; as a result, their degree of learning from the process could be curtailed. More specifically, based on the nonsignificant overall impact of the attempt to motivate through challenge, the influencing agents may fail to rely on this method of motivation in a future circumstance when it would be highly advisable to invoke its use (for example, if the subordinates to be influenced overall were high in self-esteem).

More generally, what is being suggested here is that managers—as agents of organizational change—need to distinguish between two types of unsuccessful influence attempts. In the first, there is no change on the average as a function of the influence attempt; moreover, employees' reactions exhibit little variability around the average. In the second, there also is no mean change; however, this lack of mean change belies the fact that employees' reactions vary considerably around the mean such that, when taken together, they cancel one another. In the latter case, the change agent may overlook situational and/or individual difference variables (for example, self-esteem) that moderate the impact of the influence attempt on employees' reactions. Consequently, important information vis-à-vis future influence attempts may be lost.

*Low Self-esteem and Behavioral Plasticity: Some Closing
Comments on Limiting Conditions*

A central notion in this book stems from the results of dozens of research studies in the laboratory and the field: low SEs often are more behaviorally plastic than their high self-esteem counterparts. At this juncture it should be clear that low SEs are often but not always more susceptible than high SEs to influence by external cues. We have considered some alternative comparisons in the reactions of high and low SEs to environmental factors and noted that on certain occasions high and low SEs are equally able to be influenced, high SEs are more influenced than low SEs, and the magnitude of high and low SEs' responsivity is equal, but the direction of such responsivity varies dramatically. In addition, we have discussed some of the antecedent factors that produce results inconsistent with the plasticity hypothesis, including the lack of theoretical fit between external factors and self-esteem, constraining situations, the presence of esteem-threatening cues, and whether external cues directly (versus indirectly) prescribe a behavioral course of action. All the while, I have tried not to lose sight of some of the practical implications of the fact that low SEs are not always more behaviorally plastic than high SEs.

The purpose of this discussion has been to prevent the reader from overgeneralizing—especially after reading chapters 3 and 4—the extent to which self-esteem and behavioral plasticity are inversely related. To be sure, that relationship is a powerful one, largely because the hypothesized mediators of the relationship, such as uncertainty and need for approval and self-presentation concerns, are such basic elements in the fabric of social and organizational life. However, other events, such as those that threaten employees' self-esteem, also occur with varying degrees of regularity in the workplace; if and when they do, they may elicit results at odds with the plasticity hypothesis.

Finally, a word about the methodology of future research on this issue: the delimiting conditions of the plasticity hypothesis need to be explored in the organizational setting. Chapter 3, in which it was initially suggested that low SEs are more prone to influence, was based primarily on the results of laboratory experiments. Chapter 4 provided additional evidence in field studies and laboratory analogues of organizational behavior. The research evidence in chapter 5 on delimiting conditions, except for a few rare exceptions (for example, Carroll & Tosi 1970), has come primarily from laboratory studies. Thus, future research on delimiting conditions in the actual organizational context is clearly warranted and will serve at least two important purposes: to add external validity to the research that already has been performed, particularly if the results parallel those obtained in the previous studies; and to make clearer the organizational implications of the fact that low SEs are often but not always more behaviorally plastic than high SEs.

The Adaptive Value of Behavioral Plasticity

Chapters 3 and 4 clearly demonstrated low SEs to be more behaviorally plastic than high SEs across a wide variety of situations, although there are exceptions to this general principle. Even when low SEs do exhibit greater plasticity, their greater susceptibility to influence is not always maladaptive for themselves and/or the organization. Mental health professionals are quick to point out the perils of low self-esteem and its concomitant plasticity. In various ways, our culture advises us to "be independent," "do your own thing," and not to be buffeted around willy-nilly by environmental factors. Moreover, many of the research findings presented in previous chapters are consistent with this credo. For example, a number of studies show that negative feedback or failure saps the subsequent motivation and performance level of low SEs, whereas high SEs are more resistant to the adverse impact of negative feedback (Brockner, Derr & Laing 1987; Shrauger & Sorman 1977). In addition, it has been shown that role conflict (Mossholder, Bedeian & Armenakis 1981) and unsupportive peer group interaction (Mossholder, Bedeian & Armenakis 1982) have negative impact on the work performance of low but not high SEs. Clearly, in such instances it would have been far more adaptive for the employee to be resistant to the impact of the environmental event.

Still, it would be misleading to say that low SEs' greater plasticity always is maladaptive. Instead, I wish to argue that as a general rule, behavioral plasticity is neither adaptive nor maladaptive. Rather, in certain situations successful adaptation requires individuals to be resistant to the impact of environmental input; in other situations, successful adaptation mandates employees to be open to external input. Low SEs' greater plasticity may stand them in much better stead than that of high SEs in the latter than the former situations. It is also worth mentioning that adaptation can be considered from the point of view of the individual (as I have hitherto done) and/or the organization. That is, do organizations always want their members to be high in self-esteem? Or might there be some circumstances under which organizations may wish their members to have low self-esteem, along with its concomitant susceptibility to influence by external forces? The analysis of the adaptive value of behavioral plasticity will consider the perspectives of the individual and the organization.

Based on the assumption that our culture tends to value high self-esteem and its associated resistance to influence, I will take the devil's advocate position and discuss the perils of such resistance and the virtues of plasticity. In this way, it should be possible to remove any unilateral value judgment about whether it is better to be susceptible or resistant to influence by external events. Indeed, one need go no further than the research findings presented in chapters 3 and 4 to see that low SEs' greater plasticity can be adaptive under certain conditions, which are considered here.

Information Search and Task Performance

One of the factors that renders low SEs' particularly susceptible to influence is their relatively high sense of uncertainty about the correctness of their own beliefs and behaviors. Such uncertainty motivates low SEs to search their environment for information relevant to their beliefs and behaviors. Question: is being a greater seeker of environmental input adaptive or maladaptive? It probably depends on whether successful task performance is contingent upon the quantity and/or quality of the information search. Recent research on strategic decision making at the organizational level of analysis (Fredrickson 1984; Fredrickson & Mitchell 1984) nicely illustrates this point. These authors explored the relationship between decision-making "comprehensiveness"— that is, the extent to which an organization attempts to be exhaustive or inclusive in making and integrating strategic decisions (which includes information search)—and organizational performance. The relationship between comprehensiveness and performance was determined to be contingent upon environmental stability. For an industry in a stable environment, there was a positive correlation between comprehensiveness and performance, however, just the opposite was observed for an industry in an unstable environment. Thus, under certain conditions it is adaptive to engage in prolonged information search prior to making strategic decisions, whereas in other instances it is not.

That point can be extended to the individual level of analysis in the context of the relationship between self-esteem, information search, and task performance. If low SEs do engage in greater information search due to their sense of uncertainty, then they should outperform their high self-esteem counterparts in those instances in which degree of information search is positively related to problem-solving efficiency (see Weiss and Knight 1980, for supportive results). To repeat, low SEs' style of information search is not necessarily more adaptive than high SEs'. Rather, the relative efficacy of the two groups' styles of information acquisition may be contingent on contextual factors, such as the nature of the task.

Modeling

Two mediators of behavioral plasticity could account for the tendency of low SEs to be more susceptible to the influence of a model than their high self-esteem counterparts. First, a basic tenet in the modeling literature (Bandura 1977) is that observers are more likely to imitate the behavior of a model when they are uncertain about how to act themselves. Low SEs tend to be more uncertain than high SEs about the appropriateness of their behavior and thus may be more heavily influenced by the actions of a model. Second, a basic finding in research on attitude similarity and attraction (Byrne 1971) is that people tend to like others who are similar rather than dissimilar to themselves. Low SEs, who tend to need the esteem of others (Jones 1973), may make themselves more similar to models and, thus, presumably more likable. For these two reasons, low SEs probably are more apt than high SEs to be influenced by (or imitate) the behavior of relevant models.

But, what is the adaptive value of imitating the behavior of others? It probably depends on the adaptive value of the behavior that is being imitated. For example, consider the study by Weiss (1977) on the moderating effect of self-esteem in the modeling of leadership behavior. In that study it was shown that supervisors who were low, but not those who were high, in self-esteem modeled the leadership behavior of their direct superior to the extent that their superior was high in competence, success, and reward power. It seems that low SEs made better use of the actions of the models; after all, in order to get ahead it is important to attend to the behavior of models who are successful, competent, and/or high in reward power.

The maladaptive consequences of low SEs' greater tendency to imitate models could arise if low SEs also were shown to be affected by inappropriate behavior models. Whether that is true is an important empirical question to be addressed by future research. Suffice it to say that at least under some conditions low SEs' greater susceptibility to the influence of a behavior model may elicit positive outcomes for the individual and/or the organization.

Peer-group Interaction

PGI has been shown to have a much more marked impact on the work performance and attitudes of low than high self-esteem employees (Mossholder, Bedeian & Armenakis 1982); low SEs' greater plasticity can be dysfunctional to the extent that the PGI is unsupportive. Indeed, nursing employees who were low in self-esteem performed worse than their high self-esteem counterparts in the face of an unsupportive PGI. In a more optimistic vein for low SEs, however, that same study revealed that low self-esteem employees actually performed better than high SEs when the PGI was supportive. Thus, at least for this sample of employees, it was advantageous to be low rather than high in self-esteem when they were surrounded in their work group by supportive peers.

Self-relevance of Evaluative Feedback

A third mediator of low SEs' greater plasticity is their greater propensity to view negative feedback as self-revealing or self-diagnostic. For example, many studies (Zuckerman 1979) have shown that low SEs are more likely than high SEs to attribute failure experiences to internal causes. Perhaps because of their tendency to view negative feedback as a reflection of the "true self," low SEs often exhibit reduced task persistence and performance subsequent to failure feedback. Quite often, being negatively affected by failure feedback is dysfunctional to the individual and / or the organization. Indeed, our culture preaches the value of persistence in times of difficulty (for example, "If at first you don't succeed. . . .").

Nevertheless, there are undoubtedly instances in which it is functional for workers to lower their persistence at a particular task subsequent to receiving negative performance feedback. That is, there may be circumstances in which increased effort—which high SEs often exhibit subsequent to an initial failure—does not lead to better performance. For example, if workers do not possess the requisite level of ability or if the task inherently is quite difficult, then it may not matter how much harder they try subsequent to failure. Increased effort under such conditions is akin to "beating one's head against the wall," a response that may be far less adaptive than withdrawal from the task at hand.

Consider, for example, the results of a study by McFarlin, Baumeister, and Blascovich (1984). In this laboratory experiment, subjects of varying degrees of self-esteem worked on several problems, which, unbeknownst to them, were insoluble. The external cue consisted of problem-solving "advice" that subjects were given beforehand. Half were advised that the best strategy for the task was to give up and move on when faced with a difficult puzzle (quit condition), whereas the other half were told that the best approach was to persist with each problem until it was solved (persist condition).

Table 5–3
Mean Time Spent on Insoluble Problems as a Function of Self-esteem
and Advice
(in seconds)

	Advice	
Self-esteem	*Persist*	*Quit*
High	311.33	217.36
Low	355.55	168.11

Source: McFarlin, Baumeister & Blascovich 1984.
Note: Higher scores reflect greater persistence.

Low SEs were more behaviorally plastic, persisting longer in the persist condition and shorter in the quit condition than their high self-esteem counterparts (see table 5–3). What about the adaptive value of low SEs' greater susceptibility to influence? Given that the task was insoluble, low SEs responded in a less functional manner than high SEs in the persist condition. However, in the quit condition, high SEs exhibited more of what the authors called "nonproductive persistence" than their low self-esteem counterparts. As additional evidence that low SEs responded more adaptively than high SEs in the quit condition, it was found that over time high SEs increased whereas low SEs decreased their degree of persistence at the insoluble problems.

Thus, high SEs are more apt to respond with increased persistence in the face of failure, a tendency that often serves them well. Just as surely, however, persistence in the face of failure may be dysfunctional under certain conditions (Brockner & Rubin 1985; Janoff-Bulman & Brickman 1980; Staw, Sandelands & Dutton 1981). Further thought and research is needed to compare the responses of high and low self-esteem persons in organizational settings in which increased persistence may be nonproductive. For example, if low SEs exhibit reduced persistence at the task at hand, then in what activity, if any, do they engage instead? Imagine a scenario in which workers must perform a variety of activities in order for the organization to accomplish its mission. One such example is provided by the university, in which the faculty must perform research, teaching, and service—and do all three effectively—in order for the organization to flourish. Suppose two faculty members—one high and one low in self-esteem—receive consistently negative teaching ratings. Increased persistence in this case could take the form of spending more time preparing for class, or increasing the amount of student contact outside of class. According to research on the effect of self-esteem on postfailure persistence, the high self-esteem faculty member may be more apt than the one low in self-esteem to increase the amount of effort devoted to improved teaching. Is such heightened persistence adaptive? Might not such individuals (and the entire organization) be better served if they accepted the fact that their teaching was mediocre and spent increased time on other organizationally relevant activities) for example, research and service)? More generally, the point here is that the adaptive value of increased persistence following failure is situation-specific; thus, the fact that high SEs are more likely than low SEs to respond with renewed vigor subsequent to failure may or may not produce beneficial outcomes for the individual and/or the organization.

Survivors' Reactions to Layoffs

Chapter 4 discussed the results of several laboratory experiments dealing with the impact of layoffs on the work performance of those who survive the layoff. Several studies (Brockner, Davy & Carter 1985; Brockner, O'Malley, Grover, Esaki, Glynn & Lazarides 1987) have documented that layoffs actually elicited an increase in survivors' work performance. This was especially true for survivors low rather than high in chronic self-esteem, and consistent with the plasticity hypothesis.

To convey the possibility that low SEs' greater responsivity may have been the more adaptive response, the findings should be explored a bit more closely. In one study (Brockner, O'Malley, Grover, Esaki, Glynn & Lazarides, 1987), some subjects were led to believe that their jobs were insecure, that is, someone might have to be laid off and such a decision would be based in part of the quantity of their work performance in comparison to that of a coworker. Moreover, half of the participants had just witnessed the dismissal of a different coworker (layoff condition) whereas half had not (no-layoff condition). The extent to which survivors increased the quantity of their subsequent work performance are presented in table 5–4. Low SEs in the layoff condition exhibited a much greater boost in performance than low SEs in the no-layoff condition, and high SEs in the layoff condition. (High SEs actually were somewhat less productive in the layoff than no-layoff condition, although

Table 5–4
Increase in Number of Lines Proofread for Job Insecure Participants as a Function of Self-esteem and Layoff Survival

Self-esteem	Layoff	
	Yes	No
High	6.40	14.62
Low	21.36	6.00

Source: Brockner, O'Malley, Grover, Esaki, Glynn, and Lazarides 1987.

the difference did not approach significance.) Once again, subjects' job security was partially dependent upon the quantity of their output. Thus, it is reasonable to conclude that low SEs' greater reactions to the layoff were more individually adaptive, assuming, of course, that adaptivity may be defined in this context as taking steps to enhance the likelihood of job security.

Goal Instrumentality and Performance

As discussed in chapter 3, the presence of specific, difficult goals elicits heightened productivity, especially when workers are committed to, or accepting of, the goals (Locke et al. 1981). One factor that affects goal acceptance is its perceived *instrumentality,* that is, the extent to which positive outcomes are believed to be contingent upon goal attainment (Yukl & Latham 1978). Employees are likely to be more committed to goal attainment if instrumentality is high rather than low. Indeed, from the employees'—though not necessarily the organization's—point of view, it is quite adaptive for their goal commitment to be positively related to its instrumentality. After all, it may not be in the individual's best interests to work hard and attain a goal only to receive little or no extrinsic reward as a result. The fact that Yukl and Latham obtained a significant (r = .37) relationship between employees' perceived goal instrumentality and increased productivity is consistent with the stated logic.

Interestingly enough, however, Yukl and Latham further observed that the relationship between goal instrumentality and performance increase was moderated by the employees' self-esteem. Low self-esteem employees exhibited a highly significant correlation (r = .64) whereas their high self-esteem counterparts did not (r = .01). Such results can be interpreted to be consistent with others in this section: namely, low SEs' greater susceptibility to influence (by perceived goal instrumentality) was reflective of a more individually adaptive response than was that shown by the high SEs. Low SEs increased their performance to a greater extent when goal instrumentality was high rather than low; high SEs exhibited no such tendency.

Socialization

The discussion in the preceding chapter on socialization and self-esteem perhaps best illustrates how low SEs' greater plasticity can be adaptive or maladaptive, for individuals and organizations alike. Recall the basic findings discovered in the study by Jones (1986): organizations having an institutional (rather than laissez-faire) style of socialization were more likely to produce employees who had a custodial (rather than innovative) role-taking orientation; this tendency was especially pronounced among new hires who were low rather than high in self-esteem. Such results may be viewed favorably or unfavorably by both the employing organization and its employees. From the organization's point of view, the good news is that they can facilitate their employees' adoption of the status quo to the extent that the organization establishes an institutional style of socialization. Thus, new workers will learn more easily appropriate modes of behavior and values, which should enable the organization to accomplish its objectives. The down side from the organization's perspective is that the institutional style of socialization might stifle self-sufficiency, independence, and, therefore, innovation and creativity on the part of new employees; the organizational costs of such outcomes are self-evident.

From the employees' point of view, there also is both good and bad news associated with the fact that an institutional socialization style elicits a custodial role orientation. On the positive end, the institutional style of socialization goes a long way toward reducing a major source of stress among new workers, that is, uncertainty about appropriate ways to act and think. Subsidiary data in the Jones (1986) study revealed that the institutional style of socialization was associated with greater job satisfaction than was the laissez-faire style. In a more negative vein, the institutional style is less apt than the laissez-faire style to encourage new employees to figure things out for themselves. To speculate a bit, it is conceivable that the laissez-faire style forces individuals to become more self-reliant and independent not only within the context of the particular organization, but also throughout their careers; by contrast, the institutional style might "shortchange" new employees regarding their longer term career development. Studies of creativity (for example, Stein 1974) have suggested that the parents of creative scientists in research and development (R & D) laboratories reared their children in ways that forced them to learn how to solve problems independently. Perhaps the experience of autonomy— whether cultivated early in employees' lives or during their initial tenure in the organization—fosters creativity in the workplace.

If the adaptive value of low SEs' greater plasticity is situation specific, then organizations may wish to consider the level of the self-esteem resource that they have among their pool of workers. Or, are employees more apt to contribute to the achievement of organizational goals if they are high versus low in global self-esteem? Obviously, there is no easy answer to that question; the relationship between self-esteem and successful work performance is contingent on a myriad of factors. One general conclusion from the current reasoning is that human resource managers should not assume unilaterally that high self-esteem individuals make "better" employees. Some correlates of high self-esteem—such as high levels of self-confidence and, in some instances, ability— do facilitate the achievement of organizational goals. However, other attributes more typically found among low SEs—that is, those that produce behavioral plasticity—may sometimes be even more important than the correlates of high self-esteem. In matching employees to the organizational tasks at hand, personnel and human resource managers may need to strike a balance between having workers who are confident, self-assured, and self-reliant, and yet also open to the input of relevant organizational and environmental stimuli; such a balance may combine the best of the concomitants of high and low self-esteem.

For example, Morrison (1977) studied some of the personal characteristics of middle-level managers that predicted their success in adapting to changing roles. The managers who adapted successfully were significantly higher in self-esteem than were their counterparts who did not adapt as well to their changing role requirements. Moreover, the belief system of the successful adapters was considerably more "open" than that of the unsuccessful adapters. Openness was measured by the Rokeach (1960) dogmatism scale. According to Rokeach, an open belief system is one in which "the person can receive, evaluate, and act on relevant information received from the outside on its own intrinsic merits, unencumbered by irrelevant factors in the situation arising from within the person or from the outside" (Rokeach 1960, p. 57). In the Morrison (1977) study, therefore, it appeared that the greatest adaptivity was exhibited by individuals who were both high in self-esteem and open to environmental input; on the surface, at least, the latter attribute seems similar to some of the characteristics of low SEs that render them susceptible to influence by external cues.

Behavioral Plasticity: Its Relation to Other Theories of Employee Self-esteem

The processes by which individuals' self-esteem exerts influence over their work attitudes and behaviors have been a matter of considerable theoretical controversy (Dipboye 1977a; 1977b; Korman 1970, 1977). The two predominant perspectives are self-consistency theory, and self-enhancement theory.

Self-consistency Theory

In 1970, Korman hypothesized that cognitive consistency theory, which had been very much in vogue in psychology in the late 1950s (Festinger 1957; Heider 1958; Newcomb 1959; Osgood & Tannenbaum 1955), may offer a compelling analysis of work behavior. The essence of the various versions of consistency theory is that individuals are motivated to seek consistency between their beliefs, attitudes, and behaviors; moreover, any inconsistency between these self-aspects would produce a state of psychological tension that needed to be reduced by a change in cognition and/or behavior. In attempting to extend consistency theory to the organizational setting, Korman offered the following hypothesis: "all other things being equal, individuals will engage in and find satisfying those behavioral roles which will maximize their sense of cognitive balance or consistency" (p. 32).

Self-esteem was defined by Korman as the extent to which workers see themselves as competent, need-satisfying individuals. Workers' self-esteem at a given point in time was believed to be a confluence of their global self-esteem, as well as specific situational factors (task competence, informal relationships). The ultimate utility of the theory, of course, is its ability to explain work behavior. Toward that end, Korman suggested that the following findings could be accounted for by consistency theory: the tendency for high SEs to outperform low SEs (presumably such performance differences would enable both groups to maintain consistency in their self-evaluation); the tendency for high SEs to exhibit a stronger positive correlation between work performance and job satisfaction (presumably successful performance is more consistent, and unsuccessful performance more inconsistent with high SEs' self-cognitions that they are competent, need-fulfilling persons than would be the case for low SEs); and the greater tendency for high SEs to choose occupations that are congruent with their needs and abilities (once again, presumably the tendency to choose a career for which one is well suited is consistent with high SEs' tendencies to be a competent, need-satisfying person).

Self-consistency versus Behavioral Plasticity. There are at least three key differences between self-consistency and the perspective offered by behavioral plasticity. First, Korman's definition of self-esteem refers to individuals' beliefs about their degree of competence and tendency to be need fulfilling; nowhere in this conceptualization is it explicitly stated that high SEs like themselves more than their low self-esteem counterparts.

This distinction, while subtle, lends itself to the second difference, pertaining to the breadth of the two theoretical perspectives: the key psychological events that go on inside the minds (and hearts) of high versus low SEs that produce differences in their customary modes of thought, feeling, and behavior. According to self-consistency theory, workers' primary motive is to seek consistency; according to behavioral plasticity, individuals need to be differentiated on the basis of three psychological factors: how much they are uncertain about the correctness or appropriateness of their beliefs and/or behaviors. Degree of uncertainty should affect the extent to which they rely on external cues to guide themselves; the extent to which they like themselves. Degree of self-liking should be (inversely) related to the extent to which they are dependent upon the receipt of positive evaluations from others; and the extent to which they view negative feedback as self-diagnostic. The tendency to do so may well influence the impact of such feedback on subsequent behavior. In short, the plasticity analysis tries to present a picture of the nature of high versus low self-esteem, by highlighting more than one element.

Third, the two perspectives appear to differ in their explanatory utility.

Korman proposed three major differences between high and low self-esteem persons: compared to low SEs, high SEs should be more apt to perform well, exhibit a stronger performance-satisfaction relationship, and choose occupations that are congruent with their needs and abilities. The research evidence has lent strong support only to the third proposition, and, as suggested in chapter 3, this finding can be explained just as easily by plasticity as by consistency theory. The evidence on the first two hypotheses simply does not lend strong support to either. There are some laboratory and field studies showing a positive relationship between self-esteem and performance. However, researchers very often obtain no difference in performance as a function of self-esteem, and under certain conditions (Brockner & Hulton 1978; Mossholder, Bedeian & Armenakis 1982; Weiss & Knight 1980) it has been shown that low SEs outperform high SEs.

Even more damaging to the consistency position are the myriad of studies showing that low SEs' work performance is highly susceptible to influence by external factors. That is, if low SEs seek to perform more poorly than high SEs in order to maintain a consistent self-view, then why is the performance of the former group so easily manipulable—up to and sometimes beyond the level of the latter group—by performance-relevant factors? The self-esteem effects that consistency theory purports to explain simply have not been obtained in many studies. The relationship of self-esteem to occupational choice can be explained readily by plasticity as well as consistency theory. Furthermore, plasticity theory can account for a wide range of findings about which consistency theory is apparently mute.

Finally, one other difference in the tone of the two theories should be mentioned. Compared to the plasticity analysis, consistency theory does not, at least explicitly, emphasize the joint and interactive effects of self-esteem and organizational and environmental factors on work behaviors. Instead, consistency theory has much more of a "main effect" quality to it (for example, high SEs should outperform low SEs, or high SEs should choose more need-congruent occupations than low SEs). Given recent theoretical trends toward person-situation interactionism in personality, social, and organizational psychology (Mischel 1973; Weiss & Adler 1984), the underemphasis on external factors in Korman's (1970) theory—apart from those believed to influence perceived competence at the task at hand—is unfortunate.

Self-enhancement Theory

Like self-consistency theory, self-enhancement theory suggests that differences in the work behavior of high and low SEs stem from a superordinate motivational process. In sharp contrast to consistency theory, however, that motive is not to be self-consistent, but rather to enhance, maintain, or recover a positive self-evaluation. Self-enhancement theory posits that individuals need to feel high self-esteem (see chapter 7 for further detail). An important corollary of this theory is that the strength of the need for self-enhancement is directly related to the extent to which this need has been thwarted in the past. Thus, low SEs are more likely to strive toward self-enhancement than their high self-esteem counterparts.

Self-enhancement Versus Self-consistency. Self-enhancement theory (Dipboye 1977a, 1977b) was proposed as an alternative explanation of many of the findings that had been explained by Korman (1970) as supportive of consistency theory. Unfortunately, very few studies in the organizational psychology literature have pitted the two against one another a priori in an empirical test of their predictive accuracy. The two theories have been compared, however, in social psychological studies dealing with the effect of self-esteem and interpersonal evaluations on interpersonal attraction (Jones 1973). In the prototypical study, subjects of varying levels of self-esteem are evaluated either favorably or unfavorably by another person, and then are asked to evaluate that person themselves. Consistency theory predicts that high SEs would like the positive evaluator more than the negative evaluator, and that this tendency would be reduced or even reversed among low SEs. Enhancement theory also posits that high SEs would like the positive evaluator more than the negative one, but that low SEs, who are in greater need of positive evaluation, will especially like the positive evaluator and especially dislike the negative evaluator. The bulk of the empirical evidence in this body of research favored enhancement over consistency theory.

   Although the strongest empirical tests of consistency versus enhancement theory have not been performed in the organizational context, it seems clear that Jones's (1973) findings have considerable managerial implications. To cite just one, it may be that low self-esteem employees' attitudes toward their job may be more affected than high SEs' by the evaluations that they receive in the workplace. If one's subordinate is suspected to be low in self-esteem, then managers should be sensitive to the possibility that the evaluation that the subordinate receives—be it in the form of informal comments or a more formal performance appraisal process—may have great impact on the subordinate's affective reactions.

   More generally, managers would be well advised to be attuned to the host of factors, apart from their subordinates' self-esteem, that affects the latter's dependency on being positively appraised. For example, employees who are newcomers to the organization, or even to their division or work group within the organization, often are in a state of uncertainty, stemming from the fact that they must "learn the ropes." A positive evaluation received from one's superior during this period of early socialization is bound to have a very favorable impact on the subordinate; moreover, the adverse impact of negative evaluations is apt to be amplified during this point in time, in both instances due to the fact that the newcomer is in a heightened state of being dependent on the receipt of positive feedback.

Self-enhancement versus Behavioral Plasticity. The key difference between these two positions is in their comprehensiveness. That is, behavioral plasticity is dependent on three factors: uncertainty, lack of self-liking, and proneness to view negative evaluations as self-diagnostic. The tendency to seek self-enhancement is (inversely) related to the second of these three factors. Indeed, one of the very factors that causes low SEs to be more plastic than high SEs is the tendency of the former group to like themselves less and, therefore, be more dependent on being positively appraised by others. This process is essentially identical to the one that mediates self-enhancement strivings.

In short, the plasticity perspective subsumes self-enhancement theory. Low SEs may be plastic because of their relatively high need for self-enhancement. However, some of the other mediators of low SEs' greater plasticity may have little to do with self-enhancement strivings. For example, consider the fact that low SEs are more likely than high SEs to imitate the behavior of models (Weiss 1977). In the modeling studies, low SEs were more imitative than high SEs even when they were not dependent upon the opinion of the model, suggesting that low SEs' susceptibility to the model's influence was due more to their uncertainty about appropriate behavior than their desire for self-enhancement. Therefore, plasticity appears to be able to account for a wider range of findings than self-enhancement theory.

Self-consistency, Self-enhancement, and Behavioral Plasticity:
Some Concluding Comments

As in any comparative theoretical analysis, it is likely that each has its domains of greater (or lesser) applicability. Shrauger (1975) has amassed a large amount of evidence suggesting that on cognitive measures such as memory, attention, and attribution, individuals respond in a manner that is consistent with their prior self-esteem. Thus, low SEs are more likely than high SEs to retain negative feedback accurately, give it more credence, and attribute it to internal factors. Shrauger (1975) also has proposed that affective reactions of high and low SEs are more likely to support self-enhancement theory. This set of findings suggests that the following unfortunate paradox may apply to low self-esteem workers: not liking themselves, they are heavily dependent upon receipt of positive feedback from their external worlds; however, low SEs' cognitive processes may make it difficult for them to perceive the very information that they so badly need.

The plasticity hypothesis, unlike self-consistency and self-enhancement theories, focuses on a confluence of motivational and cognitive processes associated with self-esteem, making it particularly well suited to predict the conditions under which low SEs will be more affected than high SEs by external factors. Like self-consistency and self-enhancement, the plasticity hypothesis does have its limiting conditions.

Finally, some mention must be made of the practical use of the comparative analysis between self-consistency, self-enhancement, and behavioral plasticity. The theoretical relevance of the comparative analysis should be clear. What about practical relevance or utility? I hereby submit that, perhaps even more than usual, we heed the famous words of Kurt Lewin, who suggested that there was nothing as practical as sound theory. After all, the role of management is to accomplish the organization's mission(s) through other people; that is, management must decide how to influence organization members to perform their tasks most efficiently. Effective management, in other words, necessitates a firm understanding of the social influence process. A basic moderator of the social influence process is employees' level of self-esteem. Thus, the following practical implications stem from the comparative theoretical analysis: high and low self-esteem employees may respond very differently to a variety of organizational events; a host of processes—not just one—could account for such tendencies; and the pattern of self-esteem differences in responsivity to external events may vary from situation to situation. In many instances, low SEs will be more easily influenced than high SEs; in other situations, low and high SEs will be equally easily influenced, but in directly opposite ways. Consequently, in order for practicing managers to predict and control employees' reactions with greater accuracy, it is important to consider whether the workplace environment includes elements to which low SEs, high SEs, or both are responsive.

The message is that organizational practitioners need to clarify their own theories of the nature of self-esteem. Just what is it, they should ask themselves, that differentiates the high versus low self-esteem employee? Having delineated their own theoretical stance, they then may wish to consider how to influence both types of workers, and whether it will be necessary to invoke different methods to do so. In earnestly thinking about the nature of their employees' self-esteem, practicing managers are bound to gain insights into the process(es) of social influence, insights that may well translate into increased managerial effectiveness.

Summary

If the plasticity hypothesis is viable, as the evidence in chapters 3 and 4 suggests, then a number of related questions arise. Three of the most important ones were considered in this chapter: whether it is always the case that low SEs are more susceptible to influence by external cues than their high self-esteem counterparts; whether being susceptible to influence is functional, for both employees and organizations; and how the theoretical position advanced in chapters 3 and 4 relates to existing theories in the organizational literature on employee self-esteem.

The analysis of the first of these three issues suggested that low SEs are not always more plastic than high SEs. Sometimes the two groups are influenced in identical ways by events in the workplace, at other times high SEs are more plastic than low SEs, whereas on other occasions the two groups differ in the direction, but not magnitude of their ability to be influenced. Some of the factors that elicit results contrary to the plasticity hypothesis (for example, constraining situations, cues that elicit individuals' active involvement in deciding how to behave, and esteem-threatening events) were discussed. The plasticity hypothesis has received strong support, but under certain workplace conditions it simply is not the case that low SEs are more affected than high SEs.

Of course, the fact that low SEs are not always more plastic than high SEs makes even more challenging the theorist's and the practitioner's task of predicting how employees' self-esteem will moderate their reactions to workplace factors. As stated in chapter 1, to predict the role of self-esteem in a given situation, one must be able to identify the key mediating variables in that situation and then determine how self-esteem relates to those mediating factors. But even more than that, the theorist and practitioner must be able to delineate the key psychological factors that are evoked by the given situation. For example, on the one hand, low SEs respond more than high SEs in those situations in which individuals' level of uncertainty about the accuracy of their beliefs and behaviors is a key determinant of their reactions (for example, Weiss & Knight 1980). On the other hand, certain esteem-threatening circumstances produce results contrary to the plasticity hypothesis, such that high SEs actively attempt to meet the challenge, whereas low SEs often withdraw from it (for example, Brockner 1985). The difficult task is to predict whether a given work situation is uncertainty producing, esteem-threatening, or otherwise one that might differentiate low and high SEs' responses to it.

The second issue discussed in this chapter referred to the functional value of behavioral plasticity. Even though low SEs often are more plastic than their high self-esteem counterparts, this is not to say that low SEs' greater susceptibility to influence invariably is dysfunctional, either to themselves or the organization. Under certain conditions, low SEs' greater tendency to withdraw in the face of negative feedback can be quite maladaptive. However, in other circumstances (for example, see the discussions on information search, modeling processes, and peer-group interaction) low SEs' greater plasticity is not at all dysfunctional. In short, low SEs often (though not always) are more plastic than high SEs; however, low SEs' greater susceptibility to influence does not always produce negative outcomes, either for themselves or the organization.

6
Antecedents of Employee Self-esteem

To this point, self-esteem has been discussed primarily as an independent variable; some of the cognitive, affective, and behavioral consequences (or, at least, correlates) of self-esteem have been delineated. It should be apparent that self-esteem—typically in interaction with situational factors—is a crucial predictor of employees' work beliefs and behaviors. Previous chapters attest to the complexity of the manner in which individuals' self-esteem relates to their workplace reactions. Chapters 3 and 4 lent strong support to the plasticity hypothesis; many studies suggested that low SEs' work behaviors were more susceptible to influence by external and social cues than were those of their high self-esteem counterparts. Chapter 5 presented evidence on the delimiting conditions of the plasticity hypothesis. Of course, employees' self-esteem is not the only individual difference predictor of their work behaviors and attitudes. One cannot help but conclude, however, that workers' self-esteem (in conjunction with contextual factors) is a significant antecedent of their thoughts and deeds. Given that self-esteem is such an important predictor of employee behavior, it is important to understand its antecedents. Accordingly, this chapter treats self-esteem primarily as a dependent rather than independent variable.

Some Organizing Concepts

The task of fully understanding the antecedents of self-esteem may be just as difficult as understanding its consequences or correlates; as will soon become apparent, many factors and processes may influence and mediate employees' self-esteem. Several basic concepts, however, serve to organize (that is, provide a taxonomy for) much of the subsequent discussion. First, I shall review empirical research that has explored some of the factors that cause (or at least predict) employee self-esteem. In some of these studies the dependent variable is global or chronic self-esteem, that is, the favorability of individuals' evaluations across situations and over time. Other studies employ specific or acute self-esteem—that is, the favorability of their evaluations in a given situation at a given point in time—as the dependent variable. Examples of the latter include employees' evaluations of themselves as workers, or, even more situation specific, their evaluations of their competence at particular tasks.

The distinction between global or chronic, and specific or acute self-esteem is similar to the "trait" versus "state" dichotomy assumed to exist for most personality variables. Thus, what individuals bring to a given situation is some sum of their general traits and their specific states. Research on perceived control, for example, has shown that individuals' locus of control is jointly determined by their generalized beliefs (that is, across situations and over time) about whether their behavior influences outcomes (Rotter 1966) as well as time and/or situation-specific factors (for example, Seligman 1975). Similarly, research on anxiety distinguishes between individuals' chronic or characteristic levels of anxiety, as well as their level of anxiety at a given time and place (Spielberger, Gorsuch & Lushene 1970). In short, the relationship of most individual difference variables to thought and behavior is based on some combination of the global and specific components of the individual difference variables. Or, as Markus and Kunda (1986) recently demonstrated, the self-concept is both stable (that is, trait-like) and malleable (that is, state-like). To predict individuals' *working self-concept*—that which influences mood and behavior at any given point in time—one must consider their customary mode of self-evaluation as well as the impact of more temporary situational factors.

In addition to the global-specific distinction, the relevant empirical research can be differentiated with regard to whether the studies dealt with work or nonwork antecedents of self-esteem. The analysis of the antecedents of self-esteem includes discussions of the nonwork causes of global self-esteem as well as the work-related variables affecting both global and specific self-esteem.

For theoretical and practical reasons, one needs to know more than the factors affecting self-esteem, regardless of whether the factors reside in the workplace, and regardless of whether it is global or specific self-esteem under consideration. It is just as, if not more, important to understand the psychological and social processes that mediate the development of self-esteem. For example, if performance appraisal is one of the factors affecting workers' self-esteem, it is critical to understand why; what are the processes that mediate the impact of the performance appraisal on individuals' self-esteem?

This chapter is organized into three major sections. The first presents a selective review of empirical research on the antecedents of self-esteem. The second section considers some of the processes that mediate the impact of work and nonwork variables on self-esteem; these processes have high generality, that is, they apply equally well to the development of global and specific self-esteem. Third, some implications of the material covered in the first two sections are discussed, and several areas are indicated in which further theory and research are needed.

Antecedents of Self-esteem

The antecedents of much of workers' global self-esteem are not rooted in the organizational setting. Many personality theorists have suggested that the formation of personality, in general, and self-esteem, in particular, takes place during the years of childhood and adolescence (Hall & Lindzey 1970; Rosenberg 1979), long before individuals enter work organizations. One even could argue that organizational practitioners need not concern themselves with the nonwork antecedents of workers' global self-esteem. After all, if these antecedents exerted influence long ago and outside of the organizational arena, then there is little that the practitioner can do to affect workers' self-esteem.

This argument is lacking, however, on three counts. First, employees' self-esteem reflects the combination of global and specific factors. While there may be little that practitioners can do to influence the nonwork determinants of employees' global self-esteem, there is much that they can do to affect the work factors that influence specific self-esteem. Second, and related to the first, workers' global self-esteem is largely but not entirely determined by their prework life experiences. Kohn and Schooler (1983) provide ample evidence that the "structural imperatives" of work conditions—job features that are inherent to the very work that individuals must perform on a day-in, day-out basis—have significant effects on a number of global personality dimensions, including self-esteem.

Third, although practitioners cannot affect the earlier nonwork determinants of employees' global self-esteem, they still may have much to learn from previous theory and research on this matter. To the extent that the antecedents of global and specific self-esteem (whether residing in the workplace or not) are mediated by a common core of processes—a notion that I and others (Rosenberg 1979) wholeheartedly endorse—practitioners may become much better equipped to influence global self-esteem by understanding its nonwork determinants.

Solano (cited in Schneider & Schmitt 1986) offers a similar point in discussing workplace determinants of creativity. Solano studied the background environments of creative people, focusing primarily on their parents' behaviors and attitudes. She then suggested that these nonwork antecedents of global creativity—such as experiencing multiple perspectives, being challenged, and being provided an appreciation for the intrinsic rewards of goal accomplishment, to name a few—may be applied to work environments in order to influence employees' creativity in that context.

Nonwork Determinants of Global Self-esteem

Global self-esteem is shaped primarily by early experiences in individuals' lives, which obviously have occurred outside the context of the work organization.

Indeed, a major concern of most personality theorists is to delineate the factors and processes that influence the development of self-esteem (Adler 1927; Freud 1953; Horney 1950; Rogers 1961; Sullivan 1953). Although there is considerable heterogeneity in the assumptions that such theorists make about the essence of human nature, most seem to agree that "early experience" has a major impact on personality development in general and self-esteem in particular (Rosenberg 1979).

In parallel to (though typically not derived from) personality theories of self-esteem, there has been a considerable amount of empirical work exploring the antecedents of self-esteem. One of the most notable works is a comprehensive study performed by Coopersmith (1967), who studied a sample of preadolescent children (ages ten to twelve) in order to establish the impact on their self-esteem of a wide range of parental factors. Before the results of the Coopersmith study are presented, several precautionary notes are in order. Perhaps most important, the basic design of the study is nonexperimental in nature. It may be that many of the factors to be described causally affected the child's self-esteem, but such notions technically are in the realm of speculation and conjecture. Second, the study was conducted in the mid-1960s and, consequently, focuses primarily on the impact of the mother's attributes and child-rearing practices—and not those of the father—on the child's self-esteem. Given the increased importance attached to the father's role in affecting personality development (Lamb 1977), the findings of Coopersmith may be incomplete. Third, the external generalizability of Coopersmith's results is of some concern in that his sample was both small ($N = 45$) and quite homogeneous (only normal white males from a primarily middle class school in central Connecticut were studied). In spite of these limitations, however, the study provides many interesting findings that may elucidate the causal antecedents of self-esteem.

To delineate the antecedents of self-esteem, it may be useful to specify the cognitions that tend to be associated with high versus low self-esteem. As mentioned in chapter 2, self-esteem refers to an evaluative construct; nonetheless, a variety of cognitions are likely to be predictive, if not determinant of individuals' self-esteem. These include:

1.   power or perceived control. Individuals' perceptions that they can control their environment—that is, that there is some contingency between their behavior and the outcomes of their behavior—typically lead to higher self-esteem. For example, it has been demonstrated repeatedly that high SEs are more internal in their locus of control (Dweck 1975; Fitch 1970) than are their low self-esteem counterparts.

2.   perceived importance, value, or significance. The more individuals are led to believe that they are valued, especially in the eyes of significant others, the greater is their self-esteem.

3.   perceived competence or expertise. The more individuals believe that they are competent or expert at a particular task, the greater is their self-

esteem. For example, many studies have shown that high SEs' task achievement expectations are greater than those of low SEs (for example, Coopersmith 1967; Shrauger 1972).

Virtually all of the variables that Coopersmith found to be predictive of self-esteem probably influenced participants' perceived control, and/or significance, and/or competence. More specifically, the following factors were shown to be positively associated with children's self-esteem:

1. the mother's self-esteem
2. the parents' marital adjustment (indicated by a lack of tension in the marriage)
3. the mother's estimate of the child's effectiveness in dealing with social, academic, and personal matters
4. the mother's estimate of the child's intelligence
5. the mother's affection for the child
6. the degree of mother-child rapport
7. the extent to which the mother was knowledgeable about her child's friends
8. the extent to which the child-rearing practices consisted of setting appropriate limits and strictly enforcing those limits, while simultaneously allowing for a range of acceptable behavior within the confines of the limits
9. the use of management practices such as restraint, denial, and isolation when the child violates rules, rather than more negative techniques, such as corporal punishment or the withdrawal of love.

Note that factors 3 and 4—the child's effectiveness and intelligence—probably affect self-esteem through the mediating cognition of perceived competence. Factors 5, 6, and 7—the mother's affection for, rapport with, and knowledge of the child—are probably mediated by perceived importance. For example, the implicit message conveyed by the mother who takes the time to learn about her child's friends is that the mother is interested in the child; in turn, the child's perception of his own importance is apt to be positively affected.

Factor 8, which is actually multifaceted, could elicit increased control, significance, and competence in the child. The setting of limits could enhance the child's "cognitive control," in that they are more apt to be able to distinguish between appropriate and inappropriate behavior. Moreover, the setting of limits could elevate perceived importance by conveying to children that they are cared about enough for the parents to set limits. Finally, the setting of limits could indirectly lead to felt competence, to the extent that the child is able to behave appropriately within the context of the limits.

Organizational scholars and practitioners both may stand to benefit—albeit in different ways—from a thorough understanding of the nonwork antecedents of global self-esteem. Given that self-esteem (in interaction with situational factors) is an important predictor of employees' attitudes and behaviors, and given that a considerable portion of employees' self-esteem is global in nature, it is theoretically important to delineate the antecedents of global self-esteem. Of course, it also is practically important to discern the antecedents of global self-esteem for those individuals who are assigned with the task of management, that is, accomplishing work through other people. While practitioners may not easily be able to influence the earlier, nonwork determinants of employees' global self-esteem, they may have greater success in affecting the workplace determinants of global and specific self-esteem; useful leads toward the latter ends may be suggested by theory and research on the nonwork antecedents of global self-esteem.

It also is worth noting that the nonwork antecedents of global self-esteem seem to influence the immediate social and psychological context (or what Rosenberg (1979) refers to as the "effective interpersonal environment") in which parents and children interact. Factors remote to that context should be less influential. For example, one might expect broad "social class" demographic variables (such as occupational status, as defined by Hollingshead and Redlich 1958, or socioeconomic status as defined by Duncan 1961) to be predictive of self-esteem. After all, this reasoning goes, children whose parents come from a higher social class are exposed to an environment having greater associations with success (and its resulting feelings of competence) than those coming from a lower social class. Note, however, that a demographic variable such as social class only is indirectly related to children's effective interpersonal environment, which incorporates the more direct determinants of their self-esteem. As Rosenberg (1979) suggested upon noting the weak (and sometimes nonexistent) relationship between social class and self-esteem among children, "if significant others neither look up to nor down on the child *by virtue of his socioeconomic status,* then adopting the viewpoint of these others, his objective socioeconomic status should have little impact upon his feeling of self-worth" (p. 137).

Moreover, individuals tend to interact with and then compare themselves to others who are in the same social class as themselves, a proposition readily derived from social comparison theory (Festinger 1954). If so, and if such social comparison processes are an important mediator of self-esteem, then individuals from a higher social class are not at a (self-esteem) comparative advantage relative to those from a lower social class.

Two factors—that social class only is related indirectly to the psychological context of parent-child interaction, and that members of different social classes tend to compare themselves within, rather than across, classes—lead to the prediction that children's social class and their global self-esteem are only weakly correlated, if at all. In fact, these are precisely the results that Coopersmith (1967) obtained. Coopersmith himself is quick to point out that his small sample size and the sample's restricted range of social class may have contributed to the nonsignificance of the results. Other studies that do not suffer from either of these difficulties did yield a positive association between social class and self-esteem (Kohn 1969; Rosenberg 1965; see Rosenberg & Pearlin 1978 for a review). However, the strength of the relationship between social class and self-esteem, while statistically significant, generally is quite weak. Commenting on this weak relationship, Coopersmith (1967) noted:

> Broad social contexts and prestige hierarchies do not have as pervasive and significant effects upon self-esteem as is generally assumed, but suggest instead that conditions in the effective interpersonal environment are employed to judge whether one is appreciated and respected (p. 94).

I am not suggesting that individuals' social class always is irrelevant to their self-esteem. Indeed, Rosenberg (1979) has shown that the association between social class and self-esteem is much stronger for adults than for children. It will be shown later in this chapter that social class has a much more direct impact on the immediate social psychological environment of adults than children; consequently, social class more strongly influences (or predicts) the self-esteem of the former than the latter.

Finally, it should be mentioned that the results of Coopersmith's (1967) research were highly representative of the findings obtained in many other studies. Some of these other studies used adolescents (rather than preteenagers) as subjects. Moreover, the relationship of both parents' attitudes and behaviors—rather than merely those of the mother—to their children's self-esteem were assessed. In addition, the participants were drawn from a wide variety of socioeconomic levels, rather than the highly restricted range employed by Coopersmith. In spite of these differences relative to the Coopersmith methodology, the results are strikingly similar: the more the parents fostered a psychological climate that heightened their children's perceptions of their competence and/or worthiness, that is, by granting them a reasonable amount of autonomy, by being supportive, and by spending "quality time" with them, the more likely were the children to develop high global self-esteem (Bachman 1970; Gecas 1971; Gecas & Schwalbe 1986; Peterson, Southworth & Peters 1983; Rosenberg 1965).

Workplace Determinants of Self-esteem

Employees' self-esteem is determined not only by early experience, but also by a variety of factors in the workplace (Kohn & Schooler 1983; Korman 1970). Most empirical studies on this issue, like those on the nonwork antecedents of global self-esteem, are plagued by the nonexperimental nature of the research design. Thus, the reader is cautioned to view research findings tentatively, awaiting the outcome of further studies that more convincingly demonstrate the causal impact of various factors on workers' self-esteem (for example, Kohn & Schooler 1983).

Much of the relevant research has been nicely summarized in a review article by Tharenou (1979), who has organized the organizational anteced-ents of self-esteem into two broad categories: those intrinsic to the work itself, and those related to the context in which the work is performed (see tables 6–1 and 6–2).

Intrinsic Job Characteristics and Self-esteem. Intrinsic job characteristics include the extent to which the job is varied, skilled, involves learning, involves participation in decision making, and is associated with role strains, such as ambiguity or overload. Almost all of the studies reported statistically signif-icant relationships between intrinsic job characteristics and self-esteem, in the predicted directions. Thus, the following conditions were shown to be posi-tively correlated with workers' self-esteem: job variety, skilled job content, job content that involved learning, participation in decision making about one's job, worker autonomy, and low role strain.

In addition to the possibility of these rather simple-minded main effect influences of job characteristics on self-esteem, there is suggestive evidence that workers' self-esteem is jointly (and interactively) determined by person, job, and organizational variables. For examples, Tharenou's (1979) review reported that the correlation between job complexity and self-satisfaction was signif-icantly greater for those high rather than low in job involvement (Vroom 1962), the relationship between job challenge and work-role esteem was greater for those desirous rather than less desirous of job challenge (Hite 1975), and man-agers whose work environments were characterized by a good fit between organizational factors (structure and climate) and task attributes (complex versus routine) had stronger feelings of competence than those whose work environments consisted of a poorer organization-task fit (Morse 1970).

Extrinsic Job Characteristics and Self-esteem. The last result suggests that it is not only the work, but also the context in which the work is performed that affects employees' self-esteem. Tharenou's (1979) review of the relevant context literature is described in table 6–2. Implicit in this review is that extrinsic characteristics can be further subdivided into two types: factors per-taining to the economic context in which the work is performed, and those relevant to the interpersonal context. Examples of the former category include pay and job level, and examples of the latter include the nature of the social relationships that exist between employees and their coworkers and supervisors.

Taken together, the results show that contextual variables influence employee self-esteem, and always in the manner that would be intuitively predicted. Thus, when significant relationships between contextual variables and self-esteem do exist, they show that higher occupational status, pay, and favorable working relationships both with one's coworkers and supervisors are associated with greater self-esteem. However, many more studies have obtained nonsignificant findings, at least in relation to the research on intrinsic characteristics; this suggests that the extrinsic or contextual variables may be less influential determinants of employee self-esteem than are the intrinsic characteristics. Additional support for this assertion stems from the results of a handful of studies, which simultaneously have explored the relative impact of intrinsic (job complexity, autonomy) and extrinsic (supervisory style, coworker interaction) factors on self-esteem. In all three instances (Beehr 1976; Hackman & Lawler 1971; Kornhauser 1965), the intrinsic characteristics were more predictive of self-esteem than were the extrinsic characteristics.

Several studies also have looked at the relative predictive power of social class and work-related factors (both intrinsic and extrinsic to the job) in explaining workers' self-esteem (for example, Staples, Schwalbe & Gecas 1984); the results of these studies are consistent with those reported already. Specifically, social class (such as occupational status) does not predict global or even specific self-esteem very well; work-related factors (such as supervising practices and work autonomy) do a much better job of predicting self-esteem. More (psychologically) distal variables such as social class may, however, have indirect effects on self-esteem if and only if they influence the immediate psychological nature of the work environment (Kohn & Schooler 1983).

There are two key points to note on the research on the antecedents of self-esteem. First, both global and specific self-esteem are induced when individuals are led to believe that they are competent, valued, and/or in control. As Coopersmith (1967) has pointed out, this does not imply that each cognition must be elicited in order for the person to experience high self-esteem. Instead, all we can offer is a much more crude hypothesis: that perceived competence and/or value and/or control are part and parcel of high self-esteem.

Second, the factors most highly correlated with individuals' self-esteem are those embedded in the individuals' immediate psychological environment, both in the past and the present. The nonwork antecedents of global self-esteem, according to Coopersmith, are found in parental-child interactions, and not as much in the broader context (for example, social class) in which such interactions occur. Similarly, the workplace antecedents of self-esteem have more to do with psychological states evoked by the individuals' transactions with their work than by the economic or social context in which the work takes place (or by the workers' social class). This is not to say, of course, that contextual variables do not matter; rather, they appear to be less influential than those affecting the immediate psychological climate.

Table 6–1
Studies of Relationships Between Intrinsic Job Characteristics and Self-esteem

Type of Self-esteem	Experimenters	Subjects	Situational Variables	Results
Global	Kohn & Schooler, 1973	3101 U.S. male workers, representative sample	Closeness of supervision, job complexity (dealing with things, ideas, people), routinization of work, time pressure	X[a]
	Kornhauser, 1965	407 male automobile workers	Job interest, job skill, routinization of work	X
	Vroom, 1962	399 male oil refinery and manufacturing workers	Job complexity (autonomy, learning, skill)	X
Work role	Beehr, 1976	651 white- and blue-collar supervisors and workers	Autonomy, role ambiguity	X
	French & Caplan, 1972	205 male administrators, scientists, and engineers	Participation, qualitative role overload	X
			Quantitative role overload	n.s.
	French, Tupper, & Mueller 1965	104 male university professors	Qualitative role overload	X

			[a]
Hackman & Lawler, 1971	208 telephone company employees	Job content (variety, autonomy, feedback, task identity)	X
Hite, 1975	Subsample of probability sample of U.S. workers	Job challenge (skill, autonomy, learning)	X
Kahn, Wolfe, Quinn, Snoek & Rosenthal, 1964	725 U.S. workers, representative sample	Role ambiguity	X
Levitan, 1970	Kibbutz workers	Autonomy	X
Margolis, Kroes & Quinn, 1975	1496 U.S. workers, representative sample	Role ambiguity, qualitative overload, participation	X
Sense of competence			
Argyris, 1960	124 manufacturing employees	Job skill	X
Gardell, 1971	303 male engineering and pulp and paper workers	Work complexity (skill, autonomy, variety, social interaction)	X
Gardell, 1973	370 lumberjacks	Work monotony (autonomy, mechanization)	X

Source: Tharenou 1979, p. 326.

[a] X indicates a significant relationship, n.s. a nonsignificant one.

Table 6–2
Studies of Relationships Between Extrinsic Job Characteristics and Self-esteem

Type of Self-esteem	Experimenters	Subjects	Situational Variables	Results
Global	Bachman & O'Malley, 1977	1608 young U.S. males, representative sample	Occupational status	X [a]
	Bowers, 1963	347 male foremen and manufacturing employees	Supervisor support	X
	Gavin, 1973	367 insurance managerial candidates	Job level	n.s.
	Ghiselli, 1963	416 white- and blue-collar workers	Occupational level	— [b]
	Jacques & Chason, 1977	805 Florida adults, representative sample	Occupational status	n.s.
	Kohn & Schooler, 1973	3101 U.S. male workers, representative sample	Job security, dirtiness of the work, job level, income, ownership	n.s.
	Kornhauser, 1965	407 male automobile workers	Job level	X
			Supervisory style, pay	n.s.
	Lefkowitz, 1967	179 manufacturing workers	Pay, seniority	n.s.

Work role	Beehr, 1976	651 white- and blue-collar supervisors and workers	Supervisor support Group support	X n.s.
	Ghiselli & Johnson, 1970	413 managers	Promotion (flat organization)	X
	Hall & Nougaim, 1968	49 young managerial trainees	Length of time in job, promotion, pay	X
	Hite, 1975	Subsample of probability sample of U.S. workers	Group support	X
	Kasl & French, 1962	725 male supervisors and manufacturing workers	Pay	X
	Klein & Weiner, 1977	54 middle managers	Pay	n.s.
	Quinn & Shepard, 1974	1496 U.S. workers, representative sample	Job level, job type	n.s.
	Porter, 1962	1958 managers of all levels	Job level	X
Sense of competence	Gardell, 1971	303 male engineering and pulp and paper workers	Social interaction, amount of pay, pay schedule	X
	Kipnis & Lane, 1962	77 Navy petty officers	Autocratic leadership style	X

Source: Tharenou 1979, p. 329.

[a] X indicates a significant relationship, n.s. a nonsignificant one.

[b] Significance level not tested.

What does the material presented thus far in the chapter have to say to organizational practitioners (for example, managers, consultants)? They should be sensitive to the cognitions of their subordinates that have the greatest relevance to the subordinates' self-esteem (that is, perceived competence, importance, and control). Moreover, they should be cognizant of the facts that many factors embedded in the work setting can influence perceived competence, importance, and control; and such factors can be influenced by managers' own work behaviors and attitudes.

Mediating Processes

Practitioners also need to attend to the processes that mediate the relationship between organizational variables and employees' self-esteem. Thus far we have delineated the essence of, and some of the predictors of, employees' global and specific self-esteem. Left unspecified are the mechanisms by which these factors affect employees' self-esteem. There are four key processes that mediate the formation and development of self-esteem (Gergen & Maraceck 1976). These processes are believed to be relevant to the onset and development of both global and specific self-esteem.

Comparison Processes: To Others, to the Self, and to the System

It is a basic truism that individuals acquire much self-knowledge, including self-esteem, by comparing themselves to appropriate standards or yardsticks. In general, self-esteem is enhanced (reduced) when people perceive that their behaviors and/or outcomes have exceeded (fallen short of) the standard(s) of comparison. Moreover, as Goodman (1977) has pointed out, the standard can be other people, the self, or the organizational system. In his influential theory of social comparison processes, Festinger (1954) argued that in the absence of objective reality (that is, nonsocial standards) individuals will seek social reality—standards conveyed primarily by similar others—for purposes of self-evaluation. For example, suppose that employees have just been given their annual merit raise, a source of feedback that could affect their self-esteem. One way for employees to evaluate whether they have been praised or criticized is to compare their raise to "relevant" others. To the extent that employees believe that their raise was greater (less) than those received by relevant others, their self-esteem should be heightened (reduced).

Empirical evidence that social comparison processes affect self-esteem can be found in a number of social-psychological studies. In one (Morse & Gergen 1970), subjects completed a self-esteem scale while waiting for a job interview in the presence of an experimental accomplice. In half of the instances, the accomplice's appearance was formidable. He was dressed in a snappy suit and carried an attaché case. As he opened the case, a set of sharpened pencils and a book of Aristotelian philosophy could be seen (Mr. Clean condition). For the remaining half, the accomplice was dressed in a torn sweatshirt, pants torn at the knees, and no shoes. He tossed his dog-eared copy of a 'trashy' novel on the table and sat in a slouched position (Mr Dirty condition). Subjects rated their self-esteem as considerably higher in the Mr. Dirty than Mr. Clean condition; presumably, subjects engaged in a social comparison process and thus evaluated themselves on the basis of their worth relative to the other person.

The fact that social comparison processes affect individuals' self-esteem may account for some interesting paradoxes in self-evaluation. The concept of *relative deprivation* (Stouffer et al., 1949) refers to the fact that individuals' affective evaluations (including self-esteem) do not vary simply as a function of one's objective condition but depend, instead, on how the objective conditions compare to certain psychological standards (Zanna, Crosby & Loewenstein 1987). For example, in my own research I have measured students' self-esteem at three private, highly selective colleges or universities (Middlebury College, Tufts University, and Columbia University) as well as at two public, less selective schools (SUNY College at Brockport and the University of Arizona). On average, the former students have a higher social class than the latter. Nevertheless, the average self-esteem level of the samples at all five schools is virtually identical. One explanation—though, of course, not the only one—is that students at the various schools compare themselves to similar others: their fellow students. If so, then the average self-esteem level of the students from the higher social class should not be any greater than that of the students from the lower social class. Similarly, many studies (Asher & Allen 1969; Rosenberg 1979), including the well-known Coleman Report (Coleman et al. 1966), have discovered that middle-class black children have lower self-esteem than lower class black children. One possible explanation is relative deprivation theory: middle-class black children, although "better off" objectively (for example, with regard to school achievement scores) than lower class black children may have compared themselves to middle-class whites (who may have been perceived by middle-class black children to have been even better off than themselves). Faring second-best in this social comparison, the self-esteem of middle-class black children plummeted. Lower class black children also probably compared themselves to similar others: lower class black children who were perceived to be just as "bad off" as they were themselves. As a result, their self-esteem would be less apt to suffer.

The notion of relative deprivation also has been employed to account for the affective reactions of women in the workplace (Crosby 1982). Although women have entered the labor market in droves over the past twenty years and have made considerable headway in previously male-dominated professions, there is still considerable evidence of sex discrimination; perhaps the most vivid demonstration of sex discrimination is that women earn significantly less money than men, even when variables relevant to salary (for example, years of training) are taken into account (Zanna, Crosby & Loewenstein 1987). And yet, women do not seem to be less dissatisfied about their jobs than men, even though they should be, according to more objective standards such as level of pay.

Crosby (1982) has suggested that social comparison processes may explain the paradox of the contented female worker. Specifically, there is considerable evidence that women (as well as men) use same-sex others as comparison targets in deciding how much they like their jobs. Thus, if women are earning less money than men, they will not necessarily feel discontented to the extent that they compare their job situations to those of other women (who presumably are also in a relatively economically disadvantaged state). Moreover, if this reasoning is correct, then women who do compare their job situations to those of men should feel less satisfied than women who use other women as targets for social comparison. In fact, Zanna, Crosby & Loewenstein (1987) found support for the latter hypothesis. Perhaps most striking about their study of the job attitudes of professional women in the late 1970s was that the women who compared themselves to men actually earned significantly more money than did the women with female referents. And yet, the former group expressed significantly less job satisfaction than the latter.

Of course, alternative explanations apart from relative deprivation theory may explain such findings. (The possibility that the former group generally is more negative in its evaluations than the latter is not one of them; the two groups did not differ in their evaluations of the job situation of women generally, nor in their evaluations of their home situations.) Moreover, the Zanna, Crosby & Loewenstein study applied the concept of relative deprivation to women's attitudes toward their jobs, not their self-esteem. Nonetheless, in light of the facts that social comparison affects self-esteem and job satisfaction and self-esteem are highly correlated (Tharenou 1979), an important task for future research is to explore the effect of relative deprivation or, more generally, social comparison processes on the self-esteem of women at work.

The Zanna, Crosby & Loewenstein (1987) study suggests that women working in male-dominated groups, organizations, or professions may suffer a blow to their self-esteem by comparing themselves to men and perceiving the totality of their job experience less favorably than the men's experience. A closely related principle of social comparison also may explain why women in male-dominated work contexts may develop lower self-esteem. It may not only be that women perceive their job situation less favorably than that of their male referents; in addition, women may suffer lower self-esteem merely as a result of being different from the majority of their (male) counterparts. Rosenberg (1979) presents evidence in favor of such a contextual dissonance hypothesis, which posits that individuals who perceive themselves to be different from the majority of those in their social contexts are prone to develop lower self-esteem. Thus, adolescents reared in a religiously dissonant context (for example, Catholics raised in a non-Catholic neighborhood, Jews raised in a non-Jewish neighborhood, and Protestants raised in a non-Protestant neighborhood) had lower self-esteem than their counterparts who were brought up in neighborhoods in which the predominant religion was the same as their own. Similar findings have been obtained with regard to the dissonance versus consonance of one's racial context; as noted already, black adolescents attending predominantly white schools had lower self-esteem than blacks who attended predominantly black schools.

Apparently, being different is not value free; in being different one runs the risk of having negative evaluations hurled one's way, typically pertaining to the dimension that differentiates the individual from the broader context. Hence, Rosenberg (1979) found that adolescents reared in neighborhoods that were religiously or racially dissonant were more likely to be teased, left out of things, or called names by other children because of their religion or race. Quite conceivably, women working in predominantly male groups, organizations, or professions—in which their context is dissonant with regard to gender—similarly are prone to having insults thrown their way because of their gender, which could have detrimental effects on their self-esteem (Kanter 1977).

The fact that social comparison processes affect employees' self-esteem has numerous managerial implications. Suppose, for example, that employees in a high-performing firm or work group seem to have self-esteem that is lower than it should be, given the group's relative degree of success. It could be that social comparison mediates this apparent paradox. More specifically, the high performers may choose one another as standards for social comparison. If so, then members of this high performing group should evaluate themselves on average as average. It may be useful for the practitioners to encourage the high performers to adopt less successful groups (either within or outside the organization) as referents so that they may (more accurately) appreciate their self-worth.

In other instances, practitioners may choose to run the risk of (at least temporarily) lowering employees' self-esteem by encouraging them to adopt referents that are superior to themselves. In certain situations, high self-esteem may engender a sense of complacency, with its resultant poor motivation. For example, suppose that the faculty at a middle-tier university are moderately productive researchers. If the group members compare themselves to similar others—that is, faculty at other middle-tier universities—then the esteem in which they hold themselves as researchers should be reasonably high. Suppose, however, that the manager (for example department chairperson or the dean)—presumably in an honest effort to boost research productivity—decided that the comparison group should be the research faculty at top-tier universities. The behavioral and psychological consequences of their shift in social comparison target could be considerable. On the one hand, research productivity may well increase as the faculty attempts to emulate the performance of those in their new reference group. On the other hand, group members' self-esteem may well suffer; this is because a considerable amount of time may be needed to elevate performance to that of the referent. During this transition period, the faculty at the middle-tier university is bound to fare second best in their comparison with the new reference group.

Moreover, if being different from others in one's work context—along dimensions that presumably are irrelevant for effective performance, such as race, religion, or gender—lowers individuals' self-esteem, then managers may need to pay greater attention to the demographic compositions of their work groups. To be the token or minority may have negative effects on self-esteem. Such effects may not have been intended by the organization; moreover, there are certain steps that the organization can take to minimize such outcomes (Heilman 1980).

Self and System Comparison Processes. Most of the theoretical and empirical work on comparison processes—perhaps stimulated by Festinger's (1954) article on social comparison—has dealt with the way in which individuals evaluate themselves in relation to other people. However, as Goodman (1977) and others have pointed out, individuals do not always choose others as targets of social comparison. Instead, or in addition, they may make a number of different self-comparisons that can profoundly affect their self-esteem. Thus, employees may compare themselves to a representation of a past or former self. For example, individuals may compare to their former selves their current level of work proficiency, pay, status, or any other factor that could affect perceived competence, control, and value. Self-esteem is likely to be positively related to the extent to which individuals perceive upward movement on any or all of those dimensions. In addition, individuals may compare their current selves with how they expected to be and aspired to be at that particular time. To the extent that they fall short of such standards of comparison, self-esteem is bound to suffer.

The fact that self-comparisons are an important determinant of self-esteem has considerable practical implications. In certain instances, managers may seek to establish that employees make self-comparisons rather than or in addition to social comparisons. For example, suppose that some employees' current work performance was below that of their fellow workers, but also much better than their past performance. In order to maintain improvement, it may be necessary for the manager to ensure that the employees compare themselves both to their current peer group and previous selves. In comparing themselves to the peer group, individuals may adopt high performance goals or standards, and, as mentioned in chapter 3, difficult goals often elicit greater work motivation than easy goals or no goals at all (Locke 1968). Moreover, by comparing themselves also to their previous selves, such individuals may be more apt to believe that goal attainment is possible and thus accept the goal (Erez & Kanfer 1983). After all, they may reason, if performance could have improved from its past to its current level, then it may continue to increase even further in the future.

A laboratory experiment by Shrauger and Sorman (1977) nicely illustrates how self-comparison processes may facilitate subsequent work motivation. In that study, subjects of varying levels of self-esteem received negative feedback about their performance at an initial task. Half of the participants were led to believe that their performance, while negative overall, had improved somewhat over time (improvement condition), whereas the remaining half of them did not discern any improvement (no-improvement condition). Participants' motivation at a subsequent task was then assessed: it was found that the feedback elicited greater motivation in the improvement than no-improvement condition, especially among the low rather than the high SEs. One explanation of these results is that participants in the improvement condition — especially low SEs—compared their current performance to their past performance and, having discerned the improvement, felt optimistic about their chances for continued success. It is especially intriguing that the increased motivation in the improvement condition occurred in spite of the fact that the overall feedback was negative. To extrapolate the meaning of such results to the managerial context, it could be that employees may maintain high motivation to the extent that they focus on any improvements that they may have made, even if their overall performance picture is rather poor.

In addition to others and the self, the organizational system can serve as a standard of comparison. System referents are organizationally determined performance yardsticks, against which the employees' behavior is compared. For example, a company might mandate that their salespersons achieve a certain quota of sales in order to receive a bonus payment. In this example, the salespersons' performance is evaluated strictly against the system referent; that is, regardless of whether other salespersons have attained the quota, their own likelihood of obtaining a bonus is directly related to whether their performance has met the standard.

To be sure, the different referents may be related to each other. For example, it could be that system standards are at least partially a function of social and personal standards. In the salesperson situation just described, the organization is apt to generate its standard on the basis of the past performance of other employees. Thus, the bonus sales quota may be set at a level that relatively few employees had achieved in the past. In addition, self-standards may become enacted into system referents. In a Management by Objectives (MBO) program, for instance, the employee has some input into his expected standard of performance. One factor that is undoubtedly brought to bear in the standard-setting process is the employees' past performance record.

Social, personal, and system referents also may interact so as to produce conflict. Blake and Mouton (1979) provide details of an American corporation that had had continuing difficulties over the years with one of its major transnational subsidiaries. The essence of this between-group conflict was whether the subsidiary had been performing adequately; as might be expected, the subsidiary believed that its performance was much better than corporate headquarters believed it to be. Although Blake and Mouton use somewhat different terminology, one cause of the conflict was the fact that the subsidiary and headquarters were employing different standards against which to compare the subsidiary's performance. As Blake and Mouton (1979) reported:

> Corporate headquarters used an ahistorical perspective, comprised of some twenty performance criteria. Excellence in each represented the performance of the best subsidiary in this farflung transnational corporation. When they looked at this particular subsidiary according to these twenty criteria, they could find area after area of performance where it was failing (p. 26).

In contrast, the subsidiary evaluated its current performance against historical standards. In none of the twenty categories used by headquarters had it failed to make progress in the past fifteen years, and on a number of them progress had been significant. From the subsidiary's point of view, performance was far better now than at any previous time. In short, corporate headquarters was employing a system referent, whereas the subsidiary was using a self-referent by which to evaluate its own performance.

The relationships between social, self, and system standards of comparison attest to some of the theoretical complexities inherent in comparison processes. Nonetheless, the more general and major practical points are worth reiterating: employees' self-esteem is determined at least in part by comparison processes; a variety of entities—other people, oneself, and the system—may serve as comparison targets; and each comparison target provides practitioners with a lever with which to influence employees' self-esteem.

Modeling Processes and Self-esteem

Modeling, a process somewhat related to social comparison, is another mechanism through which individuals acquire self-evaluative information. The most general point about modeling already has been raised in chapter 4; namely, that people learn many specific behaviors and attitudes by observing significant others. Moreover, modeling processes are ever present, both outside and within the organizational context (Bandura 1977; Davis & Luthans 1980; Manz & Sims 1981). Even more specifically, it is entirely plausible that self-attitudes (that is, self-esteem) also can be shaped, at least in part, by modeling processes (Weiss 1978). It can be tentatively proposed that employees' self-esteem is significantly affected by their observations (and subsequent modeling) of their superiors' and (perhaps to a lesser extent) coworkers' self-esteem.

In his study of the antecedents of children's self-esteem, Coopersmith (1967) observed a positive correlation between the self-esteem level of mother and child. It is quite possible that a modeling process mediated this result (although, of course, other explanations are possible). If self-esteem modeling occurs in parent-child relationships, then it also may occur in a variety of interpersonal relationships marked by status differences. Thus, students may imitate the self-esteem level of their teachers, patients may mimic the self-esteem level of their physicians and therapists and, of greatest relevance, employees may model the self-esteem level of their superiors. Note the considerable power that this reasoning assigns to managers as role models for their subordinates; even when managers are not wittingly attempting to alter the behaviors and/or attitudes of their subordinates, they may do so nonetheless merely through a more subtle process of modeling.

While employees' self-esteem may be influenced by modeling, left unstated is the mechanism by which this occurs. Exactly how might employees come to mimic the self-esteem of their superiors (or coworkers)? Clinical theorists (for example, Kohut 1971) and social psychologists alike (for example, Heider 1958) have suggested that the notion of connectedness or identification may be critical. In oversimplified form, employees may go through the following psychological process (albeit not necessarily on a conscious level): you (the superior) believe that you are good, worthwhile, competent, and so forth; I (the subordinate) am connected to you or, in Heider's (1958) terminology, you and I form a unit relationship; therefore I am good, worthwhile, competent, and so forth. Of course, a similar process also can generate low self-esteem, if the superiors convey that they hold negative self-attitudes.

Several studies on a phenomenon dubbed *basking in reflected glory* (or BIRG) suggest that the modeling of self-esteem is influenced by the degree of connectedness between observer and model (Cialdini et al. 1976; Cialdini & Richardson 1980). If the model (superior) possesses the attributes that are associated with high self-esteem (competence, importance, and control), and if the observers (subordinates) are in a unit relationship with the model—the likelihood of which is increased by the fact that the model and observer are linked at least through their formal relationship—then the observer may bask in the reflected glory of the model or experience a boost in self-esteem.

The research on BIRG has explored the conditions under which people seek to establish a unit relationship or sense of connectedness with a desirable other. In one study, it was found that undergraduate students were more apt to wear an article of clothing that announced their university identity on autumn Monday mornings if the university's football team had won rather than lost on the previous Saturday. In a second study, a separate group of students, when asked to describe the outcome of the university's most recent football game, where more apt to use the pronoun *we* when the team had won rather than lost (*we* won versus *they* lost). Presumably, students were attempting to create an association with the university and its football team when doing so would enable them to BIRG.

But what evidence is there that BIRGing is in the service of enhancing self-esteem? If individuals BIRG in order to bolster their self-esteem, then the tendency to BIRG should be heightened when individuals' self-esteem is in greater need of a boost. The results of several more recent experiments (Cialdini, personal communication, 1986; Cialdini & Richardson 1980) have shown that individuals are more apt to BIRG when they have received negative feedback (rather than no feedback) about their performance at a prior task, and they are low rather than high in global self-esteem. Note that these are precisely the circumstances under which individuals are likely to need a boost to their self-esteem.

Thus far our discussion has suggested that managers' high self-esteem (and/or its associated attributes) may rub off on their subordinates through the process underlying subordinates' tendency to BIRG. In a more negative vein, it is also entirely possible that managers who convey a sense of low self-esteem also may elicit imitation among subordinates. The modeling process may be mediated by the extent to which subordinates view themselves as being connected to, or in a unit relationship with, their superior. The cognitions that subordinates may hold under such conditions may be something like this: "You (the superior) are a loser," "You and I are connected," therefore, "I am a loser, too." Given that the last cognition could be especially esteem-threatening to subordinates, they may strive to dissociate themselves from their superior. Cialdini and his colleagues (personal communication, 1986) have shown not only that individuals strive to create the impression that they are in a unit relationship with a highly desirable other, but also that they are motivated to dissociate themselves from highly undesirable others. Moreover, the latter tendency, like the former, is most likely to happen when individuals are in need of a boost to their self-esteem.

Note the complications that could arise in organizations if individuals try to dissociate themselves from esteem-threatening others. Employees who wish to sever the tie with their undesirable, low self-esteem superiors or coworkers may succeed in feeling better about themselves. However, in so doing they may create distance between themselves and the others that interferes with their ability to perform effectively. If the nature of the work is highly interdependent and thus requires careful coordination between superior and subordinate, and among subordinates, then the work performance and attitudes of employees who have distanced themselves from others may well suffer.

BIRGing processes within business organizations have not been investigated, and thus represent an important calling for future research. One knotty conceptual issue, for example, is whether individuals BIRG in order to gain esteem in their own and/or others' eyes. It also would be important to discover whether employees bask in the reflected glory of their coworkers (as well as their superiors) and, if so, the impact of such tendencies on work behaviors and attitudes. For example, in the summer of 1985, New York State held a lottery in which twenty-one employees of a firm shared in a $13 million prize. A considerable amount of public fanfare was made about the winners. According to *The New York Times,* many of the coworkers in that organization who did not win nonetheless experienced a boost in morale, an intriguing effect that could be explained by the BIRG process.

To conclude the discussion of modeling processes, the BIRG process should be restored to its broader context: employees' self-esteem may be influenced through a process of modeling self-esteem of significant others in their work environment. Because workers are, by definition, in some sort of unit relationship (Heider 1958) with their significant others, they may be especially sensitive to the self-esteem-related cues that significant others provide. If the significant others seem to be high in self-esteem, then the employees may experience an increase in their self-esteem if the unit relationship already exists; or, they may work to strengthen the unit relationship so that they can more easily BIRG. Moreover, if the significant others appear to be low in self-esteem, then employees either may experience reduced self-esteem or seek to dissociate themselves from the significant others. The latter tendency, it is suggested, could have a fragmentary effect on interpersonal and/or intergroup relationships, which, in turn could reduce organizational effectiveness.

Upward Social Comparison as a Form of BIRG. The tendency to BIRG reflects a paradox of social comparison processes. More specifically, it previously was stated that social comparison should lead to reduced self-esteem to the extent that individuals fare second best in the comparison process. And yet, the tendency to BIRG suggests that being in the presence of a clearly superior other also may heighten self-esteem. For example, suppose that the new CEO (chief executive officer) of a *Fortune 500* company recently has replaced an individual who was given much credit for the organization's success; in short, the CEO's predecessor was a "legend in his own time." Comparisons between the present CEO and his or her predecessor are inevitable. But is it inevitable that such comparisons will decrease the self-esteem of the new CEO? Perhaps not. It is possible that the new CEO may feel honored to be mentioned in the same breath with, let alone replace, the former CEO. Such a reaction could be an example of BIRG. This example does not simply imply that a new CEO will feel higher self-esteem if replacing a legend than if not. Rather, it is being suggested that the new CEO's self-esteem may not be as low as one might predict, if such a prediction were derived strictly from social comparison theory; the tendency to BIRG could account for such an outcome.

More generally, this example calls attention to the antagonism or tension between social comparison and BIRG (or reflection) as processes that mediate self-esteem. According to Tesser (1984), both processes claim that the same factors shape individuals' self-esteem; interestingly enough, however, the same factors produce directly opposite effects depending upon whether it is the social comparison or BIRG process that is evoked. More specifically, both the quality of the other's performance and attributes, and closeness of the association or unit relationship between the individual and the other directly affect self-esteem. The greater the favorability of the other's performance and attributes and the more that the individual is in close association with the other person, the more likely it is that the reflection process will produce increased self-esteem. And yet, the very same factors—favorable performance and attributes and a close unit relationship—will produce lowered self-esteem if the comparison process is at work.

The key issue, of course, is to specify the factor(s) that affect whether the reflection versus comparison process is elicited. Tesser (1984) suggested that the key dimension is the relevance of the performance or attribute dimension to one's own self-definition. Relevance is affected in turn, by the extent to which individuals wish to evaluate themselves favorably on the performance or attribute dimension in question; in addition, relevance is inversely related to the discrepancy between one's own performance or attribute rating and that of the other party.

If relevance is high, then the comparison process is likely to be evoked. So, to return to the earlier example of the CEO, if the performance of the outgoing CEO is seen as favorable (or perhaps somewhat more favorable than that which the incoming CEO can reasonably expect to attain), then the incoming CEO is likely to view such a performance as relevant; accordingly, the social comparison process is apt to be elicited and the newcomer is likely to view his predecessor's performance as a threat to his or her own self-esteem. If, on the other hand, the predecessor was a living legend, such that his or her positive performance was widely discrepant from that which the newcomer could reasonably expect to attain, then the predecessor's performance may not be viewed as relevant to that of the incoming CEO. It is precisely under such conditions that the newcomer will engage in a reflection rather than social comparison process, with its corresponding positive impact on self-esteem.

Reflected Appraisal and Self-esteem

Perhaps the most straightforward process mediating employees' self-esteem is reflected appraisal. The essence of this process, originally proposed by the eminent sociologists Cooley (1902) and Mead (1934), is that individuals come to view themselves in the ways in which they perceive that they are viewed by significant others. The primary vehicle through which people learn others' views and evaluations is feedback; as individuals make their way through their (organizational and nonorganizational) worlds, they are forever receiving evaluative feedback, the cumulative effect of which is to shape their self-esteem.

Two factors serve to generate a taxonomy of workplace situations that provide employees with self-evaluative feedback: the source of the feedback and the direct (versus indirect) nature of the feedback. In work organizations, employees receive appraisals from the formal organization, their supervisors, peers (and, to a lesser extent, subordinates), as well as through their very transactions with the work itself. In addition, the feedback that employees often receive is quite direct; for example, one of the major purposes of the performance appraisal process is to provide individuals with information concerning the competence with which they have been doing their jobs. Perhaps no less important, although a good deal more subtle, is the indirect evaluative feedback provided by various sources within organizations. For example, an increasing number of businesses have formally reorganized employees into self-managing work groups, in which members are given both the responsibility and the autonomy for the performance of their primary tasks; the major reason to reorganize along these lines is to enhance worker productivity. However, the very fact that employees have been given increased autonomy could heighten their perceived control and/or value within the organization, especially if they are the sort of individuals who are willing and able to exercise the autonomy (Hackman & Oldham 1976). In essence, such a reorganization may have conveyed indirectly to employees that they are valued highly enough to be given the autonomy. The direct and indirect ways that various within-organization sources provide employees with evaluative feedback are discussed here.

Formal Organization. Most organizations periodically provide employees with a formal written or verbal evaluation of their job performance. The major intended purposes of performance appraisals are to enable the organization to make decisions about pay raises, promotions, demotions, and the like; provide counseling to employees so that they will continue job-relevant behaviors that they perform well and correct those aspects that warrant improvement; and provide the organization with an inventory of its human resources strengths and weaknesses.

Performance appraisals also are likely to unintentionally influence employees' self-esteem. My working hypothesis is that employees' self-esteem is directly related to the favorableness of their performance appraisals. This fairly simple working hypothesis, however, belies a number of complexities. First, the extent to which feedback elevates or depresses self-esteem is probably moderated by a host of factors. To borrow from a voluminous body of social psychological research on persuasive communications and attitude change (Hovland, Lumsdaine & Sheffield 1949), at least three categories of variables may play moderating roles: the appraiser, the appraisal, and the appraisee.

A basic tenet of persuasion research is that high credibility communicators—that is, individuals who are seen as expert and/or trustworthy—elicit greater attitude change in their targets of communication than do low credibility sources (McGuire 1968). Performance appraisals typically are conducted by employees' superiors, who often are viewed as having high credibility in employees' eyes. These facts have clear managerial implications, namely, that managers need to appreciate the power that they may wield in providing performance appraisals to their subordinates. The key trick in carrying out performance appraisals—particularly imparting negative information—is to convey information in such a way that the person being appraised clearly hears the message (so that corrective action can be taken, wherever appropriate) but does not feel too much of a threat to his self-esteem. (In reality, these two reactions may be one and the same; if employees' self-esteem is unduly threatened, they may adopt an overly defensive psychological posture that prevents them from hearing the message clearly and perhaps more important, taking corrective actions.) One reason that performance appraisals may backfire is that the appraisers are insensitive to the high credibility that they may possess in the eyes of the person being appraised; thus, receiving negative feedback from a high credibility source may be too esteem-threatening for many subordinates, causing them to close their ears.

This does not mean that appraisers should seek to lower their credibility; instead, it implies that they need to be especially sensitive to the way in which they manage the appraisal process (Beer 1986; Meyer 1977, cited in Hackman et al. 1983). Several factors may affect the extent to which the appraisal process imparts useful information without unnecessarily threatening the self-esteem of the person being appraised. First and foremost, the appraiser must be sure to mention the positive aspects of the person's performance; moreover, it may be necessary for the appraiser to go to some lengths to make the positive aspects salient. Research evidence (Livingston 1969) suggests that managers believe that they convey positive feedback to their subordinates much more frequently than subordinates report being the recipients of such evaluations. This could be because managers truly do not convey positive feedback as much as they think, or because positive feedback, even if conveyed, has much less salience than negative feedback. In either case, extra effort may be needed on the managers' part to accentuate the positive aspects of their subordinates' performances.

Second, it may be useful to provide the feedback in a personalistic, discerning fashion. Performance appraisals that are tailored to the individual's unique characteristics may minimize self-esteem threat (and the defensive posturing that impedes effective communication) through the indirect message that it conveys; namely, the person being appraised may believe that he is cared about or valued enough by the appraiser so that the appraiser would go to the pains of noting his or her individualistic qualities. So, for example, the appraiser might make a special note of the fact that a given employee speaks forthrightly at meetings or is rarely absent, if such behavior in fact differentiates him or her from coworkers.

A third factor pertains especially to the manner in which negative feedback is communicated. It is important that the focus be on the subordinate's observable aspects (behavior) rather than unobservable qualities (personality traits), for at least two reasons. First, there is more likely to be agreement between the appraiser and the person being appraised on those dimensions that both can "see." Both parties can agree that a salesman, for example, failed to meet the sales quota for a given period, however, they are far more likely to disagree about whether the salesman lacks motivation, ability, or both. Second, and very much related to the first, the person being appraised is apt to feel much less blamed and thus more likely to avoid a low self-esteem-based defensive posturing if his behavior rather than underlying character is found to be at fault (Janoff-Bulman 1979).

Characteristics of the person being appraised also may moderate the extent to which performance appraisals affect their self-esteem. One such factor is the individual's global self-esteem. In chapters 3 and 4 it was suggested that low SEs are more behaviorally plastic than high SEs. Many of the empirical studies explored the joint impact of workers' global self-esteem and evaluative feedback on their postfeedback task performance. A frequent finding was that low SEs' subsequent performance was more affected by the feedback then was high SEs' performance. In particular, low SEs' performance tended to deteriorate in the face of forceful negative evaluation (Brockner et al. 1983; Brockner, Derr & Laing 1987; French 1963; Shrauger & Sorman 1977), whereas high SEs' performance did not. One possible explanation is that the negative appraisal lowered low SEs' self-esteem, especially their expectations for subsequent performance; high SEs, in contrast, may have maintained more optimistic expectations, which enabled them to perform better at the subsequent task.

Organizational practitioners need to be aware of the complexities associated with the impact of performance appraisal on employees' self-esteem. In general, the self-esteem of the person being appraised should be directly affected by the positivity or negativity of the evaluation. This statement, however, overlooks the prospect that many factors may moderate the effect of the reflected performance appraisal on self-esteem. Finally, it should be mentioned that an organization's performance appraisal system is not the only formal aspect that may affect employees' self-esteem. As stated previously, factors such as how workers are organized to perform their duties, rules and policies, and even the physical structure of the work setting may indirectly convey to workers the organization's perception of their competence and worth. Such messages, however subtle, may have as great an impact on employees' self-esteem as the more direct appraisals that the organization metes out.

Informal Relationships. Employees' interactions with their fellow workers also may shape their self-esteem. A basic finding in group research in organizations is that group cohesiveness—defined as the extent to which employees value their membership and thus want to remain in the group—elicits greater satisfaction among group members. It is eminently possible that self-esteem is one mediator of the relationship between cohesiveness and satisfaction. That is, one determinant of group cohesiveness is the existence of supportive interpersonal relationships among group members. As Likert (1961) has pointed out, such interpersonal harmony may heighten individuals' felt importance, one of the very cognitions associated with self-esteem. Indeed, Tharenou's (1979) review of the relevant literature has uncovered a number of studies whose results are consistent with these assertions.

Whereas group cohesiveness may boost members' self-esteem and satisfaction, it may not necessarily lead to positive group outcomes (for example, heightened group performance). More specifically, Janis (1982) has suggested that cohesive groups may exhibit a pernicious decision-making process known as "groupthink." The essence of groupthink is that group members may become extremely concerned with agreeing with one another in order to maintain cohesiveness, or not to rock the boat; such a concurrence-seeking tendency, in turn, will interfere with members' ability to be level-headed, rational thinkers. Most victims of groupthink in Janis's case analyses were members of decision-making groups facing an external threat (for example, President Kennedy's Cabinet during the Bay of Pigs fiasco). Moreover, Janis has pointed out that decision makers' self-esteem is bound to be lowered by any or all of the following contextual factors: recent failures that make members' inadequacies salient, extremely difficult decision-making tasks that lower individuals' sense of competence, and being in the midst of a moral dilemma in which feasible alternatives are bound to violate ethical standards. Thus, the reason that cohesive groups may exhibit groupthink in response to these circumstances is to regain some of their lost self-esteem. As Janis (1982) wrote:

> No one is likely to be exempt from undergoing a temporary lowering of self-esteem occasionally as a result of being exposed to any one of three types of situational provocations. For all such sources of internal stress, participating in a unanimous consensus along with respected fellow members of a congenial group will bolster the decision maker's self-esteem (pp. 255–256).

In short, group cohesion and its associated decision-making tendencies (for example, concurrence seeking) are apt to heighten group members' self-esteem; the heightened self-esteem, however, may or may not be associated with an increase in the quality of the group's performance and/or decision making.

Job Enrichment. It has been shown that factors associated with the context in which employees perform their work may affect their sense of competence, control, and/or importance. The considerable amount of theory and research done since the early 1970s on job enrichment or redesign makes it clear that individuals' transactions with the work itself also may be an important antecedent of their self-esteem.

Perhaps the most notable advance in work redesign theory and research is the Job Characteristics Model proposed by Hackman and Oldham (1976). The model hypothesizes that five core job dimensions (skill variety, task identity, task significance, autonomy, and feedback) positively influence three critical psychological states (meaningfulness of the work, responsibility for work outcomes, and knowledge of results of work activities), which in turn positively affect such outcome variables as work motivation, satisfaction, and turnover. The model further suggests that the linkages between the core job dimensions and the critical psychological states, and between the critical psychological states and the outcome variables are more applicable to intrinsically motivated (high growth needs) rather than less intrinsically motivated (low growth needs) workers.

Let us explore the relationship between the core job dimensions and the critical psychological states a bit further. Hackman and Oldham (1976) have suggested that work characterized by variety and significance, and in which the employees are able to perform the whole job (rather than only one or a few of its component parts) is likely to instill a sense of importance or meaningfulness in individuals. Work in which employees are given autonomy elicits perceived responsibility for work outcomes, and work that incorporates feedback will enable employees to gain knowledge of work outcomes.

It is important to note that all three critical psychological states seem similar to the very cognitions associated with self-esteem. In particular, meaningfulness seems to be very much related to perceived importance or significance; that is, individuals' self-esteem is higher when they experience a sense of importance, and one way in which individuals may feel important is if the work that they are doing is of some psychological significance. Experienced responsibility and knowledge of results both seem to be akin to perceived control: individuals are more likely to feel in control if they are given some autonomy in work-related decisions. Moreover, the feedback-producing knowledge is apt to heighten cognitive control; by enabling employees to see the outcomes of their work activities, managers make it more possible for employees to perceive the relationship between their work behavior and its associated outcomes.

This is not to say, of course, that the core job dimensions in the Hackman and Oldham (1976) model affect self-esteem-related cognitions in a simple, one-to-one fashion. For example, work autonomy not only heightens employees' perceived control, but also provides feedback that they are valued enough to be given autonomy in the first place (Schwalbe 1986). Schwalbe also notes that the impact of work autonomy on self-esteem-related cognitions may be mediated by a variety of processes. Thus, having an autonomous job provides employees with feedback that may affect a number of self-esteem-related cognitions; for example, employees may interpret their autonomy to be a reward for their past competence. In addition, work autonomy may heighten self-esteem through comparison processes; employees' self-esteem is bound to be affected by whether they have more or less autonomy than they did in the past, and/or significant others in the workplace.

Although Schwalbe's (1986) analysis focused on the variety of esteem-related cognitions and processes that are affected by work autonomy in particular, it is possible that other core dimensions besides autonomy affect workers' self-esteem (via a variety of mediating processes). For example, jobs which build in feedback may heighten employees' perceived control and competence and could also make employees feel more valued or important through a more symbolic process; that is, the provision of feedback indirectly may convey to employees that they are valued enough to be given a job that provides them with feedback.

More generally, Schwalbe's (1986) analysis of the impact of work autonomy on self-esteem reflects the relationship between the antecedents of self-esteem, focusing in part on the factors intrinsic and extrinsic to the work itself, and the processes that mediate workers' self-esteem (see first two sections of this chapter). Schwalbe's conceptualization of the relationship between work autonomy and self-esteem is noteworthy in that it seeks to explain some of the mediating processes by which one particular antecedent factor (work autonomy) affects employees' self-esteem (see also Staples, Schwalbe & Gecas 1984). Indeed, future research on the antecedents of employees' self-esteem would do well to delineate the processes that mediate the impact of the antecedent factors. It may be that the processes mentioned in this chapter—social comparison, modeling, BIRG, reflected appraisal, and as shall be discussed in the next section, role playing—will play key mediating roles to varying degrees. Much needs to be learned, however, about the specific relationships between the antecedents of self-esteem and these key mediating processes.

The most frequently cited managerial implication of the Hackman's and Oldham's Job Characteristics Model is that employees' work motivation and job satisfaction may be heightened through job enrichment (especially if employees are high in growth needs). Another implication, less typically mentioned, is that job enrichment may influence workers' self-esteem. Indeed, an increase in self-esteem (that is, perceived control, importance, and competence) may be the very mediator through which job enrichment elicits increased motivation and/or satisfaction.

Reflected Appraisal and Self-esteem: Summary. It should be clear by now that the receipt of reflected appraisal is a fundamental process mediating employees' self-esteem. Moreover, a variety of workplace factors, including the formal organization, interpersonal relationships with superiors and coworkers, and the nature of the work itself, may affect self-esteem through the reflected or feedback appraisal process.

Role Playing and Self-esteem

A fourth process affecting self-esteem is role playing. Roles are defined as the behavioral expectations associated with occupying a particular position or job. Much of our social lives, both inside and outside the organizational context, requires us to play a variety of roles. An interesting question that has long puzzled psychologists, sociologists, and philosophers alike is, what effect does role playing (that is, behaving) have on internal processes (for example, attitudes, traits, and moods)? That is, to what extent do we "become" the roles that we play?

The process by which role playing may affect individuals' self-esteem is somewhat different from previously discussed processes such as social comparison, modeling, and reflected appraisal. In the case of social comparison, self-esteem is influenced through the psychology of contrasting one's self with a standard. In the example of modeling, self-esteem is affected through the psychology of observing others. In the instance of reflected appraisal, self-esteem is determined by evaluative feedback, typically (though not always) transmitted by other people. In the case of role playing, it is the act of performing one's work-related behaviors that may have an impact on self-esteem.

Social psychologists have long been interested in the effects of individuals' actions on their internal processes. The influential theories of cognitive dissonance (Festinger 1957) and self-perception (Bem 1972) both suggest that individuals make inferences about their internal states (for example, personality traits, attitudes, moods) on the basis of observing their behavior as well as the situation in which the behavior occurs. Although the nature of the mediating psychological process differs in dissonance and self-perception theory, both analyses posit that individuals are more likely to view their behavior as having been caused by, or reflective of, their internal states when there is little apparent situational justification for that behavior. In short, we come to know ourselves—including our self-esteem—by observing our own behavior and the context in which it occurs.

My basic hypothesis in the analysis of role playing and self-esteem is the following: the more individuals' work roles require them to act in a "high self-esteem manner"—that is, the act of doing their job elicits the cognitions that they are competent and important—the greater will be their self-esteem. Considerable empirical support for this assertion is provided by Kohn and Schooler (1983), who have shown that work roles that allow for "self-direction" have a positive effect on employees' self-esteem. The extent to which jobs allow for self-direction is a function of the substantive complexity of the work, defined as the degree to which performance of the work requires thought and independent judgment; closeness of supervision; and routinization, that is, the extent to which one's job is repetitive and predictable.

The managerial implications of the role-playing hypothesis are considerable. It suggests that managers can heighten (or dampen) their subordinates' self-esteem by ensuring that the very performance of the subordinates' work roles is associated (or not associated) with feeling competent, valued and/or in control. For example, to instill perceived competence, managers should be certain that subordinates have ample opportunity to perform those tasks that they do well. This prescription seems reasonably straightforward, but it does contain certain nuances. For one, it implies that managers need to be familiar enough with their subordinates to be aware of their areas of competence. For another, it could be that the job description does not readily lend itself to allowing the incumbents' particular strengths to manifest themselves. If so, then it may be possible to redesign the job in certain creative ways to bring out the incumbents' best.

The act of performing certain tasks could affect individuals' perceived control, which may, in turn, influence their self-esteem. So, for example, assigning greater autonomy to individuals may be one way to increase perceived control and, therefore, self-esteem. Or assigning certain individuals to play key leadership roles—whether formal or informal—may go a long way toward heightening their sense of being able to influence others, which could, in turn, elicit perceived control and high self-esteem.

As noted in the previous section on reflected appraisal and self-esteem, there are a number of complexities surrounding the basic hypothesis, such that role playing will not always affect subordinates' self-esteem in a straightforward fashion. First, it is probably not the mere act of performing the behavior associated with one's work role that affects self-esteem. Both dissonance and self-perception theory suggest that behavior has the potential to produce internal change—such as affecting self-esteem—to the extent that individuals cannot attribute the performance of the behavior to external factors. Therefore, if employees perceive that their behavior was associated with competence, importance, or control because of some external factor—such as monetary inducement, peer or supervisory pressure—then they may not experience as much of a boost to their self-esteem.

Very much related to this is the idea that individuals may view the work role itself as an external inducement; as such, behavior performed within the context of the role may have little impact on their self-esteem. For example, suppose that a manager finds it personally alien to be in a position of controlling other people. To the extent that they are able to control others, they may attribute it to an "external" factor: the work role. Indeed, it may be the very fact that they are acting within the context of the role that enables them to perform the behavior associated with the role! Such individuals are more likely to infer that they are "merely doing their jobs" than to experience a change in self-esteem. (Of course, the long-term consequences of performing a work role that is external to the individual could be a deep sense of job alienation and dissatisfaction.) In short, it is probably not the mere role playing, but rather the attributions that employees make for performing role-related behavior that dictates whether role playing affects self-esteem. The more that individuals perceive that they are personally responsible for the performance of the role-related behavior and its associated outcomes, the more likely is it that their self-esteem will be influenced by role playing.

To take an even more extreme example of how behavior change may not necessarily lead to a corresponding change in self-esteem, consider the "impostor phenomenon," which depicts the psychological experiences of many highly successful people (Harvey 1985). Intuitively, one might expect the terrific professional achievements of such individuals to elicit high self-esteem. Instead, and interestingly enough, however, many such persons—estimates run as high as 40 percent of all successful individuals in a variety of careers—are prone to feelings of fraudulence. Such individuals believe that they are not nearly as competent as their objective record would suggest, and live in dreaded fear of being "found out." The irony is that greater accomplishments do not reduce but, rather, serve to increase their feelings of being impostors; as their achievements accumulate, the fear is even greater that their "true" level of competence will someday leak out.

The impostor phenomenon (Clance & Imes 1978) should be distinguished from normal feelings of worry that employees experience when they take on a new work role, especially if there is considerable prestige associated with that role. Such anxieties tend to dissipate over time as individuals become more accustomed to their work roles. Preliminary evidence suggests that the schism between such individuals' objective accomplishments and their subjective experience of competence is mediated by the attributions that they make for their achievements. Rather than attributing success to an esteem-enhancing factor such as ability, they tend to perceive their success as being caused by external factors (for example, "the task was easy"), temporary factors ("I was lucky"), and/or internal though performance-irrelevant factors (for example, "I was likeable and/or good-looking").

The impostor phenomenon is limited to workers who have achieved a high degree of success. More generally, however, the impostor phenomenon illustrates the complex relationship between behavior and self-esteem; just because individuals play the role of being competent, important, or in control does not necessarily ensure that they will experience high self-esteem. The impostor phenomenon represents an example of how the very act of being objectively successful can elicit the feelings of uncertainty and self-doubt that are typically associated with low self-esteem.

Although attribution processes may mediate the relationship between

behavior and self-esteem, it also seems likely that the mere continuous performance of work-role-related behavior will initiate some change in self-esteem
(Kohn & Schooler 1983). As behavior is repetitively performed, it is more
likely that the behavior itself, and not necessarily the underlying attributions
for the behavior, will be salient in the individuals' minds (Heider 1958; Jones
& Harris 1967), for at least two reasons. First, most people like to think that
they are the "masters of their own ships"; as such, it is discomforting to think
that they are acting merely due to external constraints such as a work role.
Second, and at a purely perceptual level, various aspects of behavior—for example, its implications and outcomes—may be more important to individuals
than the underlying causes for the behavior; therefore, it may be the behaviors
themselves that are more likely to grab the perceiver's attention. As a result,
the perceiver may be more likely to reason that "I am what I do."

Conclusions

This chapter began with the notion (based on the evidence in chapters 2
through 5) that employees' self-esteem, in conjunction with other factors, is
an important predictor of work behaviors and attitudes. Accordingly, it is
important to delineate the antecedents of self-esteem. It was suggested that
workers' self-esteem is bound to be influenced by the factors that affect and
processes that mediate perceived competence, control, and/or importance.

Personality theorists and researchers have suggested that global self-esteem
is shaped primarily by factors and processes external to the work environment,
presumably at the early stage of individuals' development. Global and specific
self-esteem also are determined by a variety of factors in individuals' lives, many
of which reside in the organizational context. A review of research evidence
on the antecedents of global and specific self-esteem—to be interepreted with
caution given their nonexperimental nature—suggests that self-esteem is governed by the forces that impinge on the immediate psychological climate rather
than more distal contextual factors. Thus, parent-child interaction is a more
important determinant of childrens' global self-esteem than is social class, and
factors intrinsic to the work itself are more important antecedents of adults'
self-esteem than are the economic and/or social contexts in which the work
is performed.

Furthermore, it is important for organizational scholars and managers to
understand not only the factors that affect self-esteem, but also the various
processes that mediate the impact of such factors on self-esteem. Such processes include comparison, modeling, reflected appraisal, and role playing.
All other things being equal, employees are apt to experience high self-esteem
when their performance or attributes exceed those of the comparison target;
they are in the presence of a high self-esteem model, whose basis of esteem is

not threatening to the employees; they have received positive feedback from social (or nonsocial) sources; and their work roles require them to act in ways that suggest that they are competent, valued, and/or in control.

Within the discussion of each of these processes, I attempted to point out some of the more thought-provoking conceptual issues. Thus, in the analysis of comparison processes it was mentioned that a variety of entities—other people, the self, and the system—all may serve as targets of comparison. In the treatment of modeling, one possible process was discussed by which being in the presence of a high self-esteem model may enable higher self-esteem to rub off on the observer. The antagonistic nature of social comparison and BIRG as processes mediating self-esteem also was discussed. As Tesser (1984) points out, the same variables affect both social comparison and reflection, but in directly opposite ways. Whether comparison or BIRG is set in motion depends on the relevance of the others' performance or attributes to the target individual. In the analysis of both reflected appraisal and role playing, mention was made of the various factors that moderate the impact of such processes on employees' self-esteem. Finally, several managerial implications were presented; in particular, it seems likely that practitioners who are sensitive to the issues raised in this chapter will be better able to effect change in their subordinates' self-esteem, which could, in turn, lead to a host of desired behavioral and/or attitudinal outcomes.

Earlier in this chapter reference was made to Rosenberg's (1979) empirical observation that social class is more strongly related to the self-esteem of adults than children. Now that the important concepts of self-esteem development have been discussed—in particular, the notion that it is primarily the immediate social-psychological context or effective interpersonal environment that shapes self-esteem, and that processes such as social comparison, modeling, reflected appraisal, and role playing mediate the impact of the immediate social psychological context on self-esteem—we are better able to speculate about why social class seems to affect the self-esteem of adults more than children.

First, as Rosenberg (1979) has demonstrated, the individuals with whom children interact are perceived to be very similar in social class to themselves. For example, in one study of Baltimore school children, 93 percent of them said that they were equally rich (or poor) as most of their schoolmates. Thus, children coming from a higher (lower) social class compare themselves to others in that same social class. Most will fare neither better nor worse in such a comparison process, the net effect of which is to minimize the impact of social class on self-esteem. Adults, on the other hand, are more aware than are children of social class differences between themselves and comparison others. Many adults think that their social class is the same as comparison others, but that figure is far lower than the 93 percent level shown by children. Rosenberg (1979) reported that 43 percent saw themselves as either richer or poorer (that is, different) than most of their friends, 61 percent as richer or poorer than most of their relatives, and 49 percent as richer or poorer than most of their neighbors. Given that adults are more aware of social class differences between themselves and others (and that social comparison affects self-esteem), it stands to reason that adults' social class is a significant predictor of their self-esteem.

Second, the process of reflected appraisal also may explain the different association between social class and self-esteem for adults and children. For adults, significant others in their lives provide evaluative feedback based on the adults' social class; children, of course, also receive evaluative feedback from significant others, but the feedback rarely is based on their social class. Thus, for adults more than children, the favorability of their reflected appraisals are closely linked to their social class. Given that the process of reflected appraisal affects individuals' self-esteem, it is easier to understand how social class is a stronger predictor of adults' than childrens' self-esteem.

Third, the discussion of role playing suggested that the favorability of the outcomes of individuals' behavior are more likely to affect self-esteem to the extent that they view themselves (rather than external factors) as responsible for the behaviors (and/or outcomes). So, for example, if individuals perform their job well and can attribute their good performance to themselves rather than some external factor (for example, easy task, luck) they are more likely to feel high in self-esteem; on the other hand, poor performance attributed internally (rather than externally) has a more negative effect on self-esteem. This analysis can be related to the effect of social class on self-esteem. As Rosenberg (1979) has suggested, for adults, social class:

> is achieved, for the child ascribed. For the (adult) this status (high or low) is *earned*—the outcome of his efforts and actions; for the latter it is *conferred*—the product of another's accomplishment. If self-attribution theory suggests that people evaluate themselves largely in terms of their *own* behavior and its outcome, it is certainly easy to understand why social class should be more closely tied to the self-esteem of adults than of children (p. 139).

A fourth explanation is that for adults social class is more important or central to their self-definitions than it is for children. Thus, not only do others define (evaluate) adults on the basis of their social class, as noted in the discussion of reflected appraisal, but also adults do so for themselves. A basic principle in self-esteem development—dating to William James (1890)—is that individuals' self-esteem is governed, for better or worse, by their self-assessments in domains that are psychologically central (Rosenberg 1979).

In short, Rosenberg's (1979) cogent analysis suggests that it is the ways in which the processes of social comparison, reflected appraisal, and role playing "play themselves out" in indivdiuals' immediate social-psychological environment that mediates self-esteem development and change. The mediating processes are just as important in the relationship between social class and self-esteem for adults as they are for children. However, for the reasons suggested already, the mediating processes lead to a much stronger relationship between social class and self-esteem in adults than in children.

Yet another way to understand the stronger association between social class and self-esteem for adults than children is through analysis of the relationship between social class and the everyday activities of adults and children. The effect of work-related factors on self-esteem is critical to this analysis. In their study of more than 3,000 working men, Kohn and Schooler (1983) obtained a significant correlation between social class and self-esteem. The authors suggested that men's social class funnels them into occupational activities that shape their self-esteem. That is, the day-in, day-out work of higher social class men is characterized by greater "occupational self-direction," defined by Rosenberg (1979) as the "opportunity to make one's own decisions, to exercise independent judgment, to be exempt from close supervision" (p. 131). In short, occupational self-direction is likely to affect workers' sense of competence, value, and/or control, the very cognitions that influence their self-esteem. Indeed, Kohn and Schooler (1983) discovered that the relationship between social class and self-esteem disappeared when there was a control for occupational self-direction. Because children are not yet in the workforce, their social class does not channel them into occupational activities that shape self-esteem. Of course, social class still could affect children's self-esteem if it systematically channeled them into everyday activities (even if not in the realm of work) that did shape self-esteem. However, the discussion of the mediating processes of social comparison, reflected appraisal, and role playing suggest that such is not the case for children.

Future Research

Although considerable progress has been made in theory and research on the antedecents of self-esteem, there is ample room for further methodological, theoretical, and practical refinements. Some of the issues that warrant further attention are addressed here.

Methodology. Future research is badly needed on the causal antecedents of self-esteem. Most previous research efforts have employed nonexperimental designs, making it difficult to know whether certain factors truly caused change in self-esteem. Research methodologies that allow for the drawing of causal inferences—such as the longitudinal causal model employed by Kohn and Schooler (1982)—need to be employed in such investigations.

The Relationship(s) Between the Mediating Processes. Although the discussion of the processes mediating self-esteem have been fractionated into different sections, it is eminently possible for employees' self-esteem to be jointly (and perhaps interactively) determined by such mechanisms. For example, suppose that indivduals are assigned to play certain work roles that make salient their felt competence. If so, their self-esteem may rise through the process of role playing. In addition, they may receive positive feedback from their superior and/or coworkers about their competence. If so, their self-esteem would be heightened through the process of reflected appraisal. Or, to cite another example in which the mediating processes may work conjointly, it may be that comparison underlies the impact of much evaluative feedback the employees receive. Workers may receive reflected appraisals that compare them to relevant targets ("You performed better than anyone in your work group"), which could have a dramatic impact on their self-esteem.

Organizational scholars and practitioners need to attend to the fact that multiple processes may affect self-esteem. From a theoretical point of view, the precise nature of the mediating processes differs (for example, unlike modeling, role playing is concerned with the impact of individuals' own behavior on their subsequent self-esteem). From a practical point of view, the multiplicity of processes presents managers with opportunities and challenges as they attempt to effect change in their subordinates' self-esteem. The opportunity is due to the fact that managers have a variety of processes upon which to rely; the challenge stems from the fact that they must ensure that the processes are in synchrony (or at least do not conflict) with one another. For example, through role playing, subordinates may perform esteem-enhancing behavior; the feedback or reflected appraisals that they receive for performing such behavior should, at the very least, not undermine the esteem-enhancing impact of the role playing.

Functional Self-esteem: High or Low? An implicit assumption in much of the discussion in this chapter is that high self-esteem is more desirable—from the point of view of both individuals and organizations—and that, therefore, organizations and managers should do what they can to build employees' self-esteem. But is such an assumption always warranted? In chapter 5 the adaptive value of low SEs' tendency to be more plastic than their high self-esteem counterparts was discussed. The tentative conclusion reached was that the more plastic style associated with low SEs was sometimes less adaptive, but sometimes more adaptive than the lesser susceptibility to influence of high SEs. If low self-esteem does lead to more favorable individual and/or organizational outcomes under certain conditions (for example, Brockner & Hulton 1978; Mossholder, Bedeian, & Armenakis 1982; Weiss & Knight 1980), then might it be prudent for managers to induce low self-esteem under such conditions?

In addition to this prescriptive (and ethically loaded) question, there is the more descriptive matter of whether organizations actually ever try to lower individuals' self-esteem in order to achieve organizational goals. Institutions that demand rigid conformity—such as certain religious sects or the military— intentionally try to strip away individuals' ties to the outside community and/or any expressions of their own unique identities. The net effect of such tactics is to elicit some of the psychological processes associated with low self-esteem, precisely in order to make individuals more susceptible to, or conforming with, the norms of the institution. By requiring uniformity of behavior, organizations make individuals more uncertain about the correctness of their own beliefs and behaviors. By requiring individuals to sever their extra-organizational contacts, these same organizations make individuals more needy of being favorably viewed within the organization; these are precisely some of the psychological mechanisms that underlie low SEs' greater plasticity.

It is less certain whether business organizations deliberately engage in practices that elicit low self-esteem or its correlated psychological processes. The matter of whether they should do so, at least under certain conditions, raises an interesting dilemma; suppose it was organizationally adaptive for employees to be behaviorally plastic. On the one hand, to achieve such plasticity the organization could seek to reduce workers' self-esteem. On the other hand, it would be gravely ethically questionable to engage in any such practices. The phenomenological experience of low self-esteem is unpleasant. Consequently, one might wonder whether the possible organizational benefits to be gained justify the costs that individuals will incur. Perhaps the best resolution of this matter is for organizations to induce plasticity, without necessarily engendering low self-esteem. The bases of plasticity are mechanisms of social influence. This is not to say, however, that the bases by which low SEs are more plastic than high SEs are the only or even the most effective mechanisms of social influence. For example, many organizations have adopted behavior modification programs, in which employees' behavior is influenced by the meting out of rewards and punishments contingent upon individuals' work behavior (Luthans & Kreitner 1975). It is entirely possible that such behavior modification programs encourage workers to be susceptible to influence by organizational cues, without necessarily lowering their self-esteem.

Factors Moderating the Impact of the Antecedents of Self-esteem. In chapters 3 and 4 it was stressed repeatedly that self-esteem interacts with a variety of factors to affect individuals' work behaviors and/or attitudes. A similar theme also should be echoed in the discussion of the antecedents of self-esteem, namely, that self-esteem is determined by the simultaneous influence of a number of factors. This assertion has both descriptive and prescriptive implications. At the descriptive level, this notion suggests that any comprehensive "theory" of the antecedents of self-esteem needs to go beyond a simple listing of relevant factors and processes. Perhaps just as important, is a discussion of how such variables jointly, and perhaps interactively, combine to influence employees' self-esteem. For example, Morse (1975) found that the degree of fit between individuals and their tasks positively related to self-esteem; individuals whose job complexity was congruent with their personality predispositions along this dimension had a significantly greater sense of task competence than a control group. Morse (1970) also discovered the degree of fit between organizational and task characteristics to be positively correlated with felt competence.

It is possible, indeed likely, that the degree of impact of many of the determinants of self-esteem depends on the employees' global self-esteem. Based upon the discussion in chapters 3 and 4 of the relationship between self-esteem and susceptibility to influence, it may be that low SEs' specific self-esteem is more affected by the factors and processes discussed in this chapter than is that of their high self-esteem counterparts. For example, earlier it was suggested how the evaluative feedback provided in employees' performance appraisals may sharply influence their temporary or situation-specific self-esteem. In particular, the receipt of negative feedback may have quite detrimental effects. Possessing high global self-esteem may serve as a buffer against such negative feedback, thus, high SEs' specific self-esteem (and related behavior) may be relatively unaffected. The specific self-esteem and related work behaviors of low SEs may be much more adversely affected by negative feedback. Consistent with these conjectures, it has been shown that for individuals low (but not high) in global self-esteem, the greater the negativity of their performance appraisal, the worse was their subsequent performance (French 1963). This finding neatly parallels results of laboratory and field studies, which showed that failure tended to have a negative impact only on the subsequent task performance of low SEs (Brockner, Derr & Laing 1987; Brockner et al. 1983; Shrauger & Sorman 1977).

Of course, this analysis is not meant to imply that the specific self-esteem of individuals high in global self-esteem cannot be influenced by situational factors. In certain instances, their specific self-esteem may be influenced, albeit to a lesser extent than those possessing low global self-esteem. In other situations (that is, those defined as *constraining* in chapter 5) the specific self-esteem level of all individuals will be affected to a similar extent. Yet a third possibility is that certain scenarios will affect the specific self-esteem level of globally high SEs in one direction, and globally low SEs in the other. More specifically, in chapter 5 it was shown that certain esteem-threatening situations have effects on high and low SEs' behavior that are similar in magnitude but opposite in direction. For example, upon being presented with a difficult or challenging task, high SEs may increase their effort whereas low SEs may decrease their effort (Brockner 1985; Sigall & Gould 1977). The challenging task may serve as a "psychological watershed" for individuals; those who are confident of being able to achieve the task (globally high SEs) may experience a boost to their specific self-esteem as they contemplate and actually exhibit successful task performance. Those who are not confident (globally low SEs) are apt to feel low specific self-esteem as a result of not being able to meet the challenge. More generally, this last example calls attention to the self-perpetuating or cyclical nature of chronic self-esteem. High SEs tend to think and act in ways that reinforce their existing level of self-esteem (Hall 1971), whereas low SEs seemed to be trapped in a more vicious cycle of low self-esteem (Brockner & Hulton 1978).

Thus, let the manager who is attempting to influence employees' specific self-esteem beware: individuals' global self-esteem often (though not always) channels their behaviors and beliefs in directions consistent with their existing levels of self-esteem (Shrauger 1975). Moreover, although self-esteem has been divided into its roles as both an independent variable (chapters 2 through 5) and dependent variable (chapter 6), the more accurate portrayal of self-esteem views it as a continuous process, in which self-esteem is influenced by and influences work behaviors and situations.

The discussion here suggests that global and specific self-esteem may combine interactively to affect employee behavior. A related question to be addressed by future research is the interaction between global and specific self-esteem, as they affect one another. For example, at what point, or how, does change in specific self-esteem become change in global self-esteem? Two of the factors that may moderate the impact of specific self-esteem on global self-esteem are the importance and frequency of the situation-specific domain. Change in specific self-esteem may translate into change in global self-esteem if the domain is important and/or frequently encountered. Both moderator variables may help explain why work conditions affect personality, including global self-esteem (Kohn & Schooler 1983). For many adults, work is an important specific domain in their lives. Furthermore, the conditions in their work worlds are those to which they are frequently exposed. So powerful is the effect of work on personality, argue Kohn and Schooler, that work-produced change in personality often generalizes to the nonwork areas in individuals' lives. For example, if working conditions provide employees with self-direction, they come to value self-direction in their work as well as nonwork activities. Future research needs to delineate the workplace factors that moderate the relationship between specific and global self-esteem.

Finally, a central theme in the field of organizational behavior is that effectiveness—whether measured at the individual, group, or organizational levels of analysis—is a function of the degree of fit or congruence between the various component parts of the organization (that is, the people, the nature of the work, and informal and formal organizational arrangements; Nadler & Tushman 1980). If managers do try to influence their subordinates' self-esteem—in the service of increasing effectiveness—then they must be certain that such self-esteem change is in synchrony with any changes produced in other component parts of the organization. For example, suppose that managers aspire to raise subordinates' self-esteem. If so, they should also try to ensure that the organization provides the kind of environment in which high SEs function most effectively. Since high SEs respond well to challenging tasks (for example, Sigall & Gould 1977), then the key to managerial effectiveness in this example is not only to raise subordinates' self-esteem, but also to ensure that their work is challenging. In short, it should not be forgotten that even a dimension as fundamental as self-esteem must be treated within the context of (that is, in interaction with) a wide range of organizational events, factors, and processes.

7
Self-esteem Maintenance and Enhancement

his chapter departs temporarily from the focus on either the antecedents or consequences of the trait of self-esteem, and considers instead
the role of self-esteem maintenance and enhancement as a motivational process. The primary assumption is that employees are motivated to
maintain a positive self-evaluation, that is, they desire to think, feel, and act
in ways that either enhance or protect their self-esteem.

An important theoretical issue is the extent to which individuals are concerned with satisfying their self-esteem motives in their own and/or in others'
eyes. It seems reasonable that both private and public esteem needs are
important; neither one unilaterally predominates over the other in the organizational setting. Thus, this chapter discusses how a variety of employees'
work behaviors are in the service of satisfying their public and/or private self-
esteem needs. In addition, attention will be paid to the behavioral and
psychological strategies in which employees engage—whether consciously or
not—in order to heighten their public and/or private esteem. The relationship between employees' current level of self-esteem and their self-esteem
maintenance processes is also discussed; given the individual difference orientation of the previous chapters, it is important to consider the relationship
between individuals' extant self-esteem and their self-esteem maintenance
activities. Finally, the practical implications of employees' self-esteem maintenance motive will figure prominently throughout the chapter.

Self-esteem Maintenance: A Private and Public Affair

The key general assumption in this chapter is that employees are motivated
to maintain positive self-esteem. Thus, they seek situations or outcomes that
provide a boost to their self-esteem, and avoid situations or outcomes that
may lower their self-esteem. For several reasons, individuals' work environments provide extremely fertile ground for studying the processes through
which individuals attempt to maintain their self-esteem. First, the work role

is central to many individuals' private definitions of their self-concepts; for such persons it is important that their evaluations of themselves in the workplace be favorable.

Second, and perhaps just as important, is that for a variety of reasons employees are particularly concerned with gaining self-esteem in the eyes of others in the work organizations. For example, tangible organizational rewards, such as promotions and pay raises, are usually tied to the extent to which one is favorably evaluated by superiors. In addition, workers may be motivated to win the esteem of their peers in order to gain their acceptance or at least avoid their rejection. It could be that employees' desire to gain public esteem ultimately is in the service of enhancing their private self-esteem. As mentioned in chapter 6, a critical antecedent of self-esteem is reflected appraisal; that is, individuals come to see themselves through the eyes of others (for example, Cooley 1902; Mead 1934). If so, then individuals' public esteem motivation may reflect the more underlying desire for private esteem.

A variety of individuals' work behaviors, such as help seeking, bargaining, decision making, and task performance, are sharply affected by individuals' need for self-esteem. The most important and general practical implication of the discussion in the next section is that managers need to recognize that such employee behaviors are affected significantly by individuals' need for positive self-evaluation; having recognized this fact, managers then will be in a far better position to manage such behaviors effectively.

Self-esteem Motivation and Employee Behavior

The Help Seeker's Dilemma

Consider the following examples of this dilemma.

1. A new employee (Person A) realizes that there is much to learn from fellow group members about how to work most effectively. Some of this information can be obtained by simple observation; other details, however, are much more difficult to pick up by merely observing coworkers. Indeed, by directly seeking the help of the fellow group members, the new employee will become much more proficient at his or her tasks.

2. Like Person A, Person B is a newcomer to the organization, but unlike Person A, Person B is extremely competent in the technical aspects of the job. Still, Person B could benefit considerably if she could acquire knowledge that her supervisor is likely to possess, for example, information about the power structure in the organization or about the production process in one of the firm's competitors in the industry.

3. Person C has recently returned from a national conference, during

which he had lunch with one of his former classmates at business school. In their conversation, Person C learned that his friend had just participated in a training and development program that had benefited his work performance tremendously. Person C suspects that his own work record could be dramatically improved if he too were to complete a similar training program; moreover, he knows that the program will be offered in his city in the not too distant future and he is thinking about requesting his organization to cover his expenses so that he can attend.

All three of these examples capture the essence of the help-seeker's dilemma. In each instance the target person needs to enlist the help of others; Person A needs the assistance of coworkers, Person B wants the help of her boss, and Person C requires the aid of his organization. In fact, if the individuals can acquire the help that they are seeking, then they are likely to be far more valuable to their respective work groups and organizations. For this reason they are motivated to seek others' aid.

However, and herein lies the other side of the help-seeker's dilemma—the very fact that they are seeking help may seem incompatible with their motivation for positive self-esteem. Seeking aid from others has the potential to elicit feelings of incompetence and dependency, both of which can dampen self-esteem. How help seekers cope with this dilemma is (or should be) of considerable concern to managers. At one extreme, the help seekers may be able to acquire the needed information or assistance and consequently become more productive workers. At the other extreme, the individuals may, because of "pride," not seek help, and as a result incur the (opportunity) costs of not improving their current level of productivity.

Social-psychological research since the early 1970s has suggested that the need for positive self-esteem mediates individuals' resistance to seeking help. For example, help-seeking resistance is greater under the following conditions.

1. When individuals are led to believe prior to the help-seeking opportunity that successful task performance is reflective of their intelligence rather than their eye-hand coordination (Morse 1972). It seems likely that participants' need to perform well (and thus maintain positive self-esteem) is greater in the former than in the latter condition.

2. When the available help must be requested, rather than merely offered by the donor (Broll, Gross & Piliavin 1974). Presumably, having to ask for help further heightens the salience of one's felt incompetence and/or dependence.

3. When the recipient knows beforehand that he or she will not be provided with any opportunity to reciprocate the help. If recipients are not given the opportunity to reciprocate the favor, then they have less of an opportunity to prove that they are neither incompetent nor dependent (Baumeister 1982).

Taken together, these three findings suggest that individuals may not seek help in order to avoid a blow to their self-esteem.

The tendency to avoid feedback also may be understood as a behavior reflective of employees' need for self-esteem. That is, when employees seek help from others (coworkers, supervisors, the organization) the substance of their help seeking often takes the form of requesting feedback. They may inquire about the most appropriate behaviors to achieve a goal (referent information, in the terminology of Herold and Greller 1977) and/or about how well they have performed such behaviors (appraisal information, as labelled by Herold and Greller). In their insightful analysis of feedback-seeking behaviors, Ashford and Cummings (1983) have suggested that employees rely on two broad categories of feedback-seeking strategies: monitoring (observing relevant information in the work environment) and inquiring (directly asking relevant others for feedback). Moreover, Ashford and Cummings hypothesized that feedback seeking is inversely proportional to the costs associated with doing so. One of the costs that they identify are "face loss" costs, which seem especially relevant to this discussion. In asking for feedback, employees may be exposing themselves to the very sorts of (face loss) risks associated with requesting help more generally: appearing weak, dependent, and/or incompetent. Rather than to run such risks, employees may prefer to avoid the feedback and, in so doing, miss out on possibly useful opportunities for behavioral change.

Employees' need for self-esteem not only may reduce their help-seeking tendencies, but also affect their reactions in situations in which assistance already has been offered. Numerous studies have shown that the person receiving the help (that is, the recipient) develops negative attitudes toward the help giver when the assistance threatens the recipient's self-esteem (Gergen et al. 1975; Gross & Latané 1974). The negative reaction of the person receiving help may seem especially paradoxical from the help giver's point of view and could set the stage for an escalating conflict between the two parties. The help giver, after all, has provided aid to the other, and may expect to be appreciated for his or her efforts. The person receiving the help, on the other hand, whose self-esteem has just been lowered, may feel resentful rather than appreciative toward the help giver. The recipient may perceive that the help giver is insensitive to the fact that the offer of assistance was threatening to the recipient's self-esteem; the help giver probably feels angry at the recipient for "biting the hand that feeds him."

Another possible recipient reaction to esteem-threatening aid—and one that also could fuel the flames between the help giver and recipient—is for the recipient to perceive that the help was deserved (Gergen, Morse & Bode 1974). As Baumeister (1982) has suggested, "by asserting that the aid was deserved, the recipient implies that he or she is not helpless or incompetent and subsisting on others' handouts but rather is merely someone accepting what is rightfully his or hers" (p. 7). Such an "entitled" type of response could, of course, anger the help giver. For example, suppose that managers — who are not tuned in to these issues — offer considerable assistance to their subordinates (that is, "far and beyond the call of duty") but do so in ways that threaten the subordinates' self-esteem, that is, implying that the subordinates are incompetent and/or dependent. To protect their self-esteem, the subordinates may convince themselves that they are entitled to such managerial assistance, when in reality, they are not. This divergent view of the managers' helping behavior could cause quite a strain in the working relationship between manager and subordinates and ultimately lead to impaired group performance.

The managerial implications of the help-seekers' dilemma are considerable indeed. It may be apt to say that the help-seeker's dilemma is also the help-provider's dilemma. That is, managers and organizations should concern themselves with how to provide performance-facilitating assistance in ways that do not threaten the recipients' self-esteem. If the helping agent is able to do this, then recipients' performance should improve for at least two reasons. First, by accepting the assistance, recipients should be better equipped to perform the task at hand. Second, if there is no face loss associated with having accepted the assistance, then recipients should be less apt to develop negative attitudes toward the help giver, and/or perceive that they are entitled to the assistance, both of which can be indirectly costly by straining the relationship between the help giver and recipient.

How can managers and/or organizations provide performance-facilitating assistance in the most prudent ways? The key guiding principle is that from the recipients' point of view, seeking and/or accepting help should not be associated with feeling incompetent and/or dependent. Thus, formal and/or informal organizational factors that make help seeking an accepted type of behavior should reduce workers' reluctance to seek assistance. For example, many organizations have adopted employee assistance programs (EAPs) in order to provide workers with a wide variety of professional and personal services. The formal institutionalization of programs such as EAPs conveys an important message to employees. It suggests that it is perfectly appropriate for workers to seek help; indeed, the EAP has been developed for that exact purpose.

Of course, there are other ways to increase workers' perceptions that it is appropriate to seek help. This may be achieved through modeling processes, for example. Suppose that key actors in an organization had just taken part in a training and development program to hone their managerial and/or technical skills. By making such actions highly visible (such as through a company newsletter), the organization may reinforce the perception that it is appropriate for employees to seek assistance in order to better themselves; after all, even the key actors in this example saw fit to do so. It is, therefore, quite possible that such a help-seeking attitude may generalize to others within the organization.

In addition, to the extent that employees are reluctant to seek help, it also is important for managers and organizations to minimize the publicity and/or salience of employees' help-seeking behavior. If employees know that virtually no one else will be aware of the fact that they sought assistance, then they will not have to worry as much about any loss of public esteem — whether such concerns are rational or not — associated with requesting help. This is yet another reason for the institutionalization of a help-providing mechanism such as an EAP. If such programs exist, then employees may be more apt to think that they can seek help with little public fanfare.

Thus far, the discussion has focused on the management of employees who seek assistance from their peers, superiors, and the organization. In addition, managers may need to concern themselves with the ways in which they seek help from their subordinates. More specifically, managers' unwillingness or inability to delegate responsibility to subordinates may reflect, at least in part, the help seeker's dilemma. Managers need to delegate responsibility to their subordinates in order to perform effectively. Indeed, all of us probably are aware of managers who tried to do it all themselves, only to find that they were ineffective in trying to do so. Numerous factors may underlie managers' inability to delegate responsibility to subordinates. For example, the subordinates actually may not be willing or able to perform the tasks assigned to them. Or, managers may not fully appreciate how much more effectively they could perform by delegating responsibility appropriately.

In addition, and more germane to the present discussion, managers may not delegate responsibility to their subordinates because to do so would threaten their own need for self-esteem. Perhaps because they need to feel that they are more qualified to perform the task than their subordinates, they may fail to seek help (that is, delegate responsibility) by convincing themselves that no one else can do the job as well as they can. In many instances this may not be true; if so, then managers may be missing an important opportunity (to free themselves up) by not delegating authority. Moreover, even if it were the case that the manager were best suited to perform the task, there are indirect costs associated with their not seeking assistance in the form of delegating responsibility. Failing to delegate authority can become a self-perpetuating cycle, which could lead to managerial burnout when taken to an extreme (for example, Jackson, Schwab & Schuler 1986). That is, by not seeking subordinates' assistance, managers virtually ensure that too much of the work will land on their own shoulders; such work overload, in turn, could lead to considerable personal stress and reduced efficiency.

It is not being advocated that managers should delegate responsibility to subordinates more than they currently do. Rather, it is being suggested that certain managers in certain situations may delegate authority less than is necessary for optimal performance; moreover, the need for positive self-esteem may be one of the reasons underlying managers' reluctance to delegate authority to subordinates, to the possible detriment of the manager, the subordinates, and the organization.

In a related vein, Klein (1984) noted that midlevel managers often are resistant to adopt a more participative management culture. Top management may have decided that it wishes the organization to become more participatory, and low-level employees may welcome the opportunity to have more of a say in work-related decisions. However, midlevel management—who typically are faced with the task of implementing the more participatory culture that top management envisions—often balk at the prospect. The analysis of the help-seeker's dilemma may provide one, but by no means the only, explanation of the reluctance of midlevel management; if eliciting others' participation may be viewed as a form of help seeking, then midlevel managers may be unwilling to implement a more participatory style because to do so could threaten their own self-esteem.

The analysis thus far has focused on the potentially negative (that is, esteem-lowering) effects associated with requesting aid: that workers may put forth an image of dependence and/or incompetence. To avoid casting themselves in such an unflattering way, they may fail to seek (perhaps even much needed) assistance. There is another, related reason why workers may be reluctant to request help, one that also is based on their self-esteem protection needs. This reason does not emphasize the negative consequences associated with seeking aid, but rather, the positive effects associated with not seeking aid.

More specifically, consider the possible outcomes associated with individuals' failure to seek help. Broadly speaking, the non–help seeker's ultimate outcomes could be negative (for example, poor performance) or positive (for example, good performance). If the outcomes are negative, then the individual has a handy, self-esteem-protective excuse: his or her failure to seek assistance. Such individuals can avoid making attributions for their poor performance that would be even more damaging to their self-esteem (for example, lack of intelligence, competence, or ability). Moreover, if the non–help seeker's performance outcomes are favorable, then their self-esteem also is protected, indeed enhanced. After all, they can reason to themselves (and/or significant others) that they succeeded in spite of not seeking help. If so, they must truly possess the kinds of esteem-enhancing qualities (for example, high ability) that lead to their favorable performance. In short, there are positive (that is, self-protective or self-enhancing) consequences for individuals not to seek help, regardless of the outcomes associated with their failure to do so.

This conceptualization of workers' failure to seek help is an example of a more general (and somewhat paradoxical) self-esteem protection strategy, known as *self-handicapping*. Self-handicapping refers to individuals' tendencies—whether wittingly or not—to put obstacles or impediments in their paths to successful task performance, to influence the causal attributions made (by the self and/or others) for the self-handicapper's performance (Jones & Berglas 1978). The paradox is that by self-handicapping, individuals actually may decrease their chances for successful performance, all in the service of controlling the attributions made for their performance (whether successful or not).

Consider the following examples of self-handicapping strategies in the workplace.

1. A salesman has had an intermittent history of drug and alcohol abuse. However, he has steered clear of these substances for the past year, leading his employer to believe that he has kicked the habit. He attends a meeting with the regional sales manager, who stresses the need for a considerable increase in sales during the upcoming period. The new quota is quite challenging, but not unattainable; all of the salesmen in the region will have to work at or near their top level of performance to fulfill the quota. Unfortunately, it is exactly at this time that the salesman's drug abuse problem rears its ugly head, virtually assuring that he will not be able to perform at the level necessary to succeed.

2. A large corporation has recently updated its word processing and electronic data processing capabilities, spending hundreds of thousands of dollars in new equipment. There is no question that the new technology—once its operators have learned to use it properly—will be a great boost to productivity. One of the secretaries always has been sort of a "machine-phobe," and doubts her ability to learn how to operate the new equipment. In fact, on the days that her boss provides training to all secretaries on the proper use of the new equipment the machine-phobic secretary always is absent.

In these examples, the salesman and the secretary both may be engaging in self-handicapping; both are putting obstacles in their paths, the salesman by abusing drugs and the secretary by being absent from work on crucial days. Their self-handicapping behavior, by definition, decreases their chances for successful task completion. Note, however, that such behavior also may lead to self-protective or self-enhancing attributions for their performance, regardless of the outcome. If the salesman performs poorly he can attribute it (or try to get others to attribute it) to his drug abuse problem. It is not that he lacks the ability, the salesman would like to believe (and have others believe) that it is this darned drinking problem that lead to the subpar performance. Surely, by ridding himself of this "intermittent" personal problem he will be able to operate at top efficiency. Moreover, if the salesman happens to succeed in spite of his drug abuse problem, then he can claim an unusually high level of sales ability. Could you imagine, he would like himself and/or others to wonder, how well he would do if he did not have this problem?

For her part, the secretary also cannot lose, attributionally speaking. If she does not perform as well in her job—as her failure to learn the new technology virtually ensures—then she can attribute it to her "being sick" on the days that training was provided. Such an attribution is far more self-protective than one that questions her competence or ability. If she can perform reasonably well in spite of failing to master the operation of the technology, then she can convince herself and/or try to convince important others that she really has what it takes to succeed.

The self-handicapping analysis may provide some fresh new insight into certain problem behaviors in organizations. There has been much recent attention to drug and alcohol abuse in the workplace and to certain employees' resistance to mastering the operation of new technologies. Moreover, the self-handicapping perspective may help explain other sorts of problem behaviors, such as the "injury-prone" worker, who always seems to get hurt when his/her performance is on the line. The injury-prone person can attribute poor performance to the injury, and not to a more esteem-lowering cause, such as lack of competence. If the person succeeds in spite of the injury, he or she can attribute the performance to an unusually high level of ability, an obviously esteem-enhancing attribution.

This is not to say, of course, that the self-esteem needs underlying self-handicapping are the only, or even the most important determinants of problem behaviors such as drug abuse, resistance to seeking assistance, and injury proneness. Rather, it is possible that a nontrivial portion of such behaviors may be mediated by the self-esteem maintenance needs that lead individuals to engage in self-handicapping. A growing number of studies (Berglas & Jones 1978; Smith, Snyder & Perkins 1983; Snyder et al. 1985) indicate that self-esteem maintenance needs do produce self-handicapping. In these and other studies it was found that self-handicapping occurred to a far greater extent when individuals' self-esteem needs were threatened than when they were not.

The Bargainer's Dilemma

Conflict between and within individuals, groups, and entire organizations is an ever-present aspect of organizational life. As organizations grow in size, its members are divided into increasingly specialized groups to accomplish their tasks. One frequent effect of this specialization or differentiation process is the creation of different goals, norms, and values, which could form the basis of intergroup conflict. In addition to this between-group conflict, individuals within groups always have different abilities, personalities, and values that could sow the seeds of interpersonal conflict. In short, it is inappropriate to think that conflict can be eliminated in organizations. As Thomas (1979) has suggested:

Conflict management is both a frequent and important managerial activity. In a recent survey, top and middle managers reported spending about 20 percent of their time dealing with some form of conflict. Furthermore, they indicated that conflict management skills had become more important to their performance during the past ten years, and were highly interested in learning more about conflict and its management (pp. 151–152).

Conflict is a ubiquitous aspect of organizational life. However, the effects of conflict are not necessarily negative for the organization and/or its members. It is easier to think about the negative psychological and behavioral consequences that conflict can produce. Indeed, when I ask my students to free associate about the nature and consequences of conflict, they typically say things like frustration, anger, hostility, stress, breakdown in communication, decreased group performance, and a wide variety of other negative attributes. Certainly the nature and consequences of conflict often are negative for individuals, groups, and entire organizations.

Just as surely, however, the presence of interpersonal and intergroup conflict sets the stage for quite positive consequences, if the conflict is managed appropriately. For example, the presence of conflict may call attention to existing problems in organizations, problems that should be addressed and may have otherwise gone unnoticed in the absence of the conflict. In addition, conflict between groups on how to perform a task ultimately could produce some innovative solutions. Some conflict-free groups may be too narrow in their approach to problem solving, such as those described in Irving Janis's 1982 book, *Groupthink*. Still other possible positive consequences are those attributable to the process of working through or resolving the conflict. The real issues underlying the conflict may become clearer; furthermore, the disputants may have much to learn about how they deal with others with whom they are in conflict, so as to avoid possible pitfalls in future conflictual interactions. To repeat: conflict is omnipresent in organizations. However, the consequences of conflict are neither unilaterally negative nor positive; it all depends on how the conflict is managed.

Bargaining and negotiation are especially relevant in this context, because they are key to the process of effective conflict management. Many people probably think of bargaining in organizations on a grand or collective scale, in which labor and management meet periodically to hash out differences in how employees will go about doing their work, as well as the conditions under which the work shall be performed. Consider, however, Rubin and Brown's (1975) definition of bargaining: the process whereby two or more parties attempt to settle what each shall give and take, or perform and receive (p. 2).

Given the generality of this definition, it should be apparent that bargaining processes occur across a wide variety of organizational settings as the bargainers strive to resolve their conflicts. Bargaining may occur between individuals, groups, and organizations in the working setting. Some examples are examined here.

Bargaining Between Individuals. Two scientists are working together in a research and development laboratory. In the past they have worked well together, developing several new products and processes that have helped their organization become known as an innovator in its industry. Recently, however, a number of conflicts have emerged between the two. Scientist A, who is the younger of the two, feels that Scientist B has not been contributing his fair share to several current projects. Scientist B, who served as an informal mentor to Scientist A during the latter's earlier years in the organization, feels resentful (and perhaps just a bit jealous) toward Scientist A. For these and other reasons, the two have not worked productively together for quite some time now, and the company is starting to feel the pinch in terms of reduced innovation. It is especially important for the scientists to mend their working relationship, because the two worked far better as a team than as isolated individuals. Recognizing this fact, and with some prodding from their supervisor, they have begun discussions with the hopes of ironing out the differences between them. Both sides' pride has been hurt during their period of conflict, so negotiating this interpersonal conflict promises to be no easy matter.

Bargaining Between Groups. A job candidate who is highly qualified for both a sales management and marketing management position visits a functionally organized company. The job candidate is such an attractive applicant that both subunits, sales and marketing, are highly motivated to attract her to the organization. As a result, prior to making a formal offer to the candidate, the two sides engage in a costly bidding war against one another. Clearly, it would be in the best interests of both sales and marketing—though not necessarily the candidate herself—not to bid against one another. Recognizing this, representatives of the two sides meet with one another in order to come to some agreement about how to recruit the new candidate most efficiently.

The director of market planning and director of sales of a large food products company must develop a yearly sales plan. Historically, the two groups have had differing projections, with projections for market planning almost always higher than that for sales. To elicit the highest level of motivation among subunits at lower levels of the work force, who are ultimately responsible for achieving the sales plan, it is critical that the two directors negotiate the difference between them. If the sales plan is very high (as the director of market planning would have it), then the subordinates are likely not to try very hard, out of a sense of hopelessness about being able to meet plan. If the sales plan is very low (as the director of sales would have it), then subordinates also are likely not to try very hard, but for a different reason: the sales plan is too easy, that is, not motivating enough. Thus, it is crucial that the bargaining process between the two directors produce a sales plan that is just right: difficult, but not impossible to achieve.

Bargaining Between Organizations. Organization X has been faring poorly over the past few years, prompting speculation in the business community that it will be acquired by Organization Y. The prospect of being acquired has sent shock waves throughout Organization X. For example, morale and commitment is at an all-time low because employees anticipate the loss of the old organization. Moreover, top-level management in Organization X, in discussing the acquisition with top-level management of Organization Y, find themselves feeling quite reluctant to negotiate a settlement in which they are acquired by Organization Y. Organization Y, for its part, is quite concerned that they appear to be the acquirer, rather than the acquiree. On the surface, Organization X's reticence seems unusual, because it is clearly in X's best financial interest to be acquired by Y. Similarly, Organization Y would be best served by joining forces with Organization X even if it is not in the form of an acquisition (for example, a merger also would be beneficial).

Negotiation and Self-esteem. In all four examples the individuals', groups', and organizations' performances will suffer, unless they can minimize or eliminate the conflict through the process of bargaining. In order to reach agreement (or at least reduce the chances of a potentially destructive conflict), Scientists A and B will have to change their manner of relating to one another; sales and marketing will have to stop trying to outbid one another; the two directors will have to develop a sales plan agreeable to each; and, Organization X will have to face the reality that to remain viable it may have to join forces with Organization Y. Organization Y will have to realize that it needs to link with Organization X, even if not entirely through a process of acquisition. In short, to obtain a more favorable joint outcome, each party to the conflict will need to give a little.

However — and herein lies the essence of the bargainer's dilemma — the very act of conceding or giving a little during the negotiation process may cause bargainers to suffer a blow to their self-esteem. Concessionary behavior may be perceived as a sign of weakness by the conceder, the opposing party, the conceder's constituents, or other relevant audiences. As Rubin and Brown (1975) pointed out in their extensive review of the bargaining literature, bargainers have a strong need for positive evaluation (both in their own and others' eyes). To the extent that concessionary behavior is perceived to lead to a loss of self-esteem, bargainers will be reluctant to concede. And yet, to reach a more favorable joint outcome (on dimensions other than self-esteem maintenance), it is usually necessary for bargainers to be at least somewhat concessionary.

An extensive amount of research has documented that self-esteem maintenance needs mediate much bargaining behavior, and may interfere with bargainers' ability to negotiate in ways that are most beneficial to themselves and/or their organizations. As a prime example, consider the research of Brown (1968). In that study all bargainers first were systematically exploited by their fellow bargainer (whose behavior had been programmed by the researcher). Bargainers' need for positive evaluation was experimentally varied; half were informed by an onlooking audience of peers that they had appeared foolish and weak as a result of their exploitation, whereas half were led to believe that they had looked good even while being exploited because they played fair. All bargainers were then given an opportunity to retaliate against their fellow bargainer, by behaving in an exploitative, nonconciliatory manner. As predicted, bargainers were much more retaliative if they had been made to appear foolish rather than fair. Further evidence that self-esteem maintenance needs mediated behavior comes from the retaliative subjects' self-reported explanations of their actions: 75 percent of them said that they retaliated in order not to appear weak or foolish due to their prior exploitation.

As mentioned earlier, bargainers' need for positive self-evaluation may be directed at a host of sources. It could be a purely private matter; bargainers need to look good in their own eyes. Or, as the Brown (1968) study points out, bargainers may be concerned with how they appear in the eyes of an onlooking audience. Note, however, that at least three "audiences" could be witness to a bargaining relationship: the opposing party, an onlooking audience, and the bargainers' own constituents. Brown's (1968) study explored the impact of an onlooking audience. Other organizational scholars have investigated the effect of bargainers' need to look good in their constituents' eyes on the negotiation process. For example, Neale (1984) simulated a labor-management negotiation in which some bargainers were led to be highly concerned with their constituents' opinion of their behavior, whereas others were not. Results showed that bargainers were far less concessionary in the former than the latter condition, presumably because they were more concerned with looking good in their constituents' eyes in the former condition. McKersie, Perry, and Walton (1965) studied the effect of constituent pressure on live labor-management bargaining, the 1961 Auto Workers-International Harvester contract negotiations. Both sides were highly accountable to their constituents and, probably as a consequence, were very unwilling to make concessions to the other side.

The constituents in both the simulated (Neale 1984) and live negotiations (McKersie et al. 1965) were witness to collective bargaining between labor and management, and constrained their representatives' bargaining behavior through accountability pressures. I suspect that the effect of constituent pressure on bargainers' face-saving needs may be present in a wide variety of organizational settings, not merely in the collective bargaining context.

Remember the two examples of between-group bargaining discussed at the outset of this section. In one instance representatives of two different functional areas in the same organization were competing for a job candidate; in the other they were trying to agree upon a reasonable sales plan. In both examples the representatives may be reluctant to concede to one another, not only because of the need to look in their own and one another's eyes, but also in the eyes of the constituents that they represent.

In short, self-esteem maintenance needs constrain negotiators' bargaining (that is, conflict resolution) behavior. The need for positive evaluation may channel negotiation behaviors in directions that are not necessarily in the best interests of the negotiators, their constituents, and/or the organization. For example, the Brown (1968) study showed that participants retaliated against their fellow negotiator after being made to look foolish before an audience. It is important to note that they did so at their own personal expense. Similarly, the Neale (1984) study found that constituent accountability caused bargainers to be less concessionary; however, the ultimate outcome of the bargaining process was less rather than more successful under conditions of high constituent accountability.

Managerial Implications. The anecdotal and empirical evidence presented here suggests that bargainers' self-esteem maintenance needs affect both the process and outcome of interpersonal, intergroup, and interorganizational negotiation. The more that managers and other organizational practitioners are aware of this basic fact, the more likely they may be to facilitate conflict resolution in a constructive rather than destructive manner. For example, in their own negotiations with superiors, peers, and subordinates, managers should attend to "hidden agendas" that may be affecting the dispute resolution process. One such hidden agenda is each side's self-esteem maintenance needs. What this suggests, of course, is that managers explore their own as well their fellow negotiators' need for positive evaluation, and how such needs might be affecting, or interfering with, the bargaining process. Greater attention to both negotiators' self-esteem needs may enable managers to "work through" the impediments to the negotiation process that such needs produce. To return to the example of the corporate acquisition process described earlier, it may be useful for the acquiring company to negotiate the acquisition in ways that do not threaten the acquiree's self-esteem needs. Perhaps certain aspects of the consolidation can, or at least can appear to, take on the qualities of a merger, in order to help the more dependent organization get through the emotionally difficult period of saying farewell to the good old days.

Similarly, in adjudicating conflicts between others (that is, individuals or groups), managers need to be tuned in to the possibly interfering effects of the others' self-esteem maintenance needs in the bargaining process. For example, two organizational units may be unwilling to go along with one another, not because they find one another's objective bargaining position unreasonable, but because of their fear of loss of face associated with concession (the classic bargainer's dilemma). After many hours of deliberation, for instance, the head of sales may find the head of marketing's sales plan to be reasonable. For self-esteem maintenance reasons, however, the head of sales may be unwilling to go along with the plan. A third party to this conflict (for example, the direct superior of the head of both sales and marketing) may facilitate the process by managing the disputants' self-esteem maintenance needs. Pruitt and Johnson (1970) discovered that bargainers were less apprehensive that conceding would threaten their self-esteem if their concession making was in direct response to the suggestion of a third party mediator. Interestingly, the actual suggestions of the mediator could be identical to that of the opposing bargainer. The very fact that such suggestions came from the third party, and not the opposing party, facilitates concession making because the conceder may perceive less loss of face in responding to a respected mediator than to the opposing side.

Or, managers as third parties may facilitate conflict resolution by introducing superordinate goals (Aronson 1984). Superordinate goals are common to both sides of the bargaining process; their superordinate quality makes other conflict issues—such as bargainers' need to save face concerning other points of dispute—less salient. Recall the between-group conflict described in chapter 6 in which the headquarters of an American corporation was in an ongoing battle with one of its transnational subsidiaries about how to evaluate the subsidiary's performance. Blake and Mouton (1979) reported that headquarters used an ahistorical standard whereas the subsidiary employed an historical standard. In effect, headquarters was saying to the subsidiary, "look at how poorly you are doing on the performance criteria," whereas the subsidiary's position was "look at how far we have come on the criteria." The conflict between the two sides was quite heated, partly because of each side's self-esteem maintenance needs; giving in to the other party's performance standard could entail considerable loss of face.

To facilitate conflict resolution the managerial consultants introduced a superordinate goal. As Blake and Mouton (1979) report:

> Once it becomes apparent to both sets of leaders that two different perspectives were being employed, the issue became: which perspective is more justified under the circumstances? Which perspective should be employed as the basis for assessment of performance in the future? Agreement on the perspective to be employed provided a superordinate goal useful from the standpoint of the subsidiary's self-assessment of its performance and from the standpoint of the corporation's evaluation of subsidiary performance (p. 26).

In getting the two sides to work together on developing appropriate performance standards, the consultants removed much of the heat from the prior conflict. The two sides no longer had to focus on clinging steadfastly to their prior positions—which they probably did in part out of a need for positive evaluation—and could devote attention instead to a constructive resolution of the conflict.

In other circumstances, managers as conflict mediators may introduce superordinate goals between disputants in different ways. For example, the supervisor of the sales manager and marketing manager may convey to the two sides that it will be extremely costly to both sides if they cannot resolve the conflict effectively among themselves. To take this example to an even more extreme position, the superior may suggest to the two sides that he or she does not want to become embroiled in their dispute, and that it will be extremely costly to the two sides if he or she is forced to intervene as a third party mediator or arbitrator. The superordinate goal for the two sides would thus become one of working together to reach agreement so as to avoid a heavy-handed, costly intervention by the third party. In a sense, the manager as a third party has become a "common enemy" for the conflicted parties.

The Decision Maker's Dilemma

Consider the following examples.

1. You are a financial vice president of a large organization, with responsibility for allocating resources to two corporate divisions (Consumer Products and Industrial Products). Three years ago you were primarily responsible for the decision to allocate $10 million to Research and Development funds to one of these two divisions. Now, three years later, you learn that the performance of your $10 million allocation has been quite disappointing. You now have to decide how much of $20 million you should allocate to the division that received $10 million three years ago. Moreover, you are under greater pressure from your superior to make the right decision this time around.

2. As the manager of your work group, you played a major role in the company's decision to hire several employees and assign them to your group. Unfortunately, the new recruits' performance during their first year has been quite disappointing. You now have to make several judgments about their past performance, including the amount of pay raise, if any, that they deserve. Furthermore, you must plan the future of your work group, which means that you need to predict as accurately as possible the group members' likely future levels of performance.

3. You are a newly hired MBA graduate, who has invested a considerable amount of time, money, and emotion in your chosen profession. After several years at a variety of different jobs—none of which you found particularly rewarding—you are seriously wondering whether you made the right career choice. In fact, you are strongly considering switching to another line of work. One fact that makes it especially difficult to change careers is the

magnitude of the investment you have made in attaining your current status; somehow, the thought of giving all that up is a particularly bitter pill to swallow.

All three examples capture the essence of the decision maker's dilemma: the target individuals have allocated considerable resources in the hope of achieving some goal. In each instance the decision makers have not yet achieved their goal and have received feedback that makes them question whether their goals ever will be attained. In short, the decision makers are in a sort of no man's land; on the one hand, they may wish to cut their losses and not allocate any further resources to their previously chosen course of action. After all, it would be silly to throw good money after bad. On the other hand, they may feel compelled to allocate additional resources to the poorly performing course of action to justify or make up for all that has been expended to that point; it is not uncommon for decision makers in such circumstances to perceive that they have too much invested to quit (Teger 1980).

Of these two decisions—to escalate commitment to, or withdraw from the previously chosen, though failing course of action—there is ample anecdotal and empirical evidence that individuals opt for the former, often at considerable expense to themselves and their organizations. The available evidence suggests that the need for positive self-esteem mediates such decisions to escalate commitment. Thus, the financial officer responsible for the prior resource allocation may continue to pour funds into the previously chosen division, the manager may grossly overrate the performance of the subordinates whom they were instrumental in hiring, and the young professional may relentlessly pursue his or her previously chosen profession, which has become more unrewarding with each passing day. Decision makers do not want to admit, either to themselves or important others, that their prior decision making was incorrect and that all of the resources associated with those decisions were allocated in vain. To prove to themselves and/or others the appropriateness of their prior resource allocations, they often escalate their commitment to the previous course of action. The decision to escalate commitment is in the service of self-esteem maintenance; the downside of the dilemma is that escalating commitment—or "entrapment" as it has been called elsewhere (Brockner & Rubin 1985)—can be quite costly to both individuals and organizations.

Since the late 1970s, there has been a considerable amount of research on the causes of, and process(es) underlying, entrapment (see Brockner & Rubin 1985 and Staw & Ross 1987 for reviews). Several examples are provided of the empirical research suggesting that self-esteem maintenance needs mediate escalating commitment to a failing course of action. In one study, Staw (1976) had undergraduate business students take part in a simulated organizational decision-making scenario similar to that described in example 1 at the outset of this section. Subjects played the role of the financial vice president who had to allocate anywhere from $0–20 million to a division that had received a $10 million resource allocation five years earlier. Half of the subjects were led to believe that the outcome of the prior resources allocation was favorable (positive consequences condition) whereas the other half was informed that the outcome was unfavorable (negative consequences condition).

To evaluate whether self-esteem maintenance needs mediated escalation decisions, Staw had half of the subjects make the earlier allocation decision (personal responsibility condition). The other half were informed that their predecessor in the organization had made the earlier decision (low responsibility condition). In comparing the personal and low responsibility conditions, Staw noted that the information presented to low personal responsibility subjects was identical to that given to other subjects except for the fact that the case's scenario began at a later point in time and necessitated making the second investment decision without having participated in an earlier choice. Presumably, decision makers would perceive a greater need to justify the correctness of their own, rather than someone else's, resource allocation.

The results of the study confirmed predictions (see table 7–1). Subjects allocated more resources to the previously chosen course of action in the negative than positive consequences condition, especially if they were in the high rather than low personal responsibility condition. The condition that presumably elicited the greatest threat to individuals' self-esteem—one in which they were personally responsible for a decision yielding negative outcomes—also produced the greatest degree of escalated commitment.

Several aspects of the Staw (1976) study—which has proven to be a seminal study of sorts among organizational scholars interested in escalating commitment—are worthy of mention. First, it is intriguing that the negative consequences/personal responsibility condition elicited greater escalation

Table 7–1
Amount of Money Allocated to the Previously Chosen
Alternativeas a Function of Consequences and Personal
Responsibility
(millions of dollars)

| | Personal Responsibility | |
Consequences	High	Low
Positive	9.18	8.35
Negative	13.01	9.44

Source: Staw 1976.
Note: Higher scores reflect greater escalation of commitment. (Maximum = $20 million.)

than both positive consequences conditions. After all, one might have expected decision makers to be more apt to persist with a course of action that succeeded rather than failed. Apparently, however, the force underlying self-justification subsequent to negative feedback was greater than the motive stemming from a more traditional source of reinforcement. Second, the basic result discovered by Staw has been replicated on numerous occasions, including one in which middle-level and upper-level executives served as participants (Bazerman, Schoorman & Goodman 1980).

A second study demonstrates the impact of self-esteem maintenance needs on decision making within a performance appraisal context (Bazerman, Beekun & Schoorman 1982). Undergraduate business students played the role of vice president who either was promoting and later evaluating an executive (personal responsibility condition) or merely evaluating an executive who already had been promoted by someone else (low responsibility condition). In all cases the participants were informed that the executive's performance during the two-year period of evaluation was rather negative. Consistent with expectations, subjects evaluated the executive far more favorably in the personal responsibility than low responsibility condition. For example, when subjects were personally responsible for the executive's promotion, they allocated higher pay increases and made more positive predictions concerning future performance than when subjects were not personally responsible for the executive's promotion.

Taken together, the Bazerman, Beekun & Schoorman (1982) and Staw (1976) studies suggest that decision makers are more likely to escalate their commitment to a previously chosen though poorly performing course of action if they were personally (rather than not) responsible for the initial resource allocation. Such findings suggest, in turn, that entrapment is mediated by decision makers' self-esteem maintenance needs (see also Conlon & Parks, 1987). It should be emphasized, however, that other factors besides personal responsibility also may affect decision makers' self-esteem maintenance needs and, therefore, their proneness to entrapment. For example, Fox and Staw (1979) had all subjects partake in the negative consequence/ personal responsibility condition employed by Staw (1976). The researchers then experimentally manipulated two factors, job insecurity and policy resistance, that presumably affected the extent to which decision makers were concerned with looking good in the eyes of significant others.

The job insecurity variable influenced subjects' concern about being able to retain their current position as financial vice president. Those in the insecure condition were informed beforehand that they were "temporarily assigned to fill the position . . . and that you cannot expect support and assistance from your peers, especially if you do not perform well immediately" (p. 457). In contrast, subjects in the secure condition were told that their position was permanent and that "you can expect support and assistance from your peers, especially if you do not perform well immediately" (p. 457).

The policy resistance factor reflected the extent to which the board of directors were satisfied with subjects' initial funding decision. Prior to receiving negative feedback concerning the outcome of this decision, the high resistance subjects were informed that the board members were "highly skeptical of your recommendation and were firmly convinced you had recommended the wrong course of action . . . the Board reluctantly deferred to your judgment" (p. 458). The low resistance participants were told that the board members were "highly satisfied and supportive of your recommendation and were firmly convinced that you had recommended the correct course of action" (p. 458).

If self-esteem maintenance needs mediate escalation decisions, then participants should be most likely to persist with the failing course of action to the extent that their need to look good is heightened. Thus, escalated commitment should be greater when job insecurity is high rather than low, and when policy resistance is high rather than low. These were precisely the results that Fox and Staw (1979) obtained.

There is ample anecdotal and empirical evidence to suggest that decision makers' needs for positive evaluation may interfere with decision quality. Several examples have been described of this decision-making dilemma within the context of escalating commitment to a failing course of action; in this dilemma individuals have to decide whether to cut their losses—often the rational thing to do—or escalate their commitment, which is often the rationalizing thing to do. Note, however, that the notion that self-esteem maintenance motivation may interfere with decisional quality need not be limited to the context of entrapment. Janis's (1982) provocative groupthink hypothesis, which asserts that members of cohesive decision-making groups seek to maintain their collective self-esteem often at the expense of rational decision making, is quite germane to the more general notion advanced here (see chapter 6).

Practical Implications. The decision maker's dilemma posits that individuals' need for positive evaluation mediates their escalating commitment to a failing course of action. The most important practical matter in this discussion is how to reduce, if not entirely eliminate, organizational members' tendency to fall prey to this sort of psychological trap. Two general categories of organizational and managerial interventions are appropriate. First, escalating commitment to a failing course of action may be reduced to the extent that decision makers' self-esteem maintenance needs can be held in check. Second, it may be possible to influence the relationship between decision makers' self-esteem maintenance needs and their subsequent escalation decision. Even if decision makers' need for positive evaluation cannot be minimized, it still may be possible to reduce the extent to which such motives are expressed through the process of entrapment. Some examples from both categories are discussed.

Controlling Decision Makers' Self-esteem Needs. A basic assumption throughout this chapter is that organization members' need for positive self-evaluation is quite powerful; to think that such motives can be entirely eliminated is probably foolhardy. Nevertheless, organizational factors may still have a pronounced effect on the magnitude of decision makers' self-esteem needs. The Fox and Staw (1979) study, for example, implied that decision makers who feel "politically vulnerable" may be especially prone to entrapment. Political vulnerability causes decision makers to be especially concerned with maintaining their esteem in the eyes of others. More specifically, Fox and Staw discovered that the perception of job insecurity elicited greater escalation of commitment to the failing course of action; so did the belief that key others were initially resistant to the prior course of action. Both factors probably caused decision makers to feel as if they had more to prove, and they apparently proved their point by escalating commitment to the prior course of action.

Thus, organizations should be wary of situations in which decision makers perceive that they have so much to prove that they resort to escalating commitment to a failing course of action. Organizations may wish to take precautions in such situations to avoid the perils of entrapment. For example, if job insecurity increases decision makers' proneness to entrapment, then organizations should be especially concerned with developing safeguards against entrapment under conditions that are likely to engender job insecurity. To take this example one step further, much research has shown (for example, Louis 1980) that newcomers to organizations often experience considerable job insecurity, which could make them prone to exhibit entrapment. If so, then the organization may need to convince the new hires that their tendency to persist with a previously chosen (though failing) course of action is not a test of their mettle. This may be achieved by conveying to newcomers that they are not expected to perform like heroes during their early job tenure.

Moreover, as suggested by Fox and Staw (1979), individuals' esteem maintenance needs—with resultant pressures toward escalating commitment—may be balanced by performance-appraisal systems that evaluate decision makers on the basis of the process (and not merely the outcome) of their decision behavior. Typically, it is the negative outcome feedback that activates decision makers' self-justification or esteem maintenance needs. Suppose, however, that decision makers knew that their superior's evaluation of their performance was based on their adequacy of their decisional process. Thus, decision makers could be evaluated on the basis of the following criteria: astuteness of their definition and diagnosis of the problem, evidence that they had considered a variety of alternative ways of tackling the problem, and the appropriateness of the implementation of their preferred solution. If the outcome of the process is still negative—in spite of an apparently proper process, which could occur if unforeseeable factors affected the efficacy of the process—then decision makers should feel less of a need to justify their past behavior in the form of escalated commitment. Of course, this reasoning suggests that a considerable and perhaps costly revision of the organization's performance appraisal system may be necessary. However, the costs associated with a change in the appraisal system may be more than offset by the cost of savings produced by reducing decision makers' proneness to entrapment.

Controlling the Impact of Self-esteem Motivation. In the preceding section it was suggested that organizations may influence decision makers' tendency to become entrapped by affecting the level of their self-esteem maintenance needs. This section offers a different analysis of how entrapment may be reduced. Decision makers may have strong self-esteem maintenance needs, but this does not mean that such needs inevitably produce entrapment. Thus, rather than *reduce* individuals' self-esteem needs, which may be very difficult to do anyway, it may be possible for organizations to manage such needs. For example, one factor that may cause entrapment is decision makers' perception that they will be evaluated more favorably if their decision behavior is consistent rather than inconsistent over time. Inconsistent decision makers often are seen as weak-kneed, wishy-washy, and incompetent, whereas consistent ones tend to be perceived as firm, tough, and competent (Staw & Ross 1980).

Suppose, however, that organizational norms and/or reward structures favored experimentation in decision making. If decision makers believed that it was reasonable or even desirable for them to change their policies and practices in the face of negative feedback, then their proneness to entrapment may be reduced. Note than in this example the organization is not trying to reduce its decision makers' self-esteem needs. Rather, it is attempting to channel such needs into behaviors that are antithetical to entrapment.

This type of logic was pursued in an experiment by Brockner, Rubin, and Lang (1981). In this study, subjects varied in the extent to which they were concerned with looking good in the eyes of the onlooking audience. Half of the decision makers were led to believe that they could look good by persisting with the failing course of action, whereas the other half were led to believe that they could look good by withdrawing. Not surprisingly, subjects overall were less likely to become entrapped in the latter than in the former condition. Moreover, the least degree of entrapment was exhibited by decision makers who believed that they could look good by withdrawing and who were highly concerned with looking good. In short, the need for positive self-esteem actually may lead to the reduction of entrapment, provided that decision makers perceive that their self-esteem needs may be satisfied by withdrawing from, rather than escalating commitment to, the failing course of action.

It may be extremely difficult for decision makers in organizations to channel their self-esteem needs into reduced propensities toward entrapment. As mentioned, decision makers may perceive that many formal and/or informal organizational rewards are contingent upon their staying the course, and thus escalating their commitment to a previously chosen, though failing cause of action. More modestly, and perhaps more realistically, it may be that organizations can develop ways to counteract the self-esteem maintenance needs that often promote entrapment. This type of logic recognizes the inevitability of decision makers' self-esteem needs, as well as the impact that such needs may have on escalating commitment. What this type of logic also assumes is that other factors besides decision makers' self-esteem needs may influence their level of escalating commitment. If these other factors can be introduced into the decision-making context, they may block or neutralize the impact of self-esteem maintenance needs on escalating commitment.

More specifically, entrapment can be avoided or at least reduced to the extent that decision makers are prospectively rather than retrospectively focused. Optimal decision making mandates that resources be allocated to a previous course of action only if a future oriented cost-benefit analysis suggests that it is prudent to do so (Northcraft & Wolf 1984). The key is for organizations to alter the structure and/or process of decision making, so that individuals adopt the necessary future oriented (rather than past oriented) mindset. There are at least three ways with which to achieve a future oriented mindset.

Limit-setting. Prior to entering into a course of action that could prove entrapping (for example, instances in which goal attainment will require repeated, rather than one shot decision making), decision makers should set limits on the amount of resources they wish to invest in a particular course of action. Early on in the process, a new product development team may set a limit on the amount of time and/or money to allocate to a particular project. Importantly, the team should not necessarily abandon its efforts if the project has not completely reached fruition by the time that the agreed-upon resources have been exhausted. Instead, the team should agree to perform a future oriented, rational analysis of its options, independent of the fact that resources have been allocated to that point. For example, they may wish to consider matters such as how far along they truly are in the project, or how much revenue can be realistically expected. If the answers to these questions suggest that it is wise to continue, then the team should escalate its commitment to the previous course of action. Rigid adherence to the previously specified limit (that is, allocate no more resources) is not being advocated. Rather, limits may be thought of as the future points in times (and perhaps money) at which decision makers reconsider—from a prospective rather than retrospective vantage point—whether they wish to escalate commitment to the prior course of action.

Active (not Passive) Decision Making. Closely related to the preceding discusion is the notion that entrapment is less likely when resources must be allocated on an active rather than passive basis. In passive situations, resource allocations mount on an ongoing and automatic basis, unless the decision maker withdraws from the course of action. The second and third examples at the beginning of the discussion of the "Decision Maker's Dilemma" have the elements of passive investment situations. That is, the amount of time that the organization invests in the new employee's development increases continuously and automatically; unless the organization makes a conscious decision not to increase its commitment to see this employee perform well, then the magnitude of its resource allocation (at least in terms of time devoted to the individual) increases automatically. Similarly, people caught in the "career trap" also must make a deliberate decision to switch to a different line of work. Unless they do so, then the amount of time that is sunk into their present job or career increases automatically.

Active situations are structured quite differently; under such conditions the amount of resources allocated to a prior course of action increases only if individuals make an intentional decision to escalate commitment. If no such active decision to escalate occurs, then individuals are tacitly or even explicitly saying that they wish to withdraw from the course of action. The first situation mentioned at the outset of the "Decision Maker's Dilemma" is an example of an active investment situation; the financial vice president only can increase his commitment to the corporate division by consciously deciding to allocate additional resources.

As the preceding discussion implies, it is more difficult to withdraw from an entrapping course of action in which resources are allocated passively rather than actively; indeed, the results of several empirical studies support this notion (Brockner & Rubin 1985). More optimistically, this analysis suggests that resource allocation decisions that are structured actively should be less likely to lead to entrapment than those structured passively. Having decision makers set limits beforehand is one but not the only way to transform what may otherwise be a passive situation into one in which escalated commitment (if it is to occur) is the result of an active decision. A zero-based budgeting decision rule may be another way to create an active decision structure. In zero-based budgeting it is not assumed that courses of action which previously have been funded will automatically continue to receive support. Instead, continued commitment must result from a conscious decision to do so.

Devil's Advocate. Another factor that could facilitate prospectively (rather than retrospectively) based decision making is the presence of a devil's advocate; this individual's job is to keep the group focused on whether its desire to escalate commitment to a previously chosen, though failing, course of action is retrospectively or prospectively governed. The devil's advocate could be a regular group member, or it could be an outsider who is called upon periodically to attend certain group meetings. The notion that a devil's advocate may neutralize potentially faulty decision making is not limited to escalation of commitment decisions. For example, Cosier and his colleagues (Cosier 1978; Cosier & Aplin 1980; Schwenk & Cosier 1980) demonstrated in both laboratory and field studies that the devil's advocate procedure had a positive effect on the quality of strategic decisions. In addition, Janis's (1982) suggestions to counteract cohesive groups' tendencies toward groupthink include calling in outside experts on a semiregular basis, who evaluate the rationality of the group's decision-making, and the appointment of one or more devil's advocates within the group, whose purpose is to find fault with the group's favored decisions. Janis suggests that cohesive groups may make a variety of poor decisions, including the tendency to escalate commitment to a failing course of action in the service of justifying prior resource allocations. Thus, his suggestions to offset the groupthink process seem readily applicable to potential entrapment situations.

Summary. The decision maker's dilemma is whether to escalate commitment to, or withdraw from, a previously chosen though failing course of action. Anecdotal and empirical evidence suggest that the former option is often elected, often quite costly, and mediated by decision makers' self-esteem maintenance needs. Several different categories of factors were offered that could reduce individuals' entrapment proneness. First, it may be possible to reduce their self-esteem needs, which should produce a corresponding decrease in entrapment. Second, it may be possible to channel such self-esteem needs into the reduction of entrapment. If decision makers somehow can be led to believe that they will look good (in their own and/or others' eyes) by withdrawing their commitment, then entrapment should be less apt to occur when self-esteem maintenance needs are high rather than low. Finally, it was recognized that other factors apart from the need for self-esteem could influence whether decision makers escalate commitment to a prior, failing course of action. When faced with a decision to stick with a previous commitment, decision makers probably weigh both retrospective factors (for example, self-esteem motivation) and prospective factors (for example, economically based, cost-benefit issues). If the latter sorts of concerns can be made more salient, then decision makers may be less likely to rely upon the former, and thus less apt to fall prey to entrapment.

More generally, the discussion thus far has dealt with three different individual and group behaviors that are of fundamental significance in organizations: help-seeking, bargaining and negotiation, and decision making. Throughout, it was suggested that organization members' need to look good, privately and/or publicly, is a critical determinant of all three behaviors. Perhaps even more interestingly, it seems that such self-esteem needs actually may interfere with individuals' tendencies to act in ways that are simultaneously in their own and the organization's interest; thus, in the service of looking good, individuals may avoid seeking (much needed) assistance, negotiate intransigently when it would be better to be more concessionary, and escalate their commitment to, rather than withdraw from, a failing course of action. Moreover, it was suggested that the effective management of such behaviors as help seeking, bargaining, and decision making refers, at least in part, to the effective management of organizations members' needs for self-esteem. Managers need to ensure that employees' behaviors that benefit the organization also satisfy (or at least do not thwart) their needs for self-esteem.

The actions discussed here (help-seeking, bargaining, and decision making) do not constitute an exhaustive list of employee behaviors that are governed by the need for positive self-esteem. This analysis also could be applied to elucidate employee motivation and performance (see Dipboye 1977a). In many instances there is synchrony between the levels of motivation and performance that fulfill organizational goals and individuals' self-esteem needs; put more simply, those who try hard and perform well will be satisfying the goals of the organization and their own self-esteem needs.

In other instances, however, there may be a lack of congruence between the behaviors that fulfill both organizational goals and individuals' self-esteem needs. Perhaps most dramatic are those situations in which individuals actually run the risk of thwarting their own needs for positive evaluation by performing well. This speculation sounds counterintuitive, but it is far from impossible. Much social-psychological research has demonstrated that our performance is partly a function of the expectations and desires that significant others hold for our performance; if significant others expect and/or want us to succeed, then (all other things being equal) we will be more likely to try hard and perform well than if these others do not expect and/or want us to perform well. In the classroom it has been shown that children for whom teachers held high expectations performed much better than children for whom the teacher held either no expectations or negative expectations (Rosenthal & Jacobson 1968; Seaver 1973). In the work setting, it has been shown that employees for whom the organization held high expectations performed far better than those for whom the organizations did not entertain high expectations (Berlew & Hall 1966; Livingston 1969).

This reasoning can be applied to instances in which managers either expect and/or want certain employees *not* to try hard and succeed. Sounds implausible? Not really. Consider, for example, situations in which women are working in what used to be predominantly male-dominated occupations. The managers of these female employees may not expect them to perform well and convey such messages to them. This is not to say that managers' expectations are conscious, nor is it that their behavioral expressions of such unconscious expectations are blatant. It is, however, that both the managers' expectations and behaviors are real, and they place the recipient of these messages in a bind. On the one hand, the recipient may ignore (or even be motivated by) such negative expectation cues and perform up to their capability. On the other hand, they may be directly influenced by such factors and perform at a level significantly below their capability. Note that both options are potentially costly to the recipients. In the former instance, they run the risk of alienating their managers by not performing up (or in this case, down) to the managers' expectations. Such boat-rocking performance on the recipients' part could interfere with their need to be positively evaluated by the manager. In the latter instance, they may gain the approval of the manager but have to live with the fact that they failed to live up to their own personal standards.

Most readers may assume that the majority of individuals will be more likely to choose, and thus incur the costs associated with, the former rather than latter course of action. But, a study by Zanna and Pack (1975) that is conceptually related to the present discussion suggests otherwise. In this experiment, women undergraduates at Princeton University were led to believe that they were going to have a "getting acquainted" meeting with an attractive man. Half of the participants were told that the man liked traditional women (for example, those who were home-oriented, passive, dependent, and noncompetitive). The remaining half were told that the man valued nontraditional women (that is, those who were career-oriented, assertive, independent, and competitive). Half were led to believe that the man was quite attractive (and therefore, the women were likely to be concerned with making a good impression), whereas half were informed that the man was rather unappealing. Before meeting him, the women were asked to perform a cognitive task and were told that their task performance would be revealed to him prior to their meeting. The women performed much worse when they thought the man liked traditional rather than untraditional women, and especially when they thought he was attractive rather than unattractive (see table 7–2). Both groups of subjects gave the attractive man what he was looking for; but, in so doing those in the traditional preference condition performed at a level far lower than their capability.

It is not necessarily that organizations consciously convey the message that they do not expect and/or want any of its employees to try hard and perform well. As suggested earlier, such messages can be conveyed in very subtle (yet powerful) ways. Just as important, the recipients of such subtle messages from organizations do not necessarily respond to such messages on a conscious level. It seems likely, however, that subpar motivation and performance of certain individuals in certain instances could be explained by self-

Table 7–2
**Mean Number of Anagrams Solved as a Function of Male
Partner's Attractiveness and Preferences in Women**

| | Male Partner's Preferences in Women | |
| | Untraditional Women | Traditional Women |
Male Partner's Attractiveness		
Attractiveness	44.3	37.4
Unattractiveness	41.4	40.4

Source: Zanna & Pack 1975.
Note: Higher scores reflect better performance. (Maximum score = 50).

esteem maintenance needs. Like the participants in the traditional-attractive condition of the Zanna and Pack (1975) study, individuals may underachieve in the service of not alienating significant others upon whom they are dependent for positive evaluations.

Individual Differences in Self-esteem and Self-esteem Motivation

Throughout this chapter self-esteem maintenance was discussed as a basic and general motivation process; it was assumed that all employees seek positive evaluation, in their own and/or others' eyes. Given the discussion in chapters 2 through 5, which dealt with the correlates and consequences of self-esteem as an individual difference variable, it is important to consider the relationship between individuals' self-esteem and their tendency to engage in behaviors that elicit positive evaluation. One important question, for example, is whether high or low SEs are more likely to do so.

Although it is obviously important to raise this question, the ensuing answers may be far less obvious. To understand the complexity of the relationship between individual differences in self-esteem and self-esteem maintenance motivation, it is first necessary to analyze the factors that affect individuals' tendencies to engage in behaviors that produce heightened self-evaluation. Such behaviors typically are associated with positive outcomes (for example, successful task performance, social competence, and morality). To draw upon expectancy theory (Vroom 1964), workers' propensities to perform such behaviors are a joint function of (among other things) their expectations about being able to perform the behaviors (or, as Bandura 1977, has called them, self-efficacy beliefs), and values associated with being able to enact such behaviors. Employees will be most motivated to engage in behaviors that maintain or heighten self-esteem to the extent that they expect to be able to perform such behaviors and value their associated outcomes.

Thus, it is crucial to know how individuals' self-esteem is related to their expectancies about being able to perform, and the values they attach to the performance of, self-esteem-enhancing behaviors. It seems likely that self-esteem as an individual difference variable is positively correlated with the expectations described already. Indeed, part of the very essence of high self-esteem is the belief that one will be able to perform behaviors that produce positive outcomes. Empirically, this reasoning suggests that if all individuals value being able to perform the esteem-enhancing behavior, then high SEs should exhibit even more of a tendency to do so than their low self-esteem counterparts.

One general type of esteem-enhancing behavior is successful task performance under challenging or threatening conditions. It is precisely when "the chips are down" that task performance is most likely to affect employees' self-esteem; therefore, the ability to perform well under pressure is especially likely to elicit feelings of high self-esteem. Performance pressure can come in many forms, several of which will be discussed momentarily. As the method and details of the relevant studies are described, readers should not lose sight of the overarching point made by the results of these studies: that high SEs maintain more positive expectations than low SEs about their ability to perform the esteem-enhancing behavior.

In one study (Brockner 1985), subjects of varying levels of self-esteem either were overpaid or not to perform a clerical task. It seems likely that when individuals are overpaid (or put in a condition of positive inequity) the esteem-enhancing thing to do is to work harder. After all, people do not want to think of themselves as immoral souls who take more than they deserve. However, individuals' tendencies to work harder in response to overpayment may be partly a function of being able to work up to the level of equity implicit in the overpayment; high SEs should be more confident about their ability to do so than low SEs. In fact, high SEs in this study worked harder when overpaid than when they were equitably paid; low SEs, if anything, worked less hard in the overpayment than equity condition. Just as relevant to the present discussion, high SEs reported feeling much more confident than low SEs while working on the task in the overpayment condition; in sharp contrast, no such difference in confidence appeared in the equity payment condition.

Several other lines of research (discussed in chapter 5) also have suggested that high SEs maintain more positive expectations than low SEs under challenging or threatening conditions. Several studies have shown that difficult and challenging goals elicit greater productivity among high than low SEs (for example Carroll & Tosi 1970). This may be because high SEs' more favorable expectations produce greater goal acceptance, which leads, in turn, to enhanced performance. In addition, theory (for example, Carver & Scheier 1981) and research (for example, Brockner, Derr & Laing 1987) have shown that subsequent to receiving negative or failure feedback, high

SEs respond with much greater vigor than low SEs. It seems reasonable that positive inequity, difficult goals, and prior failure all elicit high performance pressure; these are precisely the conditions under which high SEs maintain more positive expectations (and perform better) than their low self-esteem counterparts.

Another study (Nadler et al. 1985) — drawn from a very different line of research — is both relevant to this discussion and the earlier one in this chapter on the help seeker's dilemma. Recall the essence of the help seeker's dilemma: on the one hand they wish to seek the help that will enable them to accomplish their objectives. On the other hand, the very act of seeking help could engender feelings of incompetence and/or dependence that lower self-esteem. One factor that could alleviate the latter sorts of feelings — and thus make help seeking more psychologically palatable — is help seekers' perception that they will be able to reciprocate the assistance to the help giver at some future point in time. Based on the present discussion of the self-esteem and expectancy relationship, it is predicted that high SEs entertain more favorable expectations about reciprocating help than their low self-esteem counterparts.

What would happen to individuals' help-seeking tendencies, however, if they were prevented (for example, by external circumstances) from reciprocating the assistance? Such a block should represent a greater blow to high SEs (who maintain more positive expectations about their abilities to reciprocate) than low SEs; thus, high SEs would exhibit less help seeking than low SEs when both groups are led to believe that they will not have the opportunity to reciprocate. The study by Nadler et al. (1985) tested (and provided support for) this reasoning. Subjects of varying levels of self-esteem were working on a task and were led to believe that a fellow participant could provide them with information that would facilitate their own task performance. Half of the subjects were told that they would have an opportunity to reciprocate the favor in the future, whereas half were told that because of "time constraints" there would be no such opportunity. As expected, high SEs were much less likely to seek help in the latter than in the former condition. The opportunity to reciprocate variable, in sharp contrast, had no effect on low SEs' help-seeking behavior.

In summary, high SEs appear to possess more favorable expectations about being able to perform esteem-enhancing behaviors than low SEs; this difference in expectations could account for at least some of the empirical evidence demonstrating that high SEs are more apt than low SEs to engage in behaviors that maintain or heighten self-esteem. Although expectations are one determinant of workers' propensities to engage in self-esteem maintenance behaviors, they are not the only one. As stated previously, the values that individuals attach to (the outcomes of) the behavior also are crucial. The relationship between individual differences in self-esteem and values probably is not similar to the self-esteem and expectancy relationship. Most people, regardless of their level of self-esteem, value being able to perform behaviors that elicit positive outcomes, leading to high self-esteem (McFarlin & Blascovich 1981). If anything, there is reason to think that low SEs attach greater value to esteem-enhancing behavioral outcomes than high SEs. As mentioned in the discussion in chapter 3 on the bases of behavioral plasticity, low SEs are in greater need (than high SEs) of esteem-enhancing feedback; therefore, they should respond more favorably to positive evaluations (and more unfavorably to negative evaluations) than high SEs; this has generally been shown to be true in research on self-esteem and interpersonal attraction (Jones 1973). This sort of result illustrates a (somewhat painful) paradox of low self-esteem: low SEs' negative expectations may make it difficult for them to produce the very (positive) outcomes that they so dearly covet.

More conservatively than positing an inverse correlation between individuals' self-esteem and the value that they attach to esteem-enhancing outcomes, it seems safe to say that the relationship between self-esteem and values is less positive than the self-esteem and expectation relationship. If so, then esteem-related situations, which minimize the role of expectations, should reduce high SEs' greater tendency to engage in self-esteem-maintaining (or enhancing) behaviors. As long as low SEs are convinced that they can perform the esteem-enhancing behavior, then they should be just as apt to do so as high SEs, because both groups attach high value to the outcomes of the behavior. Here again there is supportive research. For example, in one study (Sigall & Gould 1977), subjects of varying self-esteem levels were led to believe that the upcoming task was either easy or difficult. When the task was portrayed as difficult, high SEs expended much greater effort in preparation than did low SEs. (This finding, of course, is consistent with the immediately preceding discussion of high SEs' greater expectations under high pressure situations.) However, when the task was labeled as easy, and presumably all participants expected to succeed, low SEs' level of preparatory motivation was somewhat greater than that of high SEs.

Similarly, just as prior negative feedback elicits large differences in high and low SEs' subsequent motivation and performance, so too does positive or success feedback reduce and often entirely eliminate such differences in performance between high and low SEs (Brockner 1979b; Brockner, Derr & Laing 1987; Mossholder, Bedeian & Armenakis 1982; Shrauger & Sorman 1977). It seems likely that positive feedback causes low SEs to maintain relatively favorable expectations; provided that their expectations have been (at least temporarily) elevated to that of high SEs, the difference in subsequent responding should be reduced or even eliminated (because all individuals value being able to behave in an esteem-enhancing fashion). Finally, it is not even the case that all negative feedback dampens low SEs' subsequent motivation and performance. Failures that persist for relatively short duration and/or failures that can be attributed to external causes should pose far less of a threat to low SEs' (shaky) expectations, and so should have a far less demotivating effect than failures that are more esteem-threatening (for example, extended negative feedback, and/or internally attributed negative feedback). Many studies have yielded results that are consistent with this reasoning (Brockner & Elkind 1985; Brockner et al. 1983; Brockner & Guare 1983; Klein, Fencil-Morse & Seligman 1976).

The discussion of the relationship between individuals' self-esteem and their self-esteem maintenance and enhancement behavior has been largely theoretical: it has focused on the determinants of self-esteem-seeking behavior (expectancies and values), how chronic self-esteem relates to these two determinants, and thus some of the factors that moderate the relationship between individuals' self-esteem and their tendencies to engage in self-esteem maintenance behaviors. It is important to emphasize that this analysis is post hoc; very few studies have deliberately sought to delineate the conditions under which high SEs are more, less, or equally likely to engage in esteem-enhancing behaviors, relative to low SEs. Accordingly, the speculations mentioned already should be tested empirically in future research.

Moreover, although the discussion of this matter has been primarily theoretical, this should not be taken to mean that it is devoid of practical implications. For example, earlier in this chapter it was mentioned that the failure to seek help is in the service of avoiding self-esteem loss; also, the failure to seek aid could be organizationally and/or individually costly. To minimize such costs, it was suggested that managers be sensitive to their employees' self-esteem needs in offering assistance; workers are likely to be far more receptive to aid that is offered in ways that do not lower their self-esteem. Several concrete suggestions were offered on how to offer assistance without damaging the recipients' self-esteem.

Incorporating self-esteem as an individual difference variable suggests yet another practical implication, one that has appeared in various forms throughout this book; namely, that the efficacy of managerial and organizational interventions (in this case those designed to facilitate employees' receptivity to useful assistance) is likely to be moderated by the workers' level of self-esteem. More specifically, even if workers are led to believe that the act of seeking help will not engender lower self-esteem, there could still be differences between high and low SEs in their propensity to seek assistance. High SEs may be more willing to seek assistance than their low self-esteem counterparts because of the former group's greater self-efficacy beliefs. Low SEs may avoid seeking assistance because they do not believe that they have the capacity—even with that provided by the assistance—to accomplish the task at hand. Low SEs may wish to avoid the further loss of self-esteem associated with receiving assistance and still not being able to perform up to par.

Note that this reasoning is quite similar to that in the analysis of avoiding help as a self-handicapping strategy. Self-handicapping theorists (for example, Jones and Berglas 1978) have suggested that individuals with a shaky sense of self-esteem are most likely to employ self-handicapping strategies. Thus, it seems reasonable that low SEs, who generally possess a shakier sense of self-worth than high SEs (Rosenberg 1979), would be more apt to self-handicap. To my knowledge, this hypothesis has never been tested, and thus could serve as an impetus for future research.

Practical implications of the relationship between self-esteem as an individual difference variable and a motivational process also are inherent in the bargainer's dilemma and the decision maker's dilemma. In different ways, both dilemmas may cause us to question whether high self-esteem is unilaterally more adaptive than low self-esteem. That is, in both dilemmas employees may believe that intransigence and/or persistence is the esteem-maintaining or enhancing act. Thus, the bargainer may not want to concede to the other side, and the decision maker may be reluctant to withdraw from the previously chosen course of action because of the presumed loss of esteem associated with doing so. High SEs' greater expectations about being able to perform the esteem-enhancing behavior—that is, to bargain more toughly than the opposing side in order to extract concessions from the other, and to escalate commitment until the task has been successfully accomplished—could be perilous if such expectations are overly optimistic. Recent research in the decision sciences (for example, Bazerman 1986) has shown that under conditions of uncertainty most decision makers fall prey to the "overconfidence bias," which refers to a pervasive tendency to overestimate the soundness of their behaviors and beliefs. Thus, high SEs sometimes may be unduly optimistic about their ability to perform certain esteem-enhancing behaviors, which could produce disastrous outcomes. Indeed, in one study (Brockner & Rubin 1985), high SEs were shown to be more prone to entrapment then their low self-esteem counterparts.

Summary

This chapter dealt primarily with the maintenance of self-esteem as a basic human need, rather than with the antecedents or consequences of self-esteem as an individual difference variable. It was assumed that employees are very concerned with looking good, both publicly and privately, and that much of their behavior in organizations is in the service of seeking positive evaluations. The importance of employees' self-esteem needs is demonstrated perhaps most dramatically in instances in which they must act in ways that are otherwise costly (to themselves and/or the organization) to fullfill self-esteem needs. Four such examples were cited in this chapter: workers' reluctance to seek assistance which, if sought, might serve them quite well; disputants' unwillingness to make bargaining concessions that actually may be in their own long-term best interests; decision makers' reluctance to withdraw commitment from a previously chosen, though failing course of action; and the tendency of some workers to perform at a suboptimal level, so as not to violate the expectations or values that significant others hold for their performance.

The practical implications of these matters were stressed throughout; essentially, it was suggested that the effective management of subordinates is intimately related to managers' ability to influence the impact of subordinates' self-esteem needs on work behaviors. In general, managers have three categories of leverage points through which they can productively influence or control the impact of subordinates' self-esteem needs. As noted in the discussion of the decision maker's dilemma, in some situations managers may try to reduce workers' self-esteem needs to decrease the negative impact that such needs may have on their work behaviors. In addition, managers may try to channel workers' self-esteem needs into a constructive rather than destructive course of action. For example, recall that escalation of commitment to a previously chosen, though failing, course of action was reduced dramatically when decision makers believed that they could look good by allocating resources conservatively. Finally, managers should perform a thorough analysis of the factors that affect the employee behaviors over which they wish to gain influence. Self-esteem needs may be one, but by no means the only, such factor; if so, the effect of self-esteem needs can be nullified or minimized through forceful manipulation of these other factors. For example, escalation of commitment to a previously chosen, though failing, course of action probably is jointly determined by retrospective and prospective factors. Retrospective factors include decision makers' self-esteem needs, whereas prospective factors relate more to economically laden, cost-benefit concerns. If decision makers can be trained to attend to prospective factors, then the impact of retrospective, self-justificatory needs should be minimized.

The last portion of this chapter focused on the relationship between self-esteem as a personality variable and as a basic motivational process. Suffice it to say that studies exploring the nature of this relationship have been apparently contradictory; some studies show that high SEs are more likely to engage in esteem-enhancing behavior than low SEs, others have shown a reversal of this difference, and still others have shown no difference at all between the two groups. To make some sense of these inconclusive findings, it was proposed that employees' tendencies to engage in esteem-enhancing behavior are a joint function of their expectancies about being able to do so (that is, their self-efficacy beliefs), and values attached to responding in ways that enhance self-esteem. To understand the relationship of individuals' self-esteem to their tendency to engage in esteem-enhancing behaviors, it is thus necessary to analyze the relationship between self-esteem and both expectancies and values. It was further proposed that the relationship between self-esteem and expectancies was positive, which could account for the results of studies showing that high SEs are more likely than low SEs to perform esteem-enhancing behaviors. The correlation between self-esteem and values, however, was hypothesized to be zero (for example, Shrauger 1975) or even negative (for example, Jones 1973), which could account for those results showing a nonsignificant or negative relationship between self-esteem and the tendency to perform esteem-enhancing behavior. This post hoc explanation needs to be put to empirical test. If the reasoning is correct, then the relationship between self-esteem and esteem-enhancing behavior is likely to be moderated by factors that dictate whether expectancies or values are the primary basis for performing the esteem-enhancing behavior. If expectancies are most salient, then there should be a positive relationship between individuals' self-esteem and the extent to which they act in an esteem-enhancing behavior. If values play a more prominent role, then the correlation between these two variables should be zero or even negative. Finally, some of the practical implications of the (complex) relationship between individuals' extant self-esteem and their need for self-esteem were discussed.

8
A Future Research Agenda

T his book began by noting the general inability of self-esteem theory and research to elucidate human behavior in the organizational context. As in Weiss and Adler's (1984) analysis of personality research in organizational behavior, it was suggested at the outset that the self-esteem dimension potentially was quite significant, but that this great potential would never be realized until we scholars did more hard-nosed thinking about the role of self-esteem in the organizational context. Moreover, it was suggested that hard-nosed thinking could take at least two forms: clear articulation of the theories of human behavior in organizations, followed by the specification of how self-esteem is related (if at all) to the key factors and processes in those theories: and theoretical specification of the nature of self-esteem, and how the processes associated with self-esteem express themselves in the organizational context.

Note that both sorts of inquiries have been undertaken in this book. An example of the former includes the discussion of goal setting and performance in chapter 3. A question of considerable importance is whether self-esteem moderates the relationship between goal setting and performance. To address this issue, one first needs to delineate the mechanisms by which goals affect performance, and then consider how self-esteem relates to such mechanisms. The relationship between goals and performance is mediated by goal acceptance or commitment, which in turn is influenced by individuals' expectancies and values associated with goal attainment. Thus, self-esteem should moderate the relationship between goals and performance to the extent that it is associated with the mediators of goal acceptance.

An example of the latter conceptualization is the lengthy discussion in chapters 3 and 4 on self-esteem and behavioral plasticity. At the outset of chapter 3, it was noted that there is a core of processes that distinguishes between low and high SEs; these processes render the former group more susceptible to influence by external and social cues than the latter. The remainder of chapters 3 and 4 focused primarily on the organizational implications of low and high SEs' differential plasticity.

This concluding chapter is intended to provide a future research agenda; it is divided into five major sections. First, some of the more important, though largely unexplored, topics for consideration that were mentioned in the previous seven chapters will be reviewed.

Second, a host of methodological problems will be considered that have plagued (and continue to plague) investigators interested in the role of self-esteem in the organizational context; it will become apparent that these methodological difficulties are closely related to conceptual ambiguities concerning the nature of self-esteem.

Third, a pervasive theme in this book is that low and high self-esteem employees respond very differently to identical organizational events and interventions. Therefore, it has been suggested that managers must be sensitive to individual differences in employee self-esteem; the same intervention designed to increase work motivation, for example, may have a significant impact on one type of worker, but little (or even the exact opposite type of) effect on another. This complex state of affairs raises an important, practical question: how can managers better assess the self-esteem level of their subordinates, so as to match (or at least not mismatch) their interventions and interactions with their employees' existing self-esteem level?

Fourth, the discussions of self-esteem as a moderator variable in the organizational setting generally have assumed that employees of varying levels of self-esteem respond to their work environments. This view is accurate, though incomplete. Low and high SEs also exert influence on their work contexts (to which they then respond), a process that Weick (1979) has dubbed *enactment*. The fourth section will consider some of the ways in which low and high SEs create different work environments.

Fifth, self-esteem has been treated throughout the book strictly at the individual level of analysis. However, behavior within organizations can be subjected to three levels of analysis: the individual, the group, and the entire organization. This fact suggests that self-hood also may be analyzed at more than one level. The object of self-evaluation in the individual-level discussion has been *me*. The final section will speculate about the impact of self-evaluation on organizational phenomena when individuals view themselves as part of a collective (that is, *us*).

Future Research Highlights from Chapters 1 through 7

Each chapter in this book includes several mandates for future research, either in the form of specific key topics or more general concerns. The "punch line" in chapter 1 was that the role of self-esteem in predicting individuals' work behaviors and attitudes will receive a much fairer test in future research if such efforts are guided on reasonable, a priori, theoretical bases. Chapter 2 treated self-esteem primarily as a main effect factor. Some studies have shown that low and high SEs differ in their work behaviors and attitudes, but such results have lacked a unifying theoretical framework. Moreover, it may be that researchers who seek to establish self-esteem differences in work behaviors, but who do not take self-esteem × situation interaction effects into account, are doomed to fail. The disappointing yield of the main effect approach to self-esteem research is not at all meant to trivialize the importance of self-esteem in predicting individuals' work behaviors and attitudes. Rather, the effect of self-esteem can be considered much more fruitfully in conjunction with situational factors. (During a conversation with a colleague, who has done a considerable amount of research on the role of self-esteem in organizations, he stressed the importance of main effect differences between low and high self-esteem persons. The essence of his argument was that it would be difficult to persuade readers that self-esteem was an important predictor variable, unless it could be shown that self-esteem had influenced work behaviors "on its own," that is, as a main effect. However, in this book, it has been suggested that self-esteem and situational factors jointly and interactively influence employees' behavior. The importance of the personality variable of self-esteem still should be apparent even though it has been considered as an interactive rather than main effect determinant of individuals' work behaviors and attitudes; Magnusson & Endler 1977; Mischel 1973.)

Chapters 3 and 4 present one possible conceptualization of self-esteem × situation interactionism: the notion that for several reasons low SEs are more susceptible to influence by external (and especially social) cues than their high self-esteem counterparts. Future research needs to establish more convincing linkages between self-esteem and each of the three bases of plasticity, that is, uncertainty, need for positive evaluation, and the self-diagnosticity of negative feedback. Moreover, the organizational ramifications of the plasticity hypothesis warrant further consideration. Several examples were provided in chapters 3 and 4, but additional evidence is needed.

In a related vein, it is important to delineate the conditions under which the plasticity hypothesis is most likely to be supported. As mentioned in chapter 5, there are undoubtedly circumstances in which high SEs and low SEs are equally susceptible to influence. Even more interesting, perhaps, are those conditions under which high and low SEs are equally susceptible to influence, but in directly opposite directions. Further thought and research needs to address the range of organizational stimuli—be they aspects of the formal organization, the informal organization, or the very essence of the work itself—that elicit results congruent with the plasticity hypothesis, or any other hypothesis. For example, in chapter 5, it was suggested that the plasticity hypothesis was most relevant when the organizational situation under scrutiny allowed low SEs' greater uncertainty, need for approval, and tendency to view evaluative feedback as self-diagnostic to be expressed. In contrast, low and high SEs are most likely to be equally able to be influenced (but in diametrically opposite ways) when the situation poses a threat to the self-esteem of the two groups. Clearly, much research is consistent with these post hoc assertions, but further work is necessary to evaluate them on an a priori basis.

Chapter 5 raised two other matters to be addressed by further research; first, whether low SEs' more plastic style is more or less adaptive—for both the individual and the organization—than is high SEs' tendency to be less easily influenced. In considering this issue, future researchers simultaneously will be questioning the more traditional viewpoint positing that high self-esteem is unilaterally more adaptive than low self-esteem. Second, it was suggested that the plasticity hypothesis is the third theoretical formulation of employee self-esteem to make its way into the organizational literature; it needs to be critically (that is, empirically) evaluated against the two that already exist: the self-consistency position of Korman (1970) and the self-enhancement perspective offered by Dipboye (1977a).

Chapter 6 called attention to the need for further research on the causal antecedents of self-esteem. Almost all of the studies cited in the chapter were nonexperimental, making it very difficult to discern whether the independent variables actually had causal impact on the employees' self-esteem (Kohn & Schooler 1982). For that matter, most research on self-esteem as an independent variable (see chapters 2 through 4) is low in internal validity; it is obviously important to discern causality with greater precision in those types of studies as well (Bachman & O'Malley 1977).

Chapter 7 focused on employees' need to gain or maintain self-esteem as a motivational process that affects much of their behavior. Most intriguing are those circumstances in which this motive interferes with individuals' tendencies to act in the economic or more rational interests of the organization (and even themselves, sometimes). Accordingly, further thinking should be devoted to the practical matter of managing employees' self-esteem needs. On the theoretical fronts, chapter 7 suggests that we pay attention to at least two issues: the relationship between individuals' extant self-esteem and their tendencies to act in ways that preserve or enhance self-esteem, and the extent to which self-esteem maintenance is a private and/or public matter (Dipboye, Phillips & Shahani 1985).

This brief review reflects merely a smattering of some of the more important, previously-raised theoretical and practical questions that are worthy of further thought and empirical research. More detailed questions can be obtained in each chapter. Moreover, by no means are the arenas for further theorizing and investigation limited to these matters, as subsequent sections will attest.

Methodological and Conceptual Problems in the Measurement of Self-esteem

Most self-esteem researchers require subjects to complete a standardized self-esteem inventory. For example, my own research typically utilizes a version of the Revised Janis-Field Self-Esteem Scale (Eagly 1967; Robinson & Shaver 1973), a copy of which appears in figure 8–1. The typical procedure consists of having subjects evaluate themselves on a number of dimensions pertinent to the self-concept; the average score, usually unweighted, of each

---

It is important that you try to answer each question *frankly* and *honestly.* Please do not put your name anywhere on these pages. Please complete this page by using the following scale:

Write 1 if the statement describes you *very often.*
Write 2 if the statement describes you *fairly often.*
Write 3 if the statement describes you *sometimes.*
Write 4 if the statement describes you *once in a great while.*
Write 5 if the statement describes you *practically never.*

_____ How often do you have the feeling that there is nothing that you can do well?
_____ When you talk in front of a class or group of people your own age, how often do you feel worried or afraid?
_____ How often do you feel that you have handled yourself well at a social gathering?
_____ How often do you have the feeling that you can do everything well?
_____ How often are you comfortable when starting a conversation with people you don't know?
_____ How often do you feel self-conscious?
_____ How often do you feel that you are a successful person?
_____ How often are you troubled with shyness?
_____ How often do you feel inferior to most people you know?
_____ How often do you feel that you are a worthless individual?
_____ How often do you feel confident that your success in your future job or career is assured?
_____ How often do you feel sure of yourself when among strangers?
_____ How often do you feel confident that some day people will look up to you and respect you?
_____ In general, how often do you feel confident about your abilities?
_____ How often do you worry about how well you get along with other people?
_____ How often do you feel that you dislike yourself?
_____ How often do you feel so discouraged with yourself that you wonder whether anything is worthwhile?

Source: Robinson & Shaver 1973, pp. 79–80.

Figure 8–1. Revised Janis-Field Self-esteem Scale

participant is then taken. Subsequently, the researcher seeks to determine whether self-esteem relates to the dependent variable(s) of interest (or independent variables, if it is a study on the antecedents of self-esteem), either in isolation or in interaction with other situational or dispositional factors.

This methodology makes many questionable conceptual assumptions about the nature of self-esteem, as well as peoples' tendencies to report their self-esteem accurately, all of which may serve to undermine the validity (and hence predictive power) of the self-esteem measure. This section first calls attention to these underlying assumptions, and then offers suggestions about what future researchers may do to sharpen the measurement of global self-esteem.

Assumption 1: Self-esteem is Unidimensional

By taking one score from the inventory (typically an unweighted mean), researchers have implied that self-esteem is a unitary construct. However, there are conceptual reasons to believe that self-esteem may be multidimensional (Shavelson, Hubner & Stanton 1976), and recent empirical findings are consistent with this assertion. For example, Fleming and Watts (1980) factor-analyzed the Revised Janis-Field Scale and found that it consisted of four factors. Most of the items loaded on one of two factors: social confidence (for example, "How often do you worry about how well you get along with other people?" "How often are you troubled by shyness?") and self-regard (for example, "How often do you feel inferior to most people you know?" "How often do you feel that you dislike yourself?").

It is quite conceivable that the assessment of self-esteem as a unitary construct sharply limits its predictive power. For example, suppose that the researcher wished to study social interaction, and used the Revised Janis-Field Scale to measure self-esteem. It is possible that the social confidence subfactor is much more conceptually relevant (and therefore more highly related) to the dependent variable(s) of interest than is the self-regard subfactor. By collapsing across factors into a unitary dimension, researchers may be (inappropriately) weakening the power of their statistical tests. This is not to suggest that researchers always should test each subfactor's predictive utility; such an endeavor begins to take the form of a fishing expedition in the quest of statistical (and not necessarily theoretical or practical) significance. Rather, researchers' prior conceptualization should guide them in their mode of operationalizing self-esteem. If theoretical and/or practical considerations suggest that it may be worthwhile to explore the role of the subfactors of self-esteem, then by all means the investigator should do so.

Assumption 2: Self-esteem Is a Global Dimension

This assumption is similar to assumption one, but not identical. It suggests that even within a particular dimension (for example, social confidence), individuals' level of self-esteem is virtually invariant. However, there is no logical (or empirical) basis to make such an assumption. For instance, it is quite possible for individuals to have considerable confidence in social situations in which they are meeting others for the first time; this does not necessarily mean, however, that the same individuals will be especially comfortable when called upon to speak in front of a class or board meeting.

To remedy this problem, it may be necessary for researchers to match the globality and specificity (or chronicity and acuteness) of their self-esteem instruments to that of their other variables. More specifically, organizational scholars (and personality researchers, more generally) have learned that it is exceedingly difficult to predict employees' specific behaviors (for example, performance on a given day) on the basis of global personality dimensions such as self-esteem. If the research goal is to predict employees' specific behaviors, such as performance at a given task, then it may be necessary to construct more specific personality measures. For instance, employees might be asked about their task-specific levels of confidence. Moreover, they should complete the measure with regard to how they are feeling at that given moment, rather than how they feel in general (which is the more customary procedure).

The major pitfall of such procedures is that researchers may be continuously called upon to develop self-esteem scales that are specific to their particular interests. The validity of these proliferating measures are likely to remain suspect, because different researchers having different agendas are not likely to use identical measures. To avoid this messy state of affairs, researchers may well choose to rely on an already-validated, global self-esteem measure. If they do that, however, they should be careful to ensure that the criterion variable is at a corresponding level of globality. For example, suppose one wished to study the joint effect of some workplace intervention and global self-esteem on employee absenteeism. The dependent variable—in this case absenteeism—should be as general as possible; for instance, the time period during which individuals' absenteeism is assessed should span a long period of time, to constitute a more general measure of absenteeism. Or, suppose the study focused on some relationship between self-esteem and work performance. Rather than trying to establish the relationship between self-esteem and one measure of performance, the investigators should sample several different domains of work performance, establish an index based on these different measures, and then correlate the global index of work performance with the global measure of self-esteem. Indeed, a handful of studies have shown that specific (global) individual difference measures predict specific (global) behaviors fairly well, but that global individual difference measures do a much poorer job of predicting specific behaviors (Epstein 1979; Fishbein & Ajzen 1974; Weigel & Newman 1976).

Assumption 3: Self-esteem Is Crystallized

By focusing on research participants' mean self-esteem score, we are implicitly assuming that they rate themselves as relatively high or low in self-esteem with considerable confidence or certainty. This assumption may be unwarranted; more likely, many individuals may wrestle with whether they evaluate themselves favorably—even within specific domains—on an ongoing basis. For example, suppose one measured managers' self-confidence in a particular area of leadership. On some days and in some situations they will evaluate themselves favorably, whereas at other times they will not. This person may have a mean specific self-esteem score in this particular area of leadership, computed simply by averaging his or her responses to the relevant items; however, the average score may be relatively meaningless if it is associated with a high degree of variability. If individuals' self-esteem ratings (regardless of level of specificity) are made with low confidence or certainty, then they are not likely to be predictive of, or predicted by, other factors.

To address this issue, future researchers may wish to assess the certainty, confidence, or consistency of participants' self-evaluations. For example, it may be possible to compute not only a mean self-esteem score, but also a variance rating for each individual. This methodology would result in four groups of participants: high self-esteem/high variance, high self-esteem/low variance, low self-esteem/high variance, and low self-esteem/low variance. It can be hypothesized that the self-esteem factor is likely to be much more predictive for individuals having low rather than high variance scores.

Similarly, subjects could be required to rate not only their self-esteem, but also the certainty with which they made such ratings. This procedure was employed by Marecek and Mettee (1972), who were interested in exploring the effects of positive feedback as well as individuals' attributions for that feedback on subsequent performance. In this study, the performance of low and high SEs was differentially affected by the independent variables if and only if the participants were relatively certain of their existing level of self-esteem. In short, if individuals' self-esteem is not internally consistent or clear in their own minds (and hearts), then it is less likely that self-esteem will be predictive of, or predicted by, other key organizational variables.

Assumption 4: Individuals' Self-reports of their Self-esteem Are Valid

The truth value of this assumption is questionable for two broad sets of reasons. First, individuals may be unwilling to report their self-esteem accurately; second, they may be unable to do so. In either case, the validity and, therefore, predictive utility of the self-esteem construct is bound to suffer.

Unwillingness to Tell the Truth. The very process of completing a self-esteem measure places respondents in a face-saving dilemma. On the one hand, the evaluator has instructed them to answer as honestly as possible; on the other hand, respondents would like to believe and have others believe the best in themselves. Given that most self-esteem measures are quite transparent (for example, see figure 8–1), and given that respondents want to present themselves in a socially desirable light, it is likely that many describe themselves in terms more favorable than they hold privately.

If all participants (regardless of their self-esteem) overrate their self-esteem to a similar extent, then the problem probably is minimal. However, if individuals' tendency to represent themselves more favorably than they truly believe is related systematically to their global self-esteem, then there could be ambiguity in the interpretation of the results. For example, in several studies it has been shown that self-esteem (in conjunction with situational factors) is related to the dependent variables of interest in a curvilinear fashion (Brockner 1985; Brockner, Davy & Carter 1985; Brockner & Elkind 1985; Brockner, Hjelle & Plant 1985). The consistent finding in these studies is that low SEs respond differently from medium and high SEs, who, in turn, do not differ from one another.

This curvilinear relationship may be theoretically interesting, or it may be an artifact of the impact of self-presentation concerns on individuals' reporting of their self-esteem. More specifically, it just might be that self-esteem exerts impact on behavior in a threshold-like fashion: once individuals' self-esteem exceeds a certain level, it produces a significant shift in thought, feeling, and/or behavior. Moreover, additional increases in self-esteem above and beyond the threshold point do not produce a significant change on the dependent variable(s) of interest. In essence, this logic suggests that self-esteem (in interaction with situational factors) truly may affect thought and/or behavior in a curvilinear fashion.

On the other hand, the curvilinear impact of self-esteem could be due to a methodological artifact. It is possible that the upper third of the self-esteem distribution is actually a conglomerate of individuals who have truly high self-esteem and those who actually are low in self-esteem but who are "hiding" behind an overly-inflated report of their global self-esteem. On average, these individuals' true self-esteem may be no different from the medium SEs, yielding little difference between the middle and upper thirds of the self-esteem distributions on the relevant dependent variables.

There are at least three concrete steps that future researchers may take to increase respondents' willingness to report their global self-esteem accurately. First, it may be possible to employ self-esteem measures that are less transparent. For example, Ziller (1973) has developed a procedure in which subjects are shown a row or column of circles, and are asked to place themselves as well as a number of other people in the circles (see figure 8–2).

The high (low) self-esteem response in these instances is to insert oneself in the left (right) most circle if the circles are arranged in row, and in the top (bottom) most circle if they are arranged in a column. Ziller (1973) has reported the results of several studies lending construct validity to the measure. Note it is not being advocated that researchers abandon the more traditional measures of self-esteem in favor of Ziller's; the latter has its own problems (Robinson & Shaver 1973). The point is that it may be possible to achieve greater self-report validity with less transparent self-esteem measures; the Ziller procedure is an example of a less transparent mode of self-esteem assessment.

Second, it seems important for researchers to highlight the anonymity of the setting in which respondents complete the self-esteem measure. This may not affect individuals' private desires to rate themselves more favorably than they truly believe. However, it should reduce the extent to which individuals are motivated to present themselves favorably in the eyes of others.

Third, it may be worthwhile for self-esteem researchers to administer a

---

Item 1 Self-esteem

The circles below stand for people. Mark each circle with the letter standing for one of the people in the list. Do this in any way you like, but use each person only once and do not omit anyone.

F — someone who is flunking   S — yourself

H — the happiest person you know   Su — someone you know who is suc-
                                          cessful

K — someone you know who is kind   St — the strongest person you know

Source: Ziller 1973, p. 182.

Figure 8–2. Item from Ziller's Self-esteem Scale

chronic social desirability measure (Crowne & Marlowe 1964) to their respondents. This would enable them to distinguish between individuals whose high self-esteem is (versus is not) reflective of a generalized tendency to describe themselves in a socially desirable fashion. For example, in one study (Hewitt & Goldman 1974), the researchers administered a self-esteem and social desirability measure and discovered that they could classify their participants into three groups: low SEs, high SEs who were high in social desirability (fakers), and high SEs who were low in social desirability (true high SEs). The last group responded very differently on the dependent measure of interest from the low SEs and the fakers; the low SEs and fakers, in contrast, did not differ from one another.

Inability to Tell the Truth. For a variety of reasons, individuals may be unable to report their true self-esteem, which also should decrease the predictive power of the variable. For several reasons (for example, lack of introspection or intelligence), certain individuals simply have little access to their self-knowledge. When such persons are requested to complete self-esteem measures, the responses that they provide are not likely to be reflective of their inner souls, due to their lack of accessibility to the pertinent information about themselves. It even could be that individuals who are self-knowledgeable may not describe themselves accurately if asked to complete a self-report measure in an environment that interferes with their expression of such self-knowledge. For example, if the respondents are tired, or concerned with presenting themselves in a socially desirable fashion, then the impact of their self-knowledge on self-reported self-esteem is bound to be minimal.

The results of several studies suggest that it may be possible to counteract the latter sorts of problems. If researchers create an assessment environment that facilitates respondents' ability to gain access to their self-knowledge while completing the self-esteem measure, then the respondents may describe themselves with greater accuracy. The results of several studies are consistent with this assertion (see Pryor 1980, for a review). Subjects completed self-report inventories (that is, measures of personality and attitude) while either being induced to focus attention on themselves (self-focus condition) or not (control condition). The validity of respondents' self-reports was much greater in the former than in the latter condition. More specifically, the power of the self-report measure to predict respondents' actual behavior was considerably higher in the self-focus than in the control condition.

Similarly, certain individuals may exhibit a chronic tendency to be more self-knowing than others. For example, Fenigstein, Scheier, and Buss's (1975) Private Self-Consciousness Scale may be related to this individual difference. Items include "I reflect about myself a lot," "I'm generally attentive to my inner feelings," and "I'm always trying to figure myself out." Several studies (for example, Scheier, Buss & Buss 1978) have shown that personality assessments of individuals high in private self-consciousness—along dimensions other than private self-consciousness—are more valid than are those garnered from low private self-conscious individuals. Once again, the personality measures of the former group were much more predictive of the individuals' behavior than were those of the latter.

Such findings can be extrapolated to the self-esteem literature; it is possible that individuals will be better able to report their self-esteem to the extent that they are dispositionally self-knowledgeable. If so, then future self-esteem investigations may wish to measure respondents on measures of both self-esteem and self-knowledge (Greenwald, Bellezza & Banaji 1987). If the reasoning noted here is correct, then there may be little or no difference between low and high SEs (along the dependent variables of interest) who are not self-knowledgeable. However, the self-knowledgeable individuals may exhibit much stronger associations between their self-esteem and the key dependent (or independent) variables.

Note the hypothesized parallel impact of situationally induced and dispositional self-knowledge on self-report validity. In both instances greater self-knowledge may enable respondents to describe themselves more accurately in response to a standardized self-esteem inventory. The increased validity of such self-reports could, in turn, lead to more statistically (and possibly theoretically) significant findings than has been observed heretofore in much of the self-esteem literature.

Summary

Many of the assumptions underlying the traditional assessment of self-esteem have been questioned here. The dubious nature of these assumptions may have led many self-esteem researchers astray; that is, investigators may have obtained findings that were statistically nonsignificant, not because the theoretical underpinnings of their studies were inappropriate, but rather, because of conceptual and methodological difficulties associated with the assessment of self-esteem. For each assumption, at least one potential remedy to the problem was offered. In so doing, I wish to nudge future self-esteem researchers in the direction of obtaining results of greater statistical and, therefore, possibly theoretical and practical significance. Indeed, in light of the many questionable assumptions underlying current self-esteem measurement, it is a small wonder that any progress has been made at all.

Four final comments are in order: first, the assumptions that have been questioned in this section are by no means exhaustive. Some of the major ones have merely been explored. Left untouched, for example, is the fact that most researchers assign equal weights to each item in the overall scale, even though respondents probably grossly differentiate the importance of each item in affecting their overall self-evaluation.

Second, it is not being suggested that researchers who operate as if all four assumptions are valid cannot or will not attain statistical significance in their empirical efforts. Rather, they may underestimate the predictive power of self-esteem by not making some of the methodological changes in self-esteem assessment that would follow from questioning one or more of the four assumptions. For example, if theory suggests that certain subfactor (see assumption 2) measures of self-esteem are more relevant than others (to the other variable(s) of interest), then researchers should not proceed simply to measure self-esteem with a global, unitary measure like the one exhibited in figure 8–1. The failure to make theory-driven innovations in the assessment of self-esteem may cause researchers to commit beta or type II errors (Cook & Campbell 1979), such that they conclude that the results are less significant than they actually are.

Third, many of the measurement problems discussed already are not limited to the personality dimension of self-esteem. More generally, for example, the field of personality psychology has long been plagued by respondents' unwillingness or inability to describe themselves accurately on standardized self-report inventories. One of the purposes of this book is to make self-esteem, in particular, and personality, in general, a more respectable topic of inquiry among organizational scholars. Therefore, in addressing the difficulties associated with self-esteem measurement, theorists and researchers should consider whether similar strategies also may be employed as they study other relevant individual difference variables within the organizational context.

Fourth, it is worth noting that many other personality measures besides self-esteem—cited mainly in the clinical psychology literatures—place heavy emphasis on the favorability of individuals' self-evaluation. These include, but are not limited to anxiety (Taylor 1953), repression-sensitization (Byrne 1961), and social desirability (Crowne & Marlowe 1964). The intercorrelations between the latter three measures often are so high (in the .70–.80 range) that it has been suggested that they all tap the same underlying dimension, dubbed "negative affectivity" by Watson and Clark (1984).

Indeed, Watson and Clark's (1984) definition of negative affectivity seems to overlap considerably with self-esteem: "it reflects pervasive individual differences in negative emotionality and self-concept. High-NA individuals tend to be distressed and upset and have a negative view of self, whereas those low on the dimension are relatively content and secure and satisfied with themselves" (p. 465).

The concept of negative affectivity may be useful in future research on the role of personality in organizations. It may be that "different" personality dimensions, which emphasize the favorability of self-evaluation, are more similar than dissimilar. Thus, findings obtained in the anxiety literature may be equally applicable to those found in the self-esteem literature. Indeed, as Watson and Clark imply, such literatures actually are one and the same; the main difference resides in the label that has been attached to the personality dimension. While the differences in labels is conceptually trivial, the mere existence of different labels may have had the effect of making researchers uninformed about bodies of knowledge relevant to their research. As Watson and Clark concluded, "more researchers have not fully appreciated the extent to which all of these tests (that is, the different trait measures of negative affectivity) are intercorrelated. As a result, fairly separate and distinct literatures have developed around many of them" (1984, p. 484, parentheses added). So, for example, Brockner and Guare (1983) found that two different personality traits—self-esteem and depression—similarly moderated the effect of experimentally-manipulated attributions for poor performance on individuals' subsequent task performance. In short, Watson and Clark's identification of negative affectivity is a much-needed calling for future researchers to think more integratively about the meaning of empirical results obtained from seemingly different, but possibly quite similar, personality literatures.

Recognizing Employees' Self-esteem Levels

A pervasive theme of this book is that to understand the role of self-esteem within the organizational context one must appreciate person-situation interactionism; differences between high and low SEs must be considered in the context of relevant organizational variables. Moreover, as noted in chapters 3 through 5, self-esteem × situation interactionism can take several different forms. Chapters 3 and 4 called attention to the behavioral plasticity pattern, in which low SEs were shown to be more influenced by external and social factors than their high self-esteem counterparts. Chapter 5 discussed several limitations of the behavioral plasticity hypothesis, several of which also were consistent with self-esteem × situation interactionism; for example, under certain (that is, esteem-threatening) conditions low and high SEs were equally influenced by external cues, but in directly opposite ways.

Regardless of the specific nature of the self-esteem × situation interaction effect, the key point is that low and high SEs may respond very differently to the identical organizational stimuli. By extension, managers must ensure that organizational interventions and social interactions affecting employees are consistent (or at least not inconsistent) with the employees' self-esteem (Nadler & Tushman 1980). For example, suppose that a manager wishes to institute a goal-setting program to enhance employee motivation (Locke et al. 1981). It is entirely possible that low and high SEs will respond very differently to such a program (see chapter 3); if so, then the program may need to be "fine tuned" even further to achieve congruence with the employees' self-esteem level. Of course, to do this sort of fine tuning, managers must be able to evaluate and recognize their employees' level of self-esteem.

Based upon the material in chapter 2 through 6, it seems that managers may rely on two general strategies to make inferences about their employees' self-esteem. The first stems from viewing self-esteem as a dependent variable (see chapter 6). The prescription is straightforward: if certain factors (for example, work autonomy) and processes (for example, reflected appraisal, role playing) have been shown to determine self-esteem, then managers should seek information about their subordinates along these dimensions. Suppose that while recruiting an employee, a manager learns from reliable sources that the employee had the kind of background—both in and out of the workplace—that fosters high self-esteem. If so, then the recruiting manager can make a more informed decision about the prospective employee, which includes his or her likely level of self-esteem. The discussions in chapter 6 on the antecedents of self-esteem suggest some of the kinds of information that may enable managers to make predictions about an employee's level of self-esteem. Data about the employee's past, including family background and prior work history and conditions, as well as information about the work environment for the present position, may generate more accurate judgments about the employee's self-esteem.

The second strategy for judging employee self-esteem is based in the conceptualization of self-esteem as an independent variable. At first blush, the task of identifying employees' self-esteem by use of this strategy seems simple: if certain behaviors are known to be the consequences of self-esteem (for example, task performance), then one could make reasonable inferences about individuals' self-esteem by observing those behaviors and attitudes that are believed to be the consequences of self-esteem. Note that such an approach is consistent with viewing self-esteem on a main effect basis; however, the main effect approach (of self-esteem and most other personality variables) simply has not stood the test of time in the organizational literatures. Far more fruitful would be a person-situation interactionist approach to identifying employee self-esteem, which mandates that the joint effects of self-esteem and contextual factors on behavior are explored. By observing employees' behavior, and by making reasonable estimates of the nature of the employees' work situations, managers might be able to make more informed judgments about employees' levels of self-esteem.

More specifically, suppose the situation were one that allowed employees' degree of uncertainty to affect behavior. This could occur, for example, if the employee were exposed to models for appropriate behavior. In chapter 4 it was shown that low self-esteem employees are more apt (than high SEs) to imitate the work values and behaviors of a relevant model, presumably because the former group was more uncertain about the appropriateness of their own behaviors and values (Brockner, O'Malley, Hite & Davies 1987; Weiss 1977, 1978). Or, suppose that the context elicited the expression of individuals' need for approval. This could occur if employees' attitudes toward an evaluator were studied as a function of the evaluator's attitudes toward the employees. Much research has shown that low SEs express greater liking for a positive evaluator and greater disliking for a negative evaluator than do high SEs (Jones 1973), presumably because of the former group's greater need for approval.

The previous two categories of situations were those that typically provide support for the behavioral plasticity hypothesis; low SEs are much more influenced in the manners described above than are their high self-esteem counterparts. Other kinds of situations produce a different sort of variation in the reactions of high and low SEs. As discussed in chapter 5, situations that are esteem-threatening often elicit considerable responsivity in high versus low SEs, but in directly opposite ways. For example, employees' psychological and behavioral reactions to negative feedback may provide insights into their levels of self-esteem. Much research has shown that high SEs respond to negative feedback with an active, defensive rejection of the feedback; low SEs, in sharp contrast, are often buffeted around willy-nilly by the feedback. Specifically, high SEs are likely to attribute negative feedback to external, unstable, and specific causes, whereas low SEs tend to attribute such feedback to internal, stable, and global factors (Fitch 1970; Tennen & Herzberger 1987; Zuckerman 1979). Moreover, high SEs often use negative feedback as a springboard for increased subsequent performance, whereas low SEs often respond by withdrawing—either mentally or behaviorally—from the task at hand (Brockner, Derr & Laing 1987; Brockner et al. 1983; Shrauger & Sorman 1977). Interestingly, these and other studies (Campbell & Fairey 1985) have shown that the two self-esteem groups are much less apt to differ in their psychological and behavioral reactions to positive feedback.

Much can be learned about employees' self-esteem by careful observation of their reactions to a variety of different situations. The words *variety of different* are emphasized because the information gleaned from a single situation is not likely to be nearly as diagnostic about employees' self-esteem as is the evidence that converges across a number of different contexts. The word *situations* is emphasized in order to serve as a reminder that employees' behaviors are interactively determined by individual differences, such as self-esteem, as well as contextual factors; in order to make inferences about employees' self-esteem on the basis of observing their behaviors, it is also necessary to take into account relevant situational factors.

Situational Effects on Self-esteem

Both strategies for making accurate inferences about individuals' self-esteem place heavy emphasis on the perceiver's ability to learn about situational factors. Of course, the kind of information to be uncovered about the situation differs somewhat in the two strategies. In the former, it was suggested that managers need to unearth information about the variables that are known to influence their employees' self-esteem. In the latter, it was implied that practitioners must find out about those factors which, in conjunction with employees' self-esteem, influence their behaviors and attitudes.

There is yet another reason for managers to be attuned to situational factors when trying to make inferences about employees' self-esteem. This reason has more to do with assessing the average or overall level of self-esteem of the group, rather than the self-esteem of any given individual. In certain situations (for example, in a large group or organization) managers may be unable or unwilling to make accurate judgments about each employee's self-esteem; about the best that the manager may do is gauge the self-esteem level of the group on the whole. As suggested in chapter 6, employees' self-esteem is bound to fluctuate, depending on a host of organizational (or even extraorganizational) events of common concern. For example, it was suggested earlier that the work performance of high and low self-esteem employees may differ dramatically as a function of the layoffs of their coworkers (Brockner, Davy & Carter 1985). The related issue that is raised here is the following: what impact, if any, do layoffs have on the overall self-esteem level of employees who are not laid off? Under certain conditions, at least, it seems likely that survivors of layoffs also may suffer a blow to their self-esteem, at least temporarily. If so, then practitioners need to be aware of this fact and manage the workforce accordingly. For instance, several management consultants (Barton 1986) have suggested that subsequent to layoffs the surviving workforce should be assigned to perform noncomplex tasks at which they are likely to succeed. This practical prescription fits nicely with previously presented theory and research. Chapter 3 discussed how low SEs perform much better when their prior expectations are high rather than low (Sigall & Gould 1977). Given that the surviving workforce may be relatively low in self-esteem, it is critical that they approach their subsequent work with favorable expectations for success.

On a more optimistic note, it is also likely that the workforce's overall self-esteem will be relatively high in response to certain common organizational events. For example, suppose the Research and Development division of a particular organization had an especially productive year, developing many innovative products and processes. It is precisely at this time—when employees generally are feeling good about themselves—that they can be subjected to motivational inducements that have been shown to facilitate the efforts of high SEs, such as the institution of an extremely challenging goal for the upcoming year.

Pitfalls in Recognizing Employees' Self-esteem

In order to make reasonable inferences about the self-esteem level of the organization's workforce in general or of individuals in particular, practitioners should observe employees' behavior as well as the context in which it occurs; in certain settings high and low SEs should behave in predictably different ways. Thus, knowledge of behavior and situations will enable observers to "work backward" in a sense, to make inferences about employees' self-esteem. Although this particular strategy of self-esteem inference seems reasonably straightforward, it does contain at least three practical problems.

First, observers must be able to make accurate judgments about employees' behavior, especially those that are presumed to be the consequences of their self-esteem and situational factors. In addition, they must be able to make keen assessments about the nature of the situation. For example, it was suggested that high and low self-esteem workers respond in divergent ways to esteem-threatening situations, such as the receipt of negative feedback; high SEs typically respond by redoubling their efforts at the subsequent tasks at hand, whereas low SEs tend to withdraw from them. Suppose that certain employees exhibited high effort, whereas others showed low effort at a particular task. Does this mean that the former group is higher in self-esteem than the latter? Perhaps. In order to answer this question more definitively, it would be useful to evaluate the extent to which the situation were esteem threatening. The more that the former group showed greater effort than the latter in a situation known to be esteem threatening, the more confidently could one conclude that individuals' self-esteem was higher in the former than latter instance. Thus, accurate self-esteem inference also requires observers to be savvy about the nature of the situation in which the target person performs, interacts, or otherwise behaves.

Second, suppose that practitioners' inferences about employees' self-esteem are in the service of ultimately tailoring interventions and/or social interactions to employees' self-esteem level. To return to the goal-setting example, imagine that practitioners need to develop a goal-setting program that is congruent with employees' self-esteem. Suppose further, as is likely to be case, that the process of inferring self-esteem reveals considerable variability in the self-esteem level of the very individuals the practitioner wishes to influence. The practitioners' problem should be obvious; how can they tailor-make an intervention to fit employees' self-esteem when high and low SEs will respond differently to the identical intervention?

To maximize the positive impact of the intervention, it may be necessary to develop variations on the theme of the intervention to achieve congruence with employees' self-esteem. Suppose that research suggested that high SEs respond better to participatively set goals, whereas low SEs respond better to assigned goals. If so, then the goal-setting intervention should be modified to interact with employees' self-esteem in ways that heighten its positive impact on performance. Thus, even when employees' self-esteem has been identified accurately, practitioners still may face the difficult task of creating congruence between employees' self-esteem and their work environment.

Moreover, even if the practitioner were aware of what variations on the theme should be introduced to fit individual workers' self-esteem, the feasibility of being able to put such variations into practice may vary widely across situations. Certain interventions or modes of behavior do allow the influencing agent to vary his or her behavior. For example, in delivering feedback to subordinates—either in the context of a formal performance appraisal interview, or more regular, informal everyday interaction—the appraiser often can and should vary the process and/or content of the feedback in ways that fit the self-esteem of the person being appraised. Thus, the appraiser may encourage high SEs to interpret negative feedback as a challenge for their subsequent performance, in light of the evidence suggesting that high SEs often respond to challenge by increasing their efforts. Low SEs, in contrast, may be encouraged to avoid blaming their lack of ability for the negative feedback, in light of the data implying that such individuals perform most poorly in response to an internally attributed failure (see chapters 3 and 4 for relevant research).

In other situations, however, it may be far less feasible to vary the nature of the intervention or organizational stimulus to achieve congruence with employees' level of self-esteem. That is, if the natural target of the intervention is the collective (for example, the work group or the division), then any attempt to vary the intervention to fit individuals' self-esteem simply might be too unwieldy to administer. In addition, issues of equity or fair treatment are bound to arise if individuals are treated differently (as a function of their self-esteem). Influencing agents should not ignore the collectives' self-esteem under such conditions; instead, it may be more appropriate for them to make a judgment of the average or overall self-esteem level of the members of the collective and tailor their interventions accordingly.

Third, there may be a danger inherent in practitioners' attempts to achieve congruence between employees' self-esteem and their work environments. This danger stems from the fact that self-esteem and situation interactionism can be conceptualized in two very different ways. On the one hand, we have considered the interactive effect of employees' self-esteem and situational factors on relevant work outcomes (for example, task performance). A corollary of this type of interactionism is the importance of employees' self-esteem and work environments being well suited to one another. On the other hand—and herein lies the danger in practitioners' attempts to achieve such congruence—employees' self-esteem and their work environments interact to affect one another in a reciprocal fashion. In the subsequent section of this chapter, the impact of employees' self-esteem on their work environments will be discussed. More germane to the present analysis is the impact of the work environment on employees' self-esteem. It is quite possible that practitioners' attempts to structure employees' work environments to be congruent with the employees' self-esteem—presumably to elicit the most positive outcomes—also will reinforce the employees' existing levels of self-esteem. For example, suppose certain low self-esteem employees were rarely given difficult or challenging tasks; presumably, such tasks could be more profitably assigned to the high SEs, who have been shown in much previous research to respond well to challenges. Note the self-fulfilling prophecy in this example; the very fact that low SEs are not (and high SEs are) assigned to work on challenging tasks may serve to perpetuate both groups' levels of self-esteem. In short, there could be subtle costs associated with practitioners' attempts to achieve congruence or fit between employees' self-esteem and their work environments: while congruence may achieve the best short-term results, it could have the consequence of locking individuals into their existing self-esteem level (for better or for worse) over the longer haul.

One way to reduce potentially dysfunctional self-fulfilling prophecies—as in the example in which the assignment of easy goals to low SEs may reinforce their low self-esteem—is to alter the treatment of such individuals over time. More specifically, if low SEs do perform well in response to easy goals (for example, Sigall & Gould 1977), then it may be possible to "wean" them away gradually from easy to more challenging goals, and thereby enhance performance even further. Such a strategy might elicit a positive spiral of achievement and self-esteem in which low SEs' goals are made more challenging over time, as they attain less challenging goals with proficiency. It may be possible to achieve congruence between individuals' self-esteem and their work environments in the short run, without necessarily adversely locking them in to their existing level of self-esteem in the long run.

Until this point the discussion has been about the importance of, and pitfalls associated with, recognizing the self-esteem of the employees who constitute the organization's current workforce. A closely related question is to what extent should organizations concern themselves with identifying the self-esteem level of prospective employees in the selection process? Industrial psychologists and other selection specialists have long been interested in identifying the characteristics of individuals that make them more or less likely to fit—for example, perform well—within various organizations and occupations (see Schneider & Schmitt 1986, for a cogent review of this large literature).

Certainly, it cannot be said that selection specialists in organizations always should take into account the self-esteem level of those whom they hire. Rather, a more qualified prescription will be offered, one that is consistent with the person-situation interactionist viewpoint that has been presented in this book. In order to evaluate whether employees' self-esteem is an important predictor of how well they will perform in a given position, organizations first must generate accurate answers to the following two related questions. What are the central features of the job environment? Given those features, what behavioral and psychological tendencies on the part of individuals are necessary for success? Once these two questions have been answered, it then becomes appropriate to evaluate the extent to which employees' self-esteem is related to "what it takes to succeed." For instance, certain jobs (for example, many sales positions) confront employees with rejection or failure on an ongoing, daily basis. To succeed, the job incumbent must have a thick skin; that is, to remain motivated the individual must not take failure personally but rather have a generalized tendency to attribute failure to external and/or unstable and/or specific factors (Peterson & Seligman 1984). Moreover, recent research has found self-esteem to be related to individuals' attributional style, with high SEs more apt to make external attributions for failure than low SEs (Tennen and Herzberger 1987). Therefore, it stands to reason that in a rejection-laden job, high SEs should outperform low SEs, assuming, of course, that both groups have the necessary levels of ability to succeed. In fact, Seligman and Schulman (1986) reported that the attributional style of life insurance agents predicted their sales performance and turnover; as expected, those who attributed failures to external, unstable, and specific factors sold more insurance and were less likely to quit, compared to those having a more pessimistic (internal, stable, and global) attributional style. Similarly, Reed (1987) found that the self-esteem of union organizers—another group whose task is replete with rejections—also was positively correlated with their success.

Of course, many other jobs do not have as much failure or rejection built into their daily fabric. Therefore, I would expect self-esteem to be a less important predictor of successful task performance under such work conditions. Many studies have shown that self-esteem is positively correlated with subsequent performance to a greater extent if a prior rejection or negative feedback has (rather than has not) occurred (Brockner 1983; Shrauger & Sorman 1977).

More generally, expectancy theory also may provide insight into the conditions under which self-esteem should be a relevant variable to select for in "motivational testing" (Schneider & Schmitt 1986). According to expectancy theory (and as originally discussed in chapter 1), performance is a function of individuals' beliefs about the relationship between their level of effort (E) and performance (P), beliefs about the relationship between performance and outcome (O), and value attached to the outcomes. As Hollenbeck et al. (1987) have pointed out, self-esteem is related to individuals' self-efficacy beliefs (E → P); however, unless individuals believe that P → O, and that they value the outcomes, there is little reason to expect self-esteem to predict actual performance. For any of a variety of reasons—for example, an incentive system which is perceived not to dole out rewards contingently upon performance, or the nature of the task, in which the relationship between persistence and successful task completion is not perceived to be direct (Sandelands, Brockner & Glynn in press)—the work environment may be one in which individuals do not believe that P → O, or that the outcomes are valued. Under such conditions, self-esteem is not likely to predict job performance and, therefore, should be less apt to be considered a relevant personality variable during the process of selecting employees.

In other instances certain job-specific beliefs (which may be related to global self-esteem) could be relevant during selection. For example, individuals' self-assessments of their ability to perform certain jobs could be highly correlated with performance (Schneider & Schmitt 1986) and, therefore, be considered relevant information to gather in the selection process. Of course, the predictive value of such self-assessments are bound to be determined by two factors: their accuracy, and the extent to which the dimension in question actually is performance-relevant. The organization's ability to make the latter judgment will be determined to a great extent by the quality of their analysis of the central features of their job environment.

In summary, individuals' self-esteem may or may not be a relevant variable to consider during the process of selection; its relevance will depend upon the situation. In those job situations in which self-esteem predicts performance, for example, it would seem worthwhile to select employees, at least in part, on the basis of their self-esteem. However, as discussed throughout this book, there are many work situations in which there is no theoretical or empirical basis to expect self-esteem to be predictive of important behaviors and/or attitudes. Under such conditions it makes less sense to select employees on the basis of their self-esteem. The latter caution is introduced to avoid a central problem that has plagued much personality research in selection studies: the theoretically indiscriminate use of personality measures as predictors, which have tended to yield (not surprisingly) discouraging results (Ghiselli 1966; Schneider & Schmitt 1986).

Of course, even if individuals' self-esteem is deemed to be performance or job relevant, selection specialists in organizations still are confronted with the challenging task of identifying job candidates' self-esteem. Schneider and Schmitt (1986) point out that a variety of procedures are available including, but not limited to interviews, references, self-assessments, and projective tests (for example, need for achievement, a trait commonly measured through projective tests, is significantly related to self-esteem); moreover, maximal predictive validity is most likely to occur when multiple sources of information, each moderately correlated with each other, are gathered.

The discussion on the relevance of self-esteem during selection was somewhat narrow; it focused on whether self-esteem is a variable that interacts with the work environment to affect employees' work behaviors and attitudes. The analysis considered the conditions under which self-esteem will (and will not) be predictive of employees' adaptation to their work environment. There is, however, a different set of reasons why job candidates' self-esteem may be a relevant variable in the selection process. More specifically, employees' characteristics (including their self-esteem) influence the very nature of the work environment. Consequently, individuals' self-esteem not only may moderate the impact of the work environment on their behaviors and attitudes, but also it may affect the work environment directly. For either reason, organizations may choose to weight heavily the self-esteem of job applicants in the selection process.

Self-esteem and the Creation of Work Environments

The relationships between employees' self-esteem and their work environments have been discussed in numerous ways throughout this book. Chapter 6, for example, considered the impact of various work-setting factors on individuals' self-esteem. In chapters 2 through 5, in which self-esteem was analyzed as an independent variable, the interactive effects of employees' self-esteem and work context variables on relevant outcome measures, such as motivation, task performance, and satisfaction, were examined. One general theme that emerged from chapters 2 through 5 is that individuals of varying levels of self-esteem react differently to identical work settings.

Note the assumption embedded in the previous sentence: that work environments are entities to which employees respond. This assertion is correct, but an incomplete characterization of the relationship between employees and their work environments. Employees not only respond to their work settings, but also they affect the very nature of the setting. Moreover, just as employees' self-esteem moderates their reactions to work environments, so too is it likely to affect the nature of those environments.

The notion that employees both affect and are affected by their work environments is hardly novel. In a recent presidential address to the Society for Industrial and Organizational Psychology, appropriately entitled "The People Make the Place," Schneider (1985) suggested that:

> It is the people behaving in them that make organizations what they are. My thesis suggests that Kurt Lewin may have overstated the case when he hypothesized that Behavior is a function of Person and Environment, i.e., $B = f(P,E)$. My thesis is that Environments are a function of Persons Behaving in them, i.e., $E = f(P,B)$ (p. 3).

Moreover, Schneider suggests that the processes of attraction, selection, and attrition give rise to organizations having "personalities" that shape employees' behavior, which, in turn, serve to create the work environment. In essence, Schneider argues that all three processes reduce the heterogeneity of the kinds of workers in a given organization. Thus, certain types of workers will be attracted to organizations in the first place, the workers that the organization selects (out of the pool of attracted candidates) are likely to be even more homogeneous than the total pool of attracted candidates, and those who remain are likely to be even more similar to one another than those whom the organization selects. The homogeneity that emerges in the organization's workforce, argues Schneider, gives rise to the creation of a particular type of work environment.

Other organizational scholars also have commented on the reciprocal influences between employees and their work environments. For example, much leadership research has focused on the effects of leaders' behaviors on subordinates' performance (Fiedler 1973). Note that this matter pertains to the reactions of subordinates to an often salient aspect of their work environments: the leaders' behavior. However, it seems reasonable that the reverse causal sequence also is possible: that subordinates' behaviors affect those of the leader (Lowin & Craig 1968) and, in so doing, serve to influence an important element of the subordinates' work environment. Weick's (1977) analysis of enactment processes also is quite relevant to this discussion; he argues that the boundary between actors (that is, employees and organizations) and their environments often is blurry, in that actors' behaviors and/or perceptions often give rise to their environments, to which the actors then respond in an ongoing, reciprocal manner. Similarly, Kohn and Schooler (1983) not only have shown that job conditions affect personality (including self-esteem; see chapter 6), but also that individuals' personality influences their job conditions. Kohn and Schooler suggest that people, "either modify their jobs or move to other jobs more consonant with their personalities. Thus, the long-term effects of personality on job conditions are considerable. The process of job affecting man and man affecting job is truly reciprocal throughout adult life" (p. 152).

Employees' self-esteem may affect their work environments (to which they then respond) in a variety of ways. First, employees' decisions about the kinds of work environments they choose for themselves has an important effect on the environment that they experience. Second, employees' interpersonal behaviors are likely to have an important impact on the kinds of social environments that they enact. Third, in various ways workers' behaviors and attitudes can affect other informal aspects of the organizations, such as norms and values. Fourth, employees' actions may have a marked impact on the formal arrangements that the organization makes to accomplish its tasks. In each instance, employees' self-esteem is one of a number of individual difference factors that affect behaviors that, in turn, influence the work environment (to which employees simultaneously are responsive).

Throughout this discussion the reader should distinguish between the effect of employees' self-esteem on the actual versus perceived work environment. In certain instances, individuals of high versus low self-esteem literally will create different work environments. In other instances, employees' self-esteem will affect their perceptions of their work environments. One factor that distinguishes between the two types of enactment is the extent to which other people are affected by the "created" environment. If other people—besides the employees whose self-esteem is at work—are affected, then it is likely that employees' self-esteem produced real change in their work environment. On the other hand, if other people are not affected, then it is more likely that employees' environmental creations were more perceptual than actual. This is not to say that perceived environmental creation are trivial; indeed, they are potentially quite powerful in the eye of the beholder. Nor is it to say that perceived creations cannot ultimately lead to change in the actual work environments. Some possible ways in which employees' self-esteem can affect their work environments are described here.

Self-esteem and Occupational Choice

Chapter 3 discussed how employees' self-esteem may relate to decisions that ultimately dictate the nature of the work environments in which they find themselves. More specifically, high SEs are more likely to choose occupations for which they perceive themselves to be better suited than their low self-esteem counterparts (Korman 1970). That is, high SEs rated the occupation that they were about to enter as more need fulfilling than low SEs rated it; moreover, high SEs viewed themselves as possessing the abilities needed to succeed in their chosen occupation to a greater extent than their low self-esteem counterparts.

There are several explanations of these findings, two of which are consistent with the more general notion that employees' self-esteem affects their work environments. First, employees' self-esteem may influence their decisions about which careers to enter. Lacking confidence in their own opinions about careers for which they are well suited, low SEs may be especially receptive to external cues (for example, parental pressure, occupational choices of friends). High SEs, in contrast, may be more likely to rely on their own opinions about what is best for them (and for what they are best suited). Second, employees' self-esteem may affect their perceptions of how well suited they are for any chosen career. Low SEs may reason—much like Groucho Marx and Woody Allen who both remarked that they would never want to join a club that accepted them as members—that any career that they have chosen to enter cannot be one for which they are well suited.

In either case, low SEs' perceptions that they are less well suited for their chosen career than high SEs could have marked impacts on their work behaviors and attitudes. Perceived incongruity between self and job could lead to reduced motivation, commitment, and satisfaction.

Self-esteem and Interpersonal Behavior

Employees' self-esteem may not only affect the work environment that they enter, but also the nature of that environment once they have entered into it. It seems reasonably straightforward that individuals' success in organizations often is dependent upon their ability to get along with others. This is not to say that employees must be liked by their coworkers; rather, they must develop relationships that enable them to accomplish their tasks, especially if the nature of the work is highly interdependent. Employees' self-esteem thus may be relevant in that it could affect the nature of the working relationships that they develop with others. In related research, Coyne and his colleagues (for example, Coyne 1976; Strack & Coyne 1982) have shown that individual differences in depression—a dimension that is closely related to self-esteem—are systematically related to the reactions elicited from other people; depressed individuals (low SEs) often generate anxiety and hostility in their interaction partners, hardly the kinds of reactions that promote smooth working relationships.

To make matters worse, low SEs generally perceive that they are less appealing than high SEs in the eyes of their interaction partners, even if the interaction partners' actual judgments show this not to be the case (Brockner & Lloyd 1986). In either case, low SEs' experience of their interpersonal environment in the work setting could interfere dramatically with their ability to accomplish their tasks, especially if the work requires coordination with coworkers. Most of the research exploring the impact of self-esteem on reactions elicited from others has taken place in social (rather than task-related) situations, far removed from the organizational context in which employees have been brought together to work. Thus, future researchers should study the extent to which low SEs elicit more negative reactions from others (and/or think that they do) in actual work settings, as well as the impact of such tendencies on employees' ability to accomplish their tasks.

Self-esteem and the Informal Organization

The preceding discussion suggests that self-esteem may influence the nature of the working relationships that develop between employees. This section considers how employees' self-esteem may influence other aspects of the informal organization, such as norms and values. For example, imagine that an organization has decided to undergo a major transformation, from a tightly controlled, top-down, to a more participatory form of management (for example, see Boyle's 1984, discussion of the sweeping organizational change at Honeywell). During such periods of major reorganization, the architects of the change typically have general notions about the outcome(s) that they would like to achieve. The specific goals are not, indeed often cannot, be etched in stone. Thus, the degree and type of participatory management that emerges subsequent to the reorganization is apt to be partially determined by employees' input into the change process; one such input is the behavior stemming from the employees' self-esteem.

More specifically, it is possible that high self-esteem employees are more likely than low SEs to take advantage of the opportunities offered by a more participatory management style. Trusting themselves, high SEs should be able to initiate the behaviors associated with greater worker participation; low SEs, in sharp contrast, may be in greater need of managerial cues for appropriate behavior, a response style that seems antithetical to that needed for greater participation.

If this logic is correct, then high self-esteem employees should respond more adaptively than low SEs to a participative work setting. Recently, Brockner and Hess (1986) explored the relationships of employees' self-esteem to their performance in quality circles (QCs). QCs are a participative management procedure in which members of a work group meet on a voluntary, regular basis on company time; their purpose is to analyze, and diagnose, and offer solutions to problems in the workplace. The solutions are then presented to upper level management, who may or may not implement them.

QCs have become widespread in American industry since the mid 1970s (Lawler & Mohrman 1985). However, to date there has been relatively little research on the factors associated with QC effectiveness. One such predictor variable, we hypothesized, was group members' self-esteem. QCs consisting of high SEs should be better able to take advantage of the autonomy offered by QCs than low SEs. Brockner and Hess (1986) observed that the mean level of group members' self-esteem was far greater in the productive than unproductive QCs (see also Griffin and Wayne 1984).

Of course, low SEs should not be discouraged from participating in QCs; to advocate that certain individuals should or should not take part in QCs is contrary to the very philosophy underlying QCs, in which participation is supposed to be voluntary. Any implicit message that the organization conveys to low SEs suggesting that they are better off not volunteering to partake in QCs could reinforce their existing level of self-esteem, a point mentioned previously in the discussion of dysfunctional self-fulfilling prophecies. What is being suggested is that the productivity of QCs is bound to vary, depending on a host of individual factors (such as self-esteem) as well as group and organizational variables. The fact that group members' self-esteem predicted QC success is theoretically noteworthy; such results ultimately may contribute to a contingency model of QC effectiveness. Such results may have practical implications, although one of the applied ramifications is not that low SEs should be discouraged from participating in QCs. Rather, it may be that QCs consisting primarily of low SEs will require extra management of individual and/or group dynamics, relative to groups comprised mainly of high SEs. For example, it may be especially important for the former group to receive clear positive feedback about any merits of its initial work to raise their expectations that they can make suggestions for workplace-related change to which management will respond favorably.

In any event, the finding that QC success was correlated with group members' self-esteem can be related to the bigger picture here: the impact of employees' self-esteem on the work environment. If employees' self-esteem affects their performance in QCs, then the continued presence of the QC program might well depend on employees' self-esteem. The presence or absence of the QC program, in turn, may affect the extent to which the architects of the reorganization are able to create a more participative work environment.

This discussion has focused specifically on the relationship between employees' self-esteem and their behavioral autonomy, and how such autonomy may affect the efficacy of a more participative management style. More generally, the point is that employees' self-esteem may affect the very behaviors that contribute mightily to the informal nature of the work environment, which, in turn, affect those employees as well as others. To cite yet another example, certain individuals who are in particularly influential positions in organizations may bring a high self-esteem, "winning" presence to the organization that somehow brings out the best in oneself and fellow employees. The Boston Celtics basketball team are such an example; Red Auerbach—formerly the coach and now the team president—reputedly has managed somehow to instill a sense of "Celtic pride" throughout the organization (Webber 1987). The likely effect of Auerbach on the culture, and therefore other employees, within the Celtics's organization is immeasurable. Indeed, many players have performed much better than they did previously in their careers, once having donned the Celtic uniform. Clearly, there are many explanations of this outcome, one of which is consistent with the present theme: that certain individuals' personalities may affect the intangible nature of the work environment, which in turn can influence the subsequent actions and attitudes of those certain individuals as well as others.

The previous discussions of feedback-seeking behavior (see chapter 4 and 7) and goal setting (see chapter 3) suggest additional ways in which workers' self-esteem may affect the informal aspect of the work environment. Ashford and Cummings (1983) hypothesized that employees not only respond to feedback reactively, but also seek feedback proactively. In particular, they may monitor their environment for cues relevant to successful task performance and/or inquire directly to sources believed to possess the needed information. It seems likely that the amount and type of feedback seeking can have a marked impact on subsequent norms concerning feedback seeking. For example, the more individuals seek feedback through inquiry, the more likely they are to develop the norm that "this is the kind of organization in which people are not afraid to ask one another for feedback." Suppose that employees' feedback-seeking behaviors were determined (at least in part) by their level of self-esteem. As suggested in chapter 4 and demonstrated in a field study by Ashford (1986), high SEs may have less to fear from the receipt of, and therefore be more likely to seek, feedback relative to low SEs. Employees' self-esteem may affect their feedback-seeking behaviors, which, in turn, may have a profound impact on a variety of norms concerning the seeking and sharing of information (DeWhirst 1971).

Studies exploring the role of self-esteem in the goal-setting process mainly have dealt with the moderating impact of self-esteem in the relationship between goals and performance. Yet another role that self-esteem may play—and one more central to the discussion of the effect of employees' self-esteem on the work environment—is its relationship to individuals' goal-setting tendencies. In many practical applications of the goal and performance relationship, workers have some input into the goal-setting process (for example, management by objectives). It seems likely that high SEs' greater self-efficacy or self-confidence will lead them to set more difficult goals than their low self-esteem counterparts; such results have been obtained (Hollenbeck & Brief 1987). It also seems likely that individuals' goal-setting behaviors are determinants, or at least reflective, of various informal aspects of the work environment. For example, the tendency to set difficult goals may establish the legitimacy of a can-do attitude, in which workers expect (or are expected) to give it their all. In their attempts to meet such difficult goals, workers may become more likely to put in extra hours (for example, work overtime, nights, and weekends), or work more cooperatively, all of which may go a long way toward shaping informal aspects of the work environment.

Self-esteem and the Formal Organization

Employees' self-esteem also may affect the formal aspects of the work environment. Reexamine the example in which the organization is trying to adopt a more participatory management style. As any organizational practitioner and scholar knows, leverage points for organizational change exist at both the informal and formal levels. Thus, in trying to bring about greater employee participation, management undoubtedly will consider the formal mechanisms at their disposal. The degree and nature of the emerging formal arrangements may well be—indeed, perhaps even should be—affected by employees' self-esteem. Imagine that the workforce consisted primarily of high SEs, who generally act more autonomously than low SEs. If so, then it may be less necessary to make sweeping changes in the formal organization to achieve greater worker participation. For example, it may not even be necessary to adopt a formal QC program, if one suspects that the employees' high self-esteem makes them just as likely to perform the work that takes place in QCs. Of course, the organization still may wish to institutionalize QCs because of the symbolic meaning associated with such a gesture. Perhaps. Nevertheless, that is quite independent of the possibility that the creation of a QC program may be unnecessary to elicit the participatory input of high SEs; they might have acted that way anyway.

Other sections of this book provide examples of how employees' self-esteem might affect formal organizational arrangements. In chapter 4 it was noted that layoffs affect the work behavior of survivors, and differentially so as a function of the survivors' self-esteem. That line of research also suggested that the formal layoff decision rule interacted with workers' self-esteem to moderate the impact of layoffs on survivors (Brockner et al. 1986). If so, then managers may wish to ensure that the formal decision rule is congruent with the majority of the survivors' self-esteem; by *congruent,* I mean that the decision rule should be one that is likely to elicit from survivors the most positive (or least negative) reactions to the layoffs.

Chapter 4 also showed that employees' self-esteem moderates their reactions to various role stressors; low SEs appear to be much more adversely affected by such stress than their high self-esteem counterparts (Mossholder, Bedeian & Armenakis 1981). Knowledge of employees' self-esteem, therefore, may affect the extent to which their formal job duties are allowed to have role strains. The higher the employees' self-esteem, the less necessary it may be for management to ensure that the formal job duties are free of role strain.

Some Concluding Comments

The notion that employees' self-esteem affects their actual (or perceived) work environments calls attention to the reciprocal nature of the relationships between the work environment and individuals' self-esteem and work behaviors. Employees' self-esteem leads them to act in ways that affect their work environments. Moreover, employees are affected by their work environments, the very setting which they partially helped to create. Finally, employees' self-esteem often moderates their reactions to their enacted work environment.

This analysis also sheds light on the self-perpetuating nature of self-esteem. Personality, social, clinical psychologists (Brockner 1983; Lecky 1945; Swann 1983) have noted that individuals' self-esteem, once developed, is very resistant to change. One basis of this resistance to change stems from the differential environments that low and high SEs enact. Several of the relationships between employees' self-esteem and their work environments discussed already demonstrate that high SEs create environments that perpetuate high self-esteem, whereas low SEs create environments that perpetuate low self-esteem. For example, the fact that high SEs choose careers for which they are well suited, whereas low SEs are less apt to, probably will produce positive career outcomes for the former group and negative ones for the latter. Such outcomes ultimately reinforce individuals' existing self-esteem levels.

Similarly, the likely effect of low SEs' tendency to elicit (and/or perceive that they have elicited) negative interpersonal reactions is continued low self-esteem; high SEs, in generally perceiving that they are attractive in the eyes of others, are bound to experience continued high self-esteem. In addition, the process of taking advantage of the increased autonomy offered by a more participative work environment should solidify high SEs' positive self-appraisals. Low SEs, who were suspected to be less likely to take advantage of increased opportunities for participation, may come face-to-face with their sense of personal inadequacy by failing to avail themselves of such opportunities.

Swann (1983) has generated an impressive array of theory and research on self-verification processes in social interaction. His basic thesis is that once individuals have developed certain self-conceptions (such as their level of self-esteem), they tend to think and act in ways that validate such self-conceptions in their social interactions. I agree wholeheartedly with Swann; in this section I have attempted to demonstrate some of the ways in employees' creations of their work environments enables them to verify their self-esteem.

Several other brief closing comments are noted here. First, the impact of employees' self-esteem on the environment is not necessarily a conscious process; no claim is being made, for instance, that low self-esteem workers deliberately and intentionally engage in self-verification. Second, it is worth emphasizing again that employees' self-esteem may affect the nature of their work environments in ways that ultimately affect other people as well as themselves; the example on self-esteem and the creation of a more participatory work environment should make this point clearly. Finally, much of this section is highly speculative, and thus awaits the validation of future empirical research. Organizational scholars (Weick 1977) are well aware that individuals create their work environments; moreover, much research (outside of the organizational context) has demonstrated that individuals' self-esteem determines the nature of their external environments (for example, Swann 1983). To date, however, there has been little empirical research that directly explores the effect of employees' self-esteem on the nature of their actual and perceived work environments.

Multiple Levels of Self-hood in Organizations

An underlying assumption throughout this book is that human behavior in work organizations can be understood at the individual level of analysis. Thus, the object (subject) of individuals' evaluation has been the *me* (*I*) of their self-concepts. And yet, organizational scholars are quick to point out that human behavior in organizations also lends itself to analysis at the group and organizational (that is, more collective) levels. As such, it may prove fruitful to study the possible essence, antecedents, and consequences of collective self-esteem within work organizations.

Note that the study of collective self-esteem can take at least two forms. In the first, the subject of the unit of analysis still is the individual, although the object of evaluation is the *us* rather than the *me* of the individual's self-concept. As Breckler and Greenwald (1986) have suggested, individuals engage in a variety of "ego tasks" in which the primary goal is to elicit favorable reactions from different audiences. (This statement is very similar to the central assertion of chapter 7 that individuals are motivated to restore, maintain, and enhance their self-esteem.) Although much research in personality and social psychology has focused on the ego tasks of the private and public selves—to gain approval in one's own eyes as well as the eyes of others—very little has explored the ego task of the "collective self," that is, achieving the goals and, therefore, experiencing the positive evaluation, of one's reference groups.

The motivating potential of the collective self represents a possibly important, and heretofore unexplored, extension of the thesis that individuals generally strive to feel good about themselves. Breckler and Greenwald (1986) suggest that one way in which individuals may do so is by achieving the goals of their internalized reference groups. Thus, in work organizations in which individuals' collective selves often are salient, it just may be that an important determinant of individuals' satisfaction of their need for self-esteem is the extent to which they have achieved the goals of their reference group(s).

A second orientation to studying collective self-esteem would make the collective both the subject and the object of evaluation. This approach rests on the possibility that collectives, just like individuals, have traits. Thus, it could be that certain groups have a greater sense of collective self-esteem than others. If so, it may be possible to study both the antecedents and consequences of collective self-esteem, just as it is possible to do so for individuals.

To speculate further, what might be the antecedents of employees' collective sense of self-esteem? Certainly, it is likely to be influenced in part by the average self-esteem level of each individual within the collective. Schneider's (1985) attraction-selection-attrition model depicts some of the processes through which individuals' personalities affect (or create) the collective personality. As Schneider puts it, "different kinds of organizations attract, select, and retain different kinds of individuals and that's why organizations look and feel different from each other" (p. 8). Thus, for example, it is possible that a collective will exhibit high self-esteem in part because the processes of attraction, selection, and retention restrict the range of the self-esteem level of the individuals in the collective.

However, the self-esteem level of individual members is not the only determinant of a group's collective self-esteem. In the model of group behavior proposed by McGrath (1964), and subsequently expanded upon by Hackman and Morris (1975) and others, a variety of inputs affect group process, which in turn affects group outputs (see figure 8–3). Collective self-esteem is one relevant output, and individuals' self-esteem is one of the relevant input factors. However, a host of additional input variables could affect the extent to which the collective evaluates itself positively or negatively.

The notion of collective self-esteem is closely related to, but not identical with, several previously researched topics at the group level of analysis. For example, group cohesiveness is typically defined as the extent to which members value their membership, and thus want to remain, in the group. In general, cohesiveness should be positively correlated with group self-esteem. However, it is possible for group members to value their membership and want to remain in the group, without necessarily feeling that "we like ourselves." If the group serves important utilitarian functions, then group members may work together cohesively in quest of is mission; however, the sense

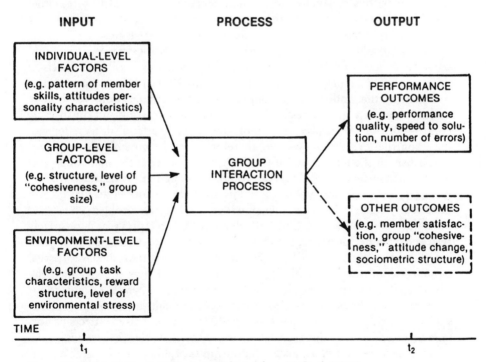

Source: Hackman & Morris 1975, p. 50. Adapted from McGrath (1964).

Figure 8–3. Model of Group Behavior

of group self-esteem may be lacking, or even if present, epiphenomenal. In short, cohesiveness refers to a belief ("I think it is important to be a member of this group") and a behavioral predisposition ("I wish to remain in this group"). Group self-esteem refers to an evaluation toward the entity ("We like ourselves").

Since the late 1970s there has been great interest in the impact of organizational and group "culture" on effectiveness (for example, Peters and Waterman 1982). Collective self-esteem refers to a specific aspect of culture: the extent to which the collective deems it normative to evaluate itself positively or negatively. Clearly, culture is a much more multifaceted subject than collective self-esteem.

Future research on collective self-esteem could explore many of the issues that have already been discussed at the individual level of analysis. In particular, we need to learn whether collective self-esteem—both at the group and organizational levels—affects employees' work behaviors and attitudes. Throughout this book individuals' self-esteem has been regarded as a significant predictor of work behaviors and attitudes, in interaction with contextual factors. It is thus reasonable to evaluate whether situational factors, either residing in the workforce or the external environment, also moderate the impact of collective self-esteem on relevant outcome measures.

It also would be important to discover whether self-esteem relates to outcome variables in parallel fashions at the individual and collective levels of analysis. For example, Staw, Sandelands, and Dutton (1981) have argued persuasively that individuals, groups, and entire organizations respond to threat in similar ways: by restricting information processing and constricting control. Of course, the precise form of such "rigidity effects" differs, depending upon the level of analysis. It, therefore, may be possible to search for parallelism in the impact of self-esteem. For instance, at the individual level of analysis low SEs seem to be more willing than high SEs to search for information prior to decision making, perhaps owing to the former group's greater uncertainty that they have the wherewithal for effective problem solving. If the nature of the task is such that the degree of information search positively relates to task performance, then low SEs should outperform high SEs, holding all other factors equal (Weiss & Knight 1980). At the collective (that is, organizational) level of analysis, Fredrickson (1984) has shown that decisional comprehensiveness—defined as "the extent to which organizations attempt to be exhaustive or inclusive in making and integrating strategic decisions" (Fredrickson & Mitchell 1984, p. 402)—also positively affects performance, provided that the external environment is stable. (Interestingly, the comprehensiveness-performance relationship is negative in an unstable environment.)

An important extension of the research on collective decision making is to determine the antecedents of comprehensiveness. It just may be that the collective's self-esteem is inversely related to comprehensiveness, just as Weiss and Knight (1980) discovered at the individual level of analysis. If so, then organizations having low collective self-esteem may perform better in stable, and worse in unstable, environments relative to organizations that are high in collective self-esteem.

Future research on collective self-esteem in work organizations may proceed profitably in a number of directions. To foreshadow a taxonomy of such efforts, I would speculate that certain efforts (for example, Breckler & Greenwald 1986) would employ the individual as the subject and the collective as the object of evaluation. For example, Greenwald, Breckler, and Wiggins (1987) recently have developed several measures of the collective self. One requires individuals to express the importance of their collective identities (for example, "being a cooperative participant in group activities," "being active in many groups"); another is more closely related to collective self-esteem, in which individuals rate how competently they have been able to enact their collective identities (for example, to what extent they are a "cooperative participant in group activities" and "active in socially important causes"). Indeed, Greenwald, Breckler, and Wiggins label the latter scale, "collective self-esteem," although it seems more like a measure of perceived competence or efficacy, rather than an evaluative rating of one's collectively based self-concept. A more evaluatively laden measure could require individuals to think about those aspects of themselves that are part of a collective (for example, member of organization X, work group Y, and the like), and then to indicate the extent to which they like or dislike the collective, keeping in mind their membership in the collective.

Other research on collective self-esteem might study the collective as both the subject and object of evaluation. Moreover, as in Breckler and Greenwald's (1986) orientation, and consistent with the more general theme of chapter 7, some may study collective self-esteem as a motivational process; others may regard collective self-esteem as a trait, focusing on both its antecedents (in a fashion parallel to chapter 6) and consequences (as in chapters 2 through 5)

Summary

This chapter was designed to build bridges between past theory and research on self-esteem at work and potential future efforts. The first section underscored some of the theoretical and practical issues which were raised initially in chapters 1 through 7. Each chapter offered several callings for further inquiry; some of the more important ones were repeated. Second, there was a discussion of some of the assumptions that investigators have made about the conceptual nature of self-esteem, all of which have interfered with our ability to assess self-esteem with maximal validity. The failings of the assumptions are noted; in addition, mention is made of how future researchers may revise these assumptions and thereby possibly increase the predictive ability of their self-esteem measures.

The third section of this chapter focused on the kind of information that managers may take into account in order to recognize their employees' level of self-esteem. The body of theory and research on the antecedents of self-esteem (see chapter 6) delineates some of the data that may be predictive of individuals' self-esteem (for example, family experience, past and current work conditions). Moreover, the research on the consequences of self-esteem (see chapters 2 through 5) suggests that more needs to be known than individuals' scores on the outcome or criterion variables to predict their self-esteem. In particular, one must observe individuals' behavior (for example, task performance) as well as the situation in which it occurs to make inferences about their self-esteem. This prescription stems from an oft-stated theme of this book: that employees' self-esteem influences their work behaviors and attitudes in conjunction with contextual factors.

The fourth part of this chapter considered a related theme of person-situation interactionism: that employees' self-esteem influences their work environment, and vice versa. Employees' self-esteem could influence their perceptions of, and hence their reactions to, the work environment. Moreover, their self-esteem may channel them into certain behaviors, which, in turn, could have a sharp influence on both formal and informal aspects of the work environment. Finally, this chapter raised the notion of collective self-esteem. Just as individuals have self-esteem, so, too, might groups and even entire organizations. Future research should analyze the essence of collective self-esteem, its antecedents, and its consequences. One particularly intriguing question is whether collective self-esteem — if it even exists — exerts impact on the collectives' work behaviors and attitudes in ways similar to the influence of individuals' self-esteem on their behaviors and attitudes.

Closing Comments

This book has explored the variety of ways in which employees' self-esteem plays an important role in organizations. The word *variety* should not go unnoticed. We have seen that self-esteem is a personality trait that, in conjunction with contextual factors, predicts employees' behaviors and attitudes. Self-esteem also has been conceptualized as a global trait and transitory state that both affects workers' reactions and is affected by their work environments. Moreover, self-esteem refers to a motivational process; employees often go to considerable pains to gain, preserve, and restore their self-esteem in their own and others' eyes. Organizational scholars and practitioners have made some empirical, theoretical, and practical headways in the study of self-esteem, but much more needs to be learned.

In discussing personality research in organizations, Weiss and Adler (1984) noted that many empirical efforts, while statistically disappointing, were not necessarily diagnostic of the true potential of personality in elucidating individuals' behavior in organizations. I heartily agree; this sentiment applies not only to studies of the antecedents and consequences of self-esteem, but also to research on self-esteem maintenance as a motivational process. In the truest sense, then, those who study self-esteem at work may find that the best is yet to come. I hope that this book stimulates scholars and practitioners at least one step forward in such productive directions.

References

Abramson, L.Y., Seligman, M.E.P., and Teasdale, J 1978. Learned helplessness in humans: Critique and reformulation. *Journal of Abnormal Psychology* 87:49–74.

Adams, J.S. 1965. Inequity in social exchange. In *Advances in experimental social psychology,* ed. L. Berkowitz, vol. 2, pp. 267–299. New York: Academic Press.

Adams, J.S., and Rosenbaum, W.B. 1962. The relationship of worker productivity to cognitive dissonance about wage inequities. *Journal of Applied Psychology* 46:161–164.

Adler, A. 1927. *Practice and theory of individual psychology.* New York: Harcourt, Brace, and World.

Adler, S. 1980. Self-esteem and causal attributions for job satisfaction. *Journal of Applied Psychology,* 65:327–332.

Aronson, E. 1968. Dissonance theory: Progress and problems. In *Theories of cognitive consistency: A sourcebook,* eds. R.P. Abelson et al., pp. 5–27. Chicago: Rand-McNally.

———. 1984. *The social animal.* San Francisco: W.H. Freeman.

Aronson, E., and Mettee, D.R. 1968. Dishonest behavior as a function of differential levels of induced self-esteem. *Journal of Personality and Social Psychology,* 9:121–127.

Asher, S., and Allen, V. 1969. Racial preference and social comparison processes. *Journal of Social Issues,* 25:157–166.

Ashford, S.J. 1986. Feedback-seeking in individual adaption: A resource perspective. *Academy of Management Journal,* 29:465–487.

Ashford, S.J., and Cummings, L.L. 1983. Feedback as an individual resource: Personal strategies of creating information. *Organizational Behavior and Human Performance,* 32:370–398.

Bachman, J.G. 1970. *Youth in transition,* Vol. 2. Ann Arbor, Mich.: Institute of Social Research.

Bachman, J.G., and O'Malley, P.M. 1977. Self-esteem in young men: A longitudinal analysis of the impact of educational and occupational attainment. *Journal of Personality and Social Psychology,* 35:365–380.

Bagozzi, R.P., and Burnkrant, R.E. 1979. Attitude organization and the attitude-behavior relationship. *Journal of Personality and Social Psychology,* 37:913–929.

Bandura, A. 1971. *Psychological modeling.* Chicago: Aldine-Atherton.

————. 1977. *Social learning theory.* Englewood Cliffs, N.J.: Prentice-Hall.

Barton, E. 1986. *Layoffs and effective management.* Paper presented at the Academy of Management Conference, Chicago.

Baumeister, R.F. 1982. A self-presentational view of social phenomena. *Psychological Bulletin,* 81:3–26.

Bazerman, M.H. 1986. *Judgement in managerial decision making.* New York: John Wiley and Sons.

Bazerman, M.H., Beekun, R.I., and Schoorman, F.D. 1982. Performance evaluation in a dynamic context: A laboratory study of the impact of a prior commitment to the ratee. *Journal of Applied Psychology,* 67:873–876.

Bazerman, M.H., Schoorman, F.D., and Goodman, P.S. 1980. A cognitive evaluation of escalation processes in managerial decision making. Unpublished manuscript, Boston University.

Beehr, T.A. 1976. Perceived situational moderators of the relationship between subjective role ambiguity and role strain. *Journal of Applied Psychology,* 61:35–40.

Beer, M. 1986. Performance appraisal. In *Handbook of organizational behavior,* ed. J.W. Lorsch, pp. 286–300. Englewood Cliffs, N.J.: Prentice-Hall.

Bem, D.J. 1972. Self-perception theory. In *Advances in experimental social psychology,* ed. L. Berkowitz, Vol. 6, pp. 2–62. New York: Academic Press.

Berglas, S., and Jones, E.E. 1978. Drug choice as a self-handicapping strategy in response to noncontingent success. *Journal of Personality and Social Psychology,* 36:405–417.

Berkowitz, L., and Lundy, R. 1957. Personality characteristics related to susceptibility to influence by peers or authority figures. *Journal of Personality,* 25:306–316.

Berlew, D.E., and Hall, D.T. 1966. The socialization of managers: Effects of expectations on performance. *Administrative Science Quarterly* 2:207–223.

Bhagat, R.S. 1982. Conditions under which stronger job performance–job satisfaction relationships may be observed: A closer look at two situational contingencies. *Academy of Management Journal,* 25:772–789.

Blake, R.R., and Mouton, J.S. 1979. Intergroup problem solving in organizations: From theory to practice. In *The social psychology of intergroup relations,* eds. W.G. Austin and S. Worchel pp. 19–32. Monterey, Ca.: Brooks/Cole.

Blonder, M.D. 1976. *Organizational repercussions of personnel cutbacks: Effects of layoffs on retained employees.* Ph.D. diss., CUNY.

Boyle, R.J. 1984. Wrestling with jellyfish. *Harvard Business Review,* 62:74–83.

Breckler, S.J., and Greenwald, A.G. 1986. *Motivational facets of the self.* In *Handbook of motivation and cognition,* eds. R.M. Sorrentino and E.T. Higgins, pp. 145–164. New York: Guilford Press.

Brehm, J.W. 1966. *A theory of psychological reactance.* New York: Academic Press.

Brehm, S.S., and Brehm, J.W. 1981. *Psychological reactance: A theory of freedom and control.* New York: Academic Press.

Brief, A.P., and Aldag, R.J. 1981. The self in work organizations: A conceptual review. *Academy of Management Review,* 6:75–88.

Brief, A.P., Burke, M.J., Atieh, J.M., Robinson, B.S., and Webster, J. (in press). Should negative affectivity remain an unmeasured variable in the study of job stress? *Journal of Applied Psychology.*

Brockner J. 1979a. Self-esteem, self-consciousness, and task performance: Replications, extensions, and possible explanations. *Journal of Personality and Social Psychology,* 37:447–461.

———. 1979b. The effects of self-esteem, success-failure, and self-consciousness on task performance. *Journal of Personality and Social Psychology,* 37:1732–1741.

———. 1983. Low self-esteem and behavioral plasticity: Some implications. In *Review of personality and social psychology,* eds. L. Wheeler and P.R. Shaver, Vol. 4, pp. 237–271. Beverly Hills, Ca.: Sage Publications.

———. 1985. The relation of self-esteem and positive inequity to productivity. *Journal of Personality,* 53:517–529.

———. 1986. [Goal setting, self-esteem, and performance.] Unpublished data, Columbia University.

———. 1988. The effects of work layoffs on survivors: Research, theory, and practice. In *Research in organizational behavior,* eds. B.M. Staw and L.L. Cummings, Vol. 10, pp. 213–255. Greenwich, Ct.: JAI Press.

Brockner, J., Davy, J., and Carter, C. 1985. Layoffs, self-esteem, and survivor guilt: Motivational, affective, and attitudinal consequences. *Organizational Behavior and Human Decision Processes,* 36:229–244.

Brockner J., Derr, W.R., and Laing, W.N. 1987. Self-esteem and reactions to negative feedback: Towards greater generalizability. *Journal of Research in Personality,* 21:318–333.

Brockner J., and Elkind, M. 1985. Self-esteem and reactance: Further evidence of attitudinal and motivational consequences. *Journal of Experimental Social Psychology,* 21:346–361.

Brockner J., Gardner, A.M., Bierman, J., Mahan, T., Thomas, B., Weiss, W., Winters, L., and Mitchell, A. 1983. The role of self-esteem and self-consciousness in the Wortman-Brehm model of reactance and learned helplessness. *Journal of Personality and Social Psychology,* 45:199–209.

Brockner J., Greenberg, J., Brockner, A., Bortz, J., Davy, J., and Carter, C. 1986. Layoffs, equity theory, and work performance: Further evidence on the impact of survivor guilt. *Academy of Management Journal,* 29:373–384.

Brockner J., Grover, S., and Blonder, M. (in press). Predictors of survivors' job commitment following layoffs: A field study. *Journal of Applied Psychology.*

Brockner J., and Guare, J. 1983. Improving the performance of low self-esteem individuals: An attributional approach. *Academy of Management Journal,* 26:642–656.

Brockner J., and Hess, T. 1986. Self-esteem and task performance in quality circles. *Academy of Management Journal,* 29:617–622.

Brockner J., Hjelle, L, and Plant, R. 1985. Self-focused attention, self-esteem, and the experience of state depression. *Journal of Personality,* 53:425–434.

Brockner J., and Hulton, A.J.B. 1978. How to reverse the vicious cycle of low self-esteem: The importance of attentional focus. *Journal of Experimental Social Psychology,* 14:564–578.

Brockner J., and Kim, D. 1987. *The effects of turnover on those who stay: A social comparison analysis.* Manuscript under editorial review.

Brockner J., and Lloyd, K. 1986. Self-esteem and likeability: Separating fact from fantasy. *Journal of Research in Personality,* 20:496–508.

Brockner J., O'Malley, M.N., Hite, T., and Davies, D. 1987. Reward allocation and self-esteem: The role of modeling and equity restoration. *Journal of Personality and Social Psychology,* 52:844–850.

Brockner J., O'Malley, M.N., Grover, S., Esaki, N., Glynn, M.A., and Lazarides, S. 1987. *The effects of layoffs, job insecurity, and self-esteem on survivors' work performance and attitudes.* Manuscript under editorial review.

Brockner J., and Rubin, J.Z. 1985. *Entrapment in escalating conflicts: A social psychological analysis.* New York: Springer-Verlag.

Brockner J., Rubin, J.Z., and Lang, E. 1981. Face-saving and entrapment. *Journal of Experimental Social Psychology,* 17:68–79.

Brockner, J., and Wallnau, L.B. 1981. Self-esteem, anxiety, and the avoidance of self-focused attention. *Journal of Research in Personality,* 15:277–291.

Broll, L., Gross, A., and Piliavin, I. 1974. Effects of offered and requested help on help seeking and reactions to being helped. *Journal of Applied Social Psychology,* 4:255–258.

Brown, B.R. 1968. The effects of need to maintain face on interpersonal bargaining. *Journal of Experimental Social Psychology,* 4:107–122.

Byrne, D. 1961. The Repression-Sensitization Scale: Rationale, reliability, and validity. *Journal of Personality,* 29:344–349.

———. 1971. *The attraction paradigm.* New York: Academic Press.

Campbell, J.D., and Fairey, P.J. 1985. Effects of self-esteem, hypothetical explanations, and verbalization of expectancies on future performance. *Journal of Personality and Social Psychology,* 48:1097–1111.

Carroll, S.J., and Tosi, H.L. 1970. Goal characteristics and personality factors in a management-by-objectives program. *Administrative Science Quarterly,* 15:295–305.

Carver, C.S., and Scheier, M.F. 1978. Self-focusing effects of dispositional self-consciousness, mirror presence, and audience presence. *Journal of Personality and Social Psychology,* 36:324–332.

———. 1981. *Attention and self-regulation: A control theory approach to human behavior.* New York: Springer-Verlag.

Cialdini, R.B., Borden, R.J., Thorne, A., Walker, M.R., Freeman, S., and Sloan, L.R. 1976. Basking in reflected glory: Three (football) field studies. *Journal of Personality and Social Psychology,* 34:366–375.

Cialdini, R.B., and Richardson, K.D. 1980. Two indirect tactics of impression management: Basking and blasting. *Journal of Personality and Social Psychology,* 39:406–415.

Clance, P.R., and Imes, S.A. 1978. The impostor phenomenon in high achieving women: Dynamics and therapeutic intervention. *Psychotherapy: Theory, Research, and Practice,* 15, (3).

Cobb, S., and Kasl, S. 1977. *Termination: The consequences of job loss.* U.S. Department of Health, Education, and Welfare, HEW Pub. No. (NIOSH) 77–224.

Coleman, J.S., Campbell, E.Q., Hobson, C.J., McPartland, J., Mood, A.M., Weinfield, F.D., and York, R.L. 1966. *Equality of educational opportunity.* Office of Education, U.S. Department of Health, Education, and Welfare. Washington, D.C.: U.S. Government Printing Office.

Conlon, E.J., and Parks, J.M. 1987. Information requests in the context of escalation. *Journal of Applied Psychology,* 72:344–350.

Cook, T.D., and Campbell, D.T. 1979. *Quasi-experimentation: Design and analysis issues for field settings.* Boston: Houghton Mifflin.

Cooley, C.H. 1902. *Human nature and the social order*. New York: Charles Scribner.

Coopersmith, S. 1967. *The antecedents of self-esteem*. San Francisco: W.H. Freeman.

Cosier, R.A. 1978. The effects of three potential aids for making strategic decisions on prediction accuracy. *Organizational Behavior and Human Performance*, 22:295–306.

Cosier, R.A., and Alpin, J.C. 1980. A critical view of dialectical inquiring as a tool in strategic planning. *Strategic Management Journal*, 1:343–356.

Coyne, J.C. 1976. Depression and the response of others. *Journal of Abnormal Psychology*, 85:186–193.

Crocker, J., Thompson, L.L., McGraw, K.M., and Ingerman, C. 1987. Downward comparison, prejudice, and evaluations of others: Effects of self-esteem and threat. *Journal of Personality and Social Psychology*, 52:907–916.

Crosby, F. 1982. *Relative deprivation and working women*. New York: Oxford University Press.

Crowne, D., and Marlowe, D. 1964. *The approval motive*. New York: Wiley.

Davis, T.R.V., and Luthans, F. 1980. A social learning approach to organizational behavior. *Academy of Management Review*, 5:281–290.

DePaulo, B., Brown, P., Ishii, S., and Fisher, J. 1981. Help that works: The effects of aid on subsequent task performance. *Journal of Personality and Social Psychology*, 41:478–487.

DeWhirst, H.D. 1971. Influence of perceived information sharing norms on communication channel utilization. *Academy of Management Journal*, 14:305–315.

Diener, C., and Dweck, C. 1980. An analysis of learned helplessness: II: The processing of success. *Journal of Personality and Social Psychology*, 39:940–952.

Dipboye, R.L. 1977a. A critical review of Korman's self-consistency theory of work motivation and occupation choice. *Organizational Behavior and Human Performance*, 18:108–126.

———. 1977b. On eliminating the alternative interpretations: A reply to Korman. *Organizational Behavior and Human Performance*, 18:129–130.

———. 1987. Self-serving reactions to feedback: A review of the literature. Manuscript under editorial review.

Dipboye, R.L., Phillips, A., and Shahani, C. 1985. *Self-serving reactions to performance feedback: An image-management approach*. Paper presented at the Academy of Management Conference, San Diego.

Dipboye, R.L., Zultowski, W.H., Dewhirst, H.D., and Arvey, R.D. 1979. Self-esteem as a moderator of performance-satisfaction relationships. *Journal of Vocational Behavior*, 15:193–206.

Duncan, O.D. 1961. A socioeconomic index for all occupations. In *Occupations and social status*, ed. A.J. Reiss, pp. 109–161. New York: Free Press.

Dweck, C.S. 1975. The role of expectations and attributions in the alleviation of learned helplessness. *Journal of Personality and Social Psychology*, 31:674–685.

Dyck, D., Vallentyne, S., and Breen, L. 1979. Duration of failure, causal attributions for failure, and subsequent reactions. *Journal of Experimental Social Psychology*, 15:122–132.

Eagly, A.H. 1967. Involvement as a determinant of response to favorable and unfavorable information. *Journal of Personality and Social Psychology*, 7:3, Whole No. 643).

Eisenberg, P., and Lazarsfeld, P.F. 1938. The psychological effects of unemployment. *Psychological Bulletin,* 35:358–390.

Ellis, R.A., and Taylor, M.S. 1983. Role of self-esteem within the job search process. *Journal of Applied Psychology,* 68:632–640.

Epstein, S. 1979. The stability of behavior: I. On predicting most of the people much of the time. *Journal of Personality and Social Psychology,* 37:1097–1127.

Erez, M., and Kanfer, F.H. 1983. The role of goal acceptance in goal setting and task performance. *Academy of Management Review,* 8:454–463.

Feather, N.T., and Barber, J.G. 1983. Depressive reactions and unemployment. *Journal of Abnormal Psychology,* 92:185–189.

Feldman, D.C., and Arnold, H.J. 1983. *Managing individual and group behavior in organizations.* New York: McGraw-Hill.

Fenigstein, A., Scheier, M.F., and Buss, A.H. 1975. Public and private self-consciousness: Assessment and theory. *Journal of Consulting and Clinical Psychology,* 43:522–527.

Festinger, L. 1954. A theory of social comparison processes. *Human Relations,* 7: 117–140.

———. 1957. *A theory of cognitive dissonance.* Stanford: Stanford University Press.

Festinger, L., and Carlsmith, J.M. 1959. Cognitive consequences of forced compliance. *Journal of Abnormal and Social Psychology,* 58:203–210.

Fiedler, F. 1973. *Leadership.* Morristown, N.J.: General Learning Press.

Fishbein, M., and Ajzen, I. 1974. Attitudes towards objects as predictors of single and multiple behavioral criteria. *Psychological Review,* 81:59–74.

Fitch, G. 1970. Effects of self-esteem, perceived performance, and choice on causal attribution. *Journal of Personality and Social Psychology,* 16:311–315.

Fleming, J.S., and Watts, W.A. 1980. The dimensionality of self-esteem: Some results for a college sample. *Journal of Personality and Social Psychology,* 39:921–929.

Fox, F.V., and Staw, B.M. 1979. The trapped administrator: Effects of job insecurity and policy resistence upon commitment to a course of action. *Administrative Science Quarterly,* 24:449–471.

Fredrickson, J.W. 1984. The comprehensiveness of strategic decision processes: Extension, observations, and future directions. *Academy of Management Journal,* 27:445 • 466.

Frederickson, J.W., and Mitchell, T.R 1984. Strategic decision processes: Comprehensiveness and performance in an industry with an unstable environment. *Academy of Management Journal,* 27:399–423.

French, J.R.P. 1963. The social environment and mental health. *Journal of Social Issues,* 19:39–56.

French, J.R.P., and Raven, B.H. 1959. The bases of social power. In *Studies in social power,* ed. D. Cartwright, pp. 150–167. Ann Arbor: Institute for Social Research.

Freud, S. 1953. *The standard edition of the complete psychological works.* London: Hogarth Press.

Gecas, V., and Schwalbe, M.L. 1986. Parental behavior and adolescent self-esteem. *Journal of Marriage and the Family,* 48:37–46.

———, and Schwalbe, M.L. 1986. Parental behavior and adolescent self-esteem. *Journal of Marriage and the Family,* 48:37–46.

Gergen, K.J., Ellsworth, P., Maslach, C., and Seipel, M. 1975. Obligation, donor resources, and reactions to aid in three cultures. *Journal of Personality and Social Psychology,* 31:390–400.

Gergen, K.J., and Maracek, J. 1976. *The psychology of self-esteem.* Morristown, N.J.: General Learning Press.

Gergen, K.J., Morse, S., and Bode, K. 1974. Overpaid or overworked: Cognitive and behavioral reactions to inequitable rewards. *Journal of Applied Social Psychology,* 4:259–274.

Ghiselli, E. 1966. *The validity of occupational aptitude tests.* New York: John Wiley.

———. 1973. The validity of aptitude tests in personnel selection. *Personnel Psychology,* 20:461–477.

Glass, D.C. 1964. Changes in liking as a means of reducing cognitive discrepancies between self-esteem and aggression. *Journal of Personality,* 32:531–549.

Goffman, E. 1959. *The presentation of self in everyday life.* Garden City, N.Y.: Doubleday, Anchor Books.

Goodman, P.S. 1977. Social comparison processes in organizations. In *New directions in organizational behavior,* eds. B.M. Staw & G.R. Salancik, pp. 97–132. Malabar, Fla.: Robert E. Krieger.

Goodman, P.S., and Atkin, R.S. 1984. Consequences of absenteeism. In *Absenteeism,* ed. P. Goodman. San Francisco: Jossey-Bass.

Greenhalgh, L. 1983. Managing the job insecurity crisis. *Human Resource Management,* 22:431–444.

Greenwald, A.G., Bellezza, F.S., and Banaji, M.R. 1987. *Self-esteem, self-consciousness, and access to self-knowledge.* Unpublished manuscript, Ohio State University.

Greenwald, A.G., Breckler, S.J., and Wiggins, E.C. 1987. Public, private, and collective selfevaluation: Measurement of individual differences. Manuscript under editorial review.

Griffin, R.J., and Wayne, S.J. 1984. *A field study of effective and less effective quality circles.* Paper presented at the Academy of Management Conference, Boston.

Gross, A., and Latané, B. 1974. Receiving help, reciprocation, and interpersonal attraction. *Journal of Applied Social Psychology,* 4:220–223.

Guion, R.M., and Gottier, R.F. 1965. Validity of personality measures in personnel selection. *Personnel Psychology,* 18:135–164.

Hackman, J.R. 1986. The design of work teams. In *Handbook of organizational behavior,* ed. J.W. Lorsch, pp. 315–342. Englewood Cliffs, N.J.: Prentice-Hall.

Hackman, J.R., and Lawler, E.E. 1971. Employee reactions to job characteristics. *Journal of Applied Psychology,* 55:259–286. Monograph.

Hackman, J.R., Lawler, E.E., and Porter, L.W. 1983. *Perspectives on behavior in organizations,* 2nd ed. New York: McGraw-Hill.

Hackman, J.R., and Morris, C.G. 1975. Group tasks, group interaction process, and group performance effectiveness: A review and proposed interpretation. In *Advances in experimental social psychology,* ed. L. Berkowitz, Vol. 8, pp. 45–99. New York: Academic Press.

Hackman, J.R., and Oldham, G.R. 1976. Motivation through the design of work: Test of a theory. *Organizational Behavior and Human Performance,* 16:250–279.

Hall, C.S., and Lindzey, G. 1970. *Theories of personality.* New York: John Wiley and Sons.

Hall, D.T. 1971. A theoretical model of career subsidentity development in organizational settings. *Organizational Behavior and Human Performance,* 6:50–76.

Hartley, J. 1980. The impact of unemployment upon the self-esteem of managers. *Journal of Occupational Psychology,* 53:147–155.

Harvey, J.C. 1985. *If I'm so successful, why do I feel like a fake?: The impostor phenomenon.* New York: St. Martin's Press.

Harvey, J., Ickes, W., and Kidd, R. 1976. *New directions in attribution research,* Vol. 1. Hillsdale, N.J.: Lawrence Erlbaum Associates.

Heider, F. 1958. *The psychology of interpersonal relations.* New York: John Wiley.

Heilman, M.E. 1980. The impact of situational factors on personnel decisions concerning women: Varying the sex composition of the applicant pool. *Organizational Behavior and Human Performance,* 26:386–395.

Herold, D. and Greller, M. 1977. Feedback: The definition of a construct. *Academy of Management Journal,* 20:142–147.

Hewitt, J., and Goldman, M. 1974. Self-esteem, need for approval, and reactions to personal evaluations. *Journal of Experimental Social Psychology,* 10:210–210.

Hite, A.L. 1975. *Some characteristics of work roles and their relationships to self-esteem and depression.* Ph.D. diss., University of Michigan.

Hollenbeck, J.R., and Brief, A.P. 1987. The effects of individual differences and goal origin on the goal setting process. Manuscript under editorial review.

Hollenbeck, J.R., Brief, A.P., Whitener, E.M., and Pauli, K.E. 1987. Personality traits and personnel selection: Increasing the predictive validity of ability tests through motivational testing. Manuscript under editorial review.

Hollenbeck, J.R., and Whitener, E.M. 1985. *Reclaiming measures of personality traits for selection: The case for self-esteem.* Paper presented at the Academy of Management Conference, San Diego.

Hollingshead, A.B., and Redlich, F.C. 1958. *Social class and mental illness: A community study.* New York: John Wiley.

Horney, K. *Neurosis and human growth.* New York: Norton.

Hovland, C.I., Lumsdaine, A.A., and Sheffield, F.D. 1949. *Experiments on mass communication.* Princeton, N.J.: Princeton University Press.

Iaffaldano, M.T., and Muchinsky, P.M. 1985. Job satisfaction and job performance: A meta-analysis. *Psychological Bulletin,* 97:251–273.

Ilgen, D.R., Fisher, C.D., and Taylor, M.S. 1979. Consequences of individual feedback on behavior in organizations. *Journal of Applied Psychology,* 64:349–371.

Jackson, S.E., Schwab, R.L., and Schuler, R.S. 1986. Toward an understanding of the burnout phenomenon. *Journal of Applied Psychology,* 71:630–640.

Jacobs, R., and Solomon, T. 1977. Strategies for enhancing the prediction of job performance from job satisfaction. *Journal of Applied Psychology,* 62:417–421.

Jahoda, M. 1982. *Employment and unemployment: A social psychological analysis.* London: Cambridge University Press.

James, W. 1890. *The principles of psychology.* Reprint. New York: Dover, 1950.

Janis, I. 1954. Personality correlates of susceptibility to persuasion. *Journal of Personality,* 22:504–518.

———. 1982. *Groupthink.* Boston Houghton Mifflin.

Janoff-Bulman, R. 1979. Characterological versus behavioral self-blame: Inquiries into depression and rape. *Journal of Personality and Social Psychology*, 37:1798–1809.

Janoff-Bulman, R., and Brickman, P. 1982. Expectations and what people learn from failure. In *Expectations and actions: Expectancy-value models in psychology*, ed. N.T. Feather. Hillsdale, N.J.: Lawrence Erlbaum.

Jones, E.E. 1964. *Ingratiation*. New York: Appleton-Century-Crofts.

Jones, E.E., and Berglas, S. 1978. Control of attributions about the self through self-handicapping strategies: The appeal of alcohol and the role of underachievement. *Personality and Social Psychology Bulletin*, 4:200–206.

Jones, E.E., and Harris, V.A. 1967. The attribution of attitudes. *Journal of Experimental Social Psychology*, 3:1–24.

Jones, G.R. 1986. Socialization tactics, self-efficacy, and newcomers' adjustments to organizations. *Academy of Management Journal*, 29:262–279.

Jones, S.C. 1973. Self and interpersonal evaluations: Esteem theories vs. consistency theories. *Psychological Bulletin*, 79:185–199.

Kanfer, R., and Hulin, C.L. 1985. Individual differences in successful job searches following lay-off. *Personnel Psychology*, 38:835–847.

Kanter, R.M. 1977. *Men and women of the corporation*. New York: Basic Books.

Kaufman, H.G., 1982. *Professionals in search of work: Coping with the stress of job loss and underemployment*. New York: John Wiley and Sons.

King, M.R., and Manaster, G.J. 1977. Body image, self-esteem, expectations, self-assessments, and actual success in a simulated job interview. *Journal of Applied Psychology*, 62:589–595.

Klein, D., Fencil-Morse, E., and Seligman, M.E.P. 1976. Learned helplessness, depression, and the attribution of failure. *Journal of Personality and Social Psychology*, 33:508–516.

Klein, J.A. 1984. Why supervisors resist employee involvement. *Harvard Business Review*, 62(5):87–95.

Kohn, M.L. 1969. *Class and conformity: A study in values*. Homewood, Ill.: The Dorsey Press.

Kohn, M.L., and Schooler, C. 1982. Job conditions and personality: A longitudinal assessment of their reciprocal effects. *American Journal of Sociology*, 87:1257–1286.

———. 1983. *Work and personality: An inquiry into the impact of social stratification*. Norwood, N.J.: Ablex.

Kohut, H. 1971. *The analysis of the self*. New York: International University Press.

Korman, A.K. 1966. Self-esteem variable in vocational choice. *Journal of Applied Psychology*, 50:479–486.

———. 1967. Self-esteem as a moderator of the relationship between self-perceived abilities and vocational choice. *Journal of Applied Psychology*, 51:65–67.

———. 1968. Task success, task popularity, and self-esteem as influences on task liking. *Journal of Applied Psychology*, 52:484–490.

———. 1969. Self-esteem as a moderator in vocational choice: Replications and extensions. *Journal of Applied Psychology*, 53:188–192.

———. 1970. Toward an hypothesis of work behavior. *Journal of Applied Psychology*, 54:31–41.

———. 1977. An examination of Dipboye's "A critical review of Korman's self-consistency theory of work motivation and occupational choice." *Organizational Behavior and Human Performance,* 18:127–128.

Kornhauser, A. 1965. *Mental health of the individual worker.* New York: Wiley.

Kram, K.E. 1983. Phases of the mentor relationship. *Academy of Management Journal,* 26:608–625.

Lamb, M.E. 1977. Father-infant and mother-infant interaction in the first year of life. *Child Development,* 48:167–184.

Latham, G.P., and Locke, E.A. 1979. Goal-setting: A motivational technique that works. *Organizational Dynamics,* 8(2):68–80.

Lawler, E.E. 1971. *Pay and organizational effectiveness: A psychological view.* New York: McGraw-Hill.

Lawler, E.E., and Mohrman, S.A. 1985. Quality circles after the fad. *Harvard Business Review,* 63(1):64–71.

Lecky, P. 1945. *Self-consistency: A theory of personality.* New York: Island Press.

Likert, R. 1961. *New patterns of management.* New York: McGraw-Hill.

Livingston, J.S. 1969. Pygmalion in management. *Harvard Business Review,* 47:81–89.

Locke, E.A. 1968. Toward a theory of task motivation and incentives. *Organizational Behavior and Human Performance,* 3:157–189.

———. 1986. *Generalizing from laboratory to field settings.* Lexington, Mass.: Lexington Books.

Locke, E.A., Shaw, K.M., Saari, L.M., and Latham, G.P. 1981. Goal setting and task performance: 1969–1980. *Psychological Bulletin,* 90:125–152.

London, M., and Klimoski, R.J. 1975. Self-esteem and job complexity as moderators of performance and satisfaction. *Journal of Vocational Behavior,* 6:293–304.

Lopez, E.M. 1982. A text of the self-consistency theory of the job performance-job satisfaction relationship. *Academy of Management Journal,* 25:335–348.

Lopez, E.M., and Greenhaus, J.H. 1978. Self-esteem, race, and job satisfaction. *Journal of Vocational Behavior,* 13:75–83.

Louis, M.R. 1980. Surprise and sense making: What newcomers experience in entering unfamiliar organizational settings. *Administrative Science Quarterly,* 25:226–251.

Lowin, A., and Craig, J.R. 1968. The influence of level of performance on managerial style: An experimental object-lesson in the ambiguity of correlational data. *Organizational Behavior and Human Performance,* 3:440–458.

Luthans, F., and Kreitner, R. 1975. *Organizational behavior modification.* Glenview, Ill.: Scott, Foresman, and Company.

Maccoby, E.E., and Jacklin, C.N. 1974. *The psychology of sex differences.* Stanford, Ca.: Stanford University Press.

Magnusson, D., and Endler, N.S. 1977. *Personality at the crossroads: Current issues in interactional psychology.* Hillsdale, N.J.: Lawrence Erlbaum.

Maier, N.R.F. 1955. *Psychology in industry.* Boston: Houghton Mifflin.

Manz, C.C., and Sims, H.P. 1981. Vicarious learning: The influence of modeling on organizational behavior. *Academy of Management Review,* 6:105–113.

Maracek, J., and Mettee, D.R. 1972. Avoidance of continued success as a function of self-esteem, level of esteem certainty, and responsibility for success. *Journal of Personality and Social Psychology*, 22:98–107.

Markus, H., and Kunda, Z. 1986. Stability and malleability of the self-concept. *Journal of Personality and Social Psychology*, 51:858–866.

McFarlin, D.B. 1985. Persistence in the face of failure: The impact of self-esteem and contingency information. *Personality and Social Psychology Bulletin*, 11: 153–163.

McFarlin, D.B., Baumeister, R.F., and Blascovich, J. 1984. On knowing when to quit: Task failure, self-esteem, advice, and nonproductive persistence. *Journal of Personality*, 52:138–155.

McFarlin, D.B., and Blascovich, J. 1981. Effects of self-esteem and performance feedback on future affective preferences and cognitive expectations. *Journal of Personality and Social Psychology*, 40:521 • 531.

McGrath, J.E. 1964. *Social psychology: A brief introduction*. New York: Holt.

McGuire, W.J. 1968. Personality and susceptibility to social influence. In *Handbook of personality theory and research*, eds. E.F. Borgatta and W.W. Lambert, pp. 140–162. Chicago: Rand-McNally.

———. 1972. Attitude change: The information-processing paradigm. In *Experimental social psychology*, ed. C.G. McClintock, pp. 108–141. New York: Holt, Rinehart, and Winston.

McKersie, R.B., Perry, C.R., and Walton, R.E. 1965. Intraorganizational bargaining in labor negotiations. *Journal of Conflict Resolution*, 9:463–481.

Mead, G.H. 1934. *Mind, self, and society*. Chicago: University of Chicago Press.

Milgram, S. 1974. *Obedience to authority*. New York: Harper.

Mischel, W. 1968. *Personality and assessment*. New York: Wiley.

———. 1973. Towards a cognitive social learning reconceptualization of personality. *Psychological Review*, 80:252–283.

Mitchell, T.R. 1979. Organizational behavior. In *Annual Review of Psychology*, eds. M.R. Rosenzweig and L.W. Porter, Vol. 4, pp. 243–281. Palo Alto, Ca.: Annual Reviews, Inc.

———. 1982. *People in organizations: An introduction to organizational behavior*. New York: McGraw-Hill.

Morrison, R.F. 1977. Career adaptivity: The effective adaptation of managers to changing role demands. *Journal of Applied Psychology*, 62:549–558.

Morse, J.J. 1970. Organizational characteristics and individual motivation. In *Studies in organizational design*, eds. J.W. Lorsch and P.R. Lawrence. Homewood, Ill.: Dorsey Press.

———. 1975. Person-job congruence and individual adjustment and development. *Human Relations*, 28:841–861.

Morse, S.J., 1972. Help, likeability, and social influence. *Journal of Applied Social Psychology*, 2:34–46.

Morse, S.J., and Gergen, K.J. 1970. Social comparison, self-consistency, and the concept of self. *Journal of Personality and Social Psychology*, 16:148–156.

Mossholder, K.W., Bedeian, A.G., and Armenakis, A.A. 1981. Role perceptions, satisfaction, and performance: Moderating effects of self-esteem and organizational level. *Organizational Behavior and Human Performance*, 28:224–234.

———. 1982. Group process-work outcome relationships: A note on the moderating impact of self-esteem. *Academy of Management Journal,* 25:575–585.

Mowday, R.T. 1979. Equity theory predictions of behavior in organizations. In *Motivation and work behavior,* eds. R.M. Steers and L.W. Porter, pp. 124–146. New York: McGraw-Hill.

Mowday, R.T., Porter, L.W., and Steers, R.M. 1982. *Employee-organization linkages: The psychology of commitment, absenteeism, and turnover.* New York: Academic Press.

Nadler, A., Mayseless, O., Peri, N. and Chemerinski, A. 1985. Effects of opportunity to reciprocate and self-esteem on help-seeking behavior. *Journal of Personality,* 53:23–35.

Nadler, D.A., and Tushman, M.L. 1980. A model for diagnosing organizational behavior. *Organizational Dynamics,* 9(2):35–51.

Neale, M.A. 1984. The effects of negotiation and arbitration cost salience on bargainer behavior: The role of the arbitrator and constituency on negotiator judgment. *Organizational Behavior and Human Performance,* 34:97–111.

Newcomb, T.M. 1959. Individual systems of orientation. In *Psychology: A study of a science,* ed. S. Koch, Vol. 3, pp. 384–422. New York: McGraw-Hill.

Northcraft, G.B., and Wolf, G. 1984. Dollars, sense, and sunk costs: A life-cycle model of resource allocation decisions. *Academy of Management Review,* 9: 225–234.

Orne, M. 1962. On the social psychology of the psychological experiment. *American Psychologist,* 28:641–651.

Osgood, C.E., and Tannenbaum, P.H. 1955. The principle of congruity in the prediction of attitude change. *Psychological Review,* 62:42–55.

Peters, T., and Waterman, R. 1982. *In search of excellence: Lessons from America's best-run companies.* New York: Harper and Row.

Peterson, C., and Seligman, M.E.P. 1984. Causal explanations as a risk factor for depression: Theory and evidence. *Psychological Review,* 91:347–374.

Peterson, G.W., Southworth, L.E., and Peters, D.F. 1983. Children's self-esteem and maternal behavior in three low-income samples. *Psychological Reports,* 52: 79–86.

Pruitt, D.G., and Johnson, D.F. 1970. Mediation as an to face saving in negotiation. *Journal of Personality and Social Psychology,* 14:239–246.

Pryor, J.B. 1980. Self-reports and behavior. In *The self in social psychology,* eds. D.M. Wegner and R.R. Vallacher, pp. 206–228, New York: Oxford University Press.

Raben, C.S., and Klimoski, R.J. 1973. The effects of expectation upon task performance as moderated by levels of self-esteem. *Journal of Vocational Behavior,* 3:475–483.

Reed, T. 1987. [Self-esteem as a predictor of success in union organizing.] Unpublished data, Columbia University.

Robinson, J.R., and Shaver, P.R. 1973. *Measures of social psychological attitudes.* Ann Arbor, Mich.: Institute for Social Research.

Rogers, C.R. 1951. *Client-centered therapy.* Boston: Houghton-Mifflin.

———. 1961. *On becoming a person.* Boston: Houghton-Mifflin.

Rokeach, M. 1960. *The open and closed mind.* New York: Basic Books.

Rosenberg, M. 1965. *Society and the adolescent self-image.* Princeton, N.J.: Princeton University Press.

———. 1979. *Conceiving the self.* New York: Basic Books.

Rosenberg, M., and Pearlin, L.I. 1978. Social class and self-esteem among children and adults. *American Journal of Sociology,* 84:53–77.

Rosenfeld, C. 1975. Job seeking methods used by American workers. *Monthly Labor Review,* 98(5):39–42.

Rosenthal, R., and Jacobson, L. 1968. *Pygmalion in the classroom: Teacher expectation and pupils' intellectual development.* New York: Hold, Rinehart, and Winston.

Rotter, J.B. 1966. Generalized expectancies for internal vs. external reinforcement. *Psychological Monographs,* 80(1):Whole No. 609.

Rubin, J.Z., and Brown, B.R. 1975. *The social psychology of bargaining and negotiation.* New York: Academic Press.

Sandelands, L., Brockner, J., and Glynn, M.A. (in press). "If at first you don't succeed, try, try again: The effects of persistence-performance contingencies, ego involvement, and self-esteem on task persistence." *Journal of Applied Psychology.*

Sarason, I.G., Smith, R.E., and Diener, E. 1975. Personality research: Components of variance attributable to the person and the situation. *Journal of Personality and Social Psychology,* 32:199–204.

Schachter, S., Ellertson, N., McBride, D., and Gregory, D. 1951. An experimental study of cohesiveness and productivity. *Human Relations,* 4:229–238.

Scheier, M.F., Buss, A.H., and Buss, D.M. 1978. Self-consciousness, self-report of aggressiveness, and aggression. *Journal of Research in Personality,* 12:133–140.

Schneider, B. 1985. *The people make the place.* Presidential Address, Society of Industrial and Organizational Psychology, Los Angeles, 1985.

Schneider, B., and Schmitt, N. 1986. *Staffing organizations.* Glenview, Ill.: Scott, Foresman, and Company.

Schwalbe, M.L. 1986. Autonomy in work and self-esteem. *The Sociological Quarterly,* 26:519–535.

Schwenk, C.R., and Cosier, R.A. 1980. Effects of the expert, devil's advocate, and dialectical inquiry methods on prediction performance. *Organizational Behavior and Human Performance,* 26:409–424.

Seaver, W.B., 1973. Effects of naturally induced teacher expectancies. *Journal of Personality and Social Psychology,* 28:333–343.

Seligman, M.E.P. 1975. *Helplessness: On depression, development, and death.* San Francisco: W.H. Freeman.

Seligman, M.E.P., Abramson, L.Y., Semmel, A., and von Baeyer, C. 1979. Depressive attributional style. *Journal of Abnormal Psychology,* 88:242–247.

Seligman, M.E.P., and Schulman, P. 1986. Explanatory style as a predictor of productivity and quitting among life insurance sales agents. *Journal of Personality and Social Psychology,* 50:832–838.

Shamir, B. 1986. Self-esteem and the psychological impact of unemployment. *Social Psychology Quarterly,* 49:61–72.

Shavelson, R.J., Hubner, J.J., and Stanton, G.C. 1976. Self-concept: Validation of construct interpretation. *Review of Educational Research,* 46:407–441.

Shrauger, J.S. 1972. Self-esteem and reactions to being observed by others. *Journal of Personality and Social Psychology,* 23:192–200.

———. 1975. Responses to evaluation as a function of initial self-perceptions. *Psychological Bulletin,* 82:581–596.

Shrauger, J.S., and Rosenberg, S. 1970. Self-esteem and the effects of success and failure feedback on performance. *Journal of Personality,* 38:404–417.

Shrauger, J.S., and Sorman, P. 1977. Self-evaluations, initial success and failure, and improvement as determinants of persistence. *Journal of Consulting and Clinical Psychology,* 45:784–795.

Sigall, H., and Gould, R. 1977. The effects of self-esteem and evaluator demandingness on effort expenditure. *Journal of Personality and Social Psychology,* 35:12–20.

Smith, T.W., Snyder, C.R., and Perkins, S.C. 1983. The self-serving function of hypochondriacal complaints: Physical symptoms of self-handicapping strategies. *Journal of Personality and Social Psychology,* 44:787–797.

Snyder, C.R., Smith, T.W., Augelli, R.W., and Ingram, R.E. 1985. On the self-serving function of social anxiety: Shyness as a self-handicapping strategy. *Journal of Personality and Social Psychology,* 48:970–980.

Snyder, M. 1981. Impression management: The self in social interaction. In *Social psychology in the 80s,* eds. L. Wrightsman and K. Deaux. Monterey, Ca.: Brooks/Cole.

Spielberger, C.D., Gorsuch, R.L., and Lushene, R.E. 1970. *Manual for the State-Trait anxiety inventory.* Palo Alto, Ca.: Consulting Psychologists Press.

Staples, C.L., Schwalbe, M.L., and Gecas, V. 1984. Social class, occupational conditions, and efficacy-based self-esteem. *Sociological Perspectives,* 27:85–109.

Staw, B.M. 1976. Knee-deep in the big muddy: A study of escalating commitment to a chosen course of action. *Organizational Behavior and Human Performance,* 16:27–44.

———. 1977. Motivation in organizations: Toward synthesis and redirection. In *New directions in organizational behavior,* eds. B.M. Staw and G.R. Salancik, pp. 55–96. Malabar, Fla.: Robert E. Krieger.

———. 1980. The consequences of turnover. *Journal of Occupational Behavior,* 1:253–273.

Staw, B.M., and Ross, J. 1980. Commitment in an experimenting society: An experiment on the attribution of leadership from administrative scenarios. *Journal of Applied Psychology,* 65:249–260.

———. 1987. Understanding escalation situations: Antecedents, prototypes, and solutions. In *Research in organizational behavior,* eds. B.M. Staw and L.L. Cummings, Vol. 9, in press. Greenwich, Ct.: JAI Press.

Staw, B.M., Sandelands, L.E., and Dutton, J.E. 1981. Threat-rigidity effects in organizational behavior. *Administrative Science Quarterly,* 26:501–524.

Steers, R.M. 1984. *Introduction to organizational behavior.* Glenview, Ill.: Scott, Foresman and Company.

Stein, M.I. 1974. *Stimulating creativity,* Vol. 1. New York: Academic Press.

Stogdill, R.M. 1972. Group productivity. *Organizational Behavior and Human Performances,* 8:26–43.

Stouffer, S.A., Suchman, E.A., Devinney, L.C., Star, S.A., and Williams, R.M., Jr.

1949. *The American soldier: Adjustment during army life,* Vol. 1. Princeton, N.J.: Princeton University Press.

Strack, S., Blaney, P.H., Ganellen, R.J., and Coyne, J.C. 1985. Pessimistic self-preoccupation, performance deficits, and depression. *Journal of Personality and Social Psychology,* 49:1076–1085.

Strack, S., and Coyne, J.C. 1982. Social confirmation of dysphoria: Shared and private reactions. Unpublished manuscript, University of California.

Sullivan, H.S. 1953. *The interpersonal theory of psychiatry.* New York: Norton.

Swann, W.B. 1983. Self-verification: Bringing social reality into harmony with the self. In *Psychological perspectives on the self,* eds. J. Suls and A.G. Greenwald, Vol. 2, pp. 33–66. Hillsdale, N.J.: Erlbaum.

Taylor, J.A. 1953. A personality scale of manifest anxiety. *Journal of Abnormal and Social Psychology,* 48:285–290.

Teger, A. 1980. *Too much invested to quit.* New York: Pergamon Press.

Tennen, H., and Eller, S. 1977. Attributional components of learned helplessness and facilitation. *Journal of Personality and Social Psychology,* 35:265–271.

Tennen, H., and Herzberger, S. 1987. Depression, self-esteem, and the absence of selfprotective attributional biases. *Journal of Personality and Social Psychology,* 52:72–80.

Tesser, A. 1984. Some effects of self-evaluation maintenance on cognition and action. In *The handbook of motivation and cognition: Foundations of social behavior,* eds. R.M. Sorrentino and E.T. Higgins, pp. 435–464. New York: Guilford Press.

Tharenou, P. 1979. Employee self-esteem: A review of the literature. *Journal of Vocational Behavior,* 15:316–346.

Tharenou, P., and Harker, P. 1984. Moderating influence of self-esteem on relationships between job complexity, performance, and satisfaction. *Journal of Applied Psychology,* 69:623–632.

Thomas, K.W. 1979. Organizational conflict. In *Organizational behavior,* ed. S. Kerr, pp. 151–181. Columbus, Ohio: Grid Publishing, Inc.

Tolman, E.L. 1935. *Purposive behavior in animals and men.* New York: Century.

Trotter, R.J. 1987. Stop blaming yourself. *Psychology Today,* 21:30–39.

Van Maanen, J., and Schein, E.H. 1979. Towards a theory of organizational socialization. In *Research in organizational behavior,* eds. B.M. Staw and L.L. Cummings, Vol. 1, pp. 209–264. Greenwich, Conn.: JAI Press.

Vroom, V.H. 1962. Ego involvement, job satisfaction, and job performance. *Personnel Psychology,* 15:159–177.

———. 1964. *Work and motivation.* New York: Wiley.

Vroom, V.H., and Yetton, P. 1973. *Leadership and decision making.* Pittsburgh: University of Pittsburgh Press.

Warr, P.B. 1983. Work, jobs, and unemployment. *Bulletin of the British Psychological Society,* 36:305–311.

Watson, D., and Clark, L.A. 1984. Negative affectivity: The disposition to experience aversive emotional states. *Psychological Bulletin,* 96:465–490.

Webber, A. 1987. Red Auerbach on management. *Harvard Business Review,* 87(2): 84–91.

Weick, K.E. 1977. Enactment processes in organizations. In *New directions in orga-*

nizational behavior, eds. B.M. Staw and G.R. Salancik, pp. 267–300. Malabar, Fla.: Robert E. Krieger.

———. 1979. *The social psychology of organizing.* Reading, Mass.: Addison-Wesley.

Weigel, R.H., and Newman, L.S. 1976. Increasing attitude-behavior correspondence by broadening the scope of the behavioral measure. *Journal of Personality and Social Psychology,* 33:793–802.

Weiner, B. 1974. *Achievement motivation and attribution theory.* Morristown, N.J.: General Learning Press.

Weiss, H.M. 1977. Subordinate imitation of supervisory behavior: The role of modeling in organizational socialization. *Organizational Behavior and Human Performance,* 19:89–105.

———. 1978. Social learning of work values in organizations. *Journal of Applied Psychology,* 63:711–718.

Weiss, H.M., and Adler, S. 1984. Personality and organizational behavior. In *Research in organizational behavior,* eds. B.M. Staw and L.L. Cummings, Vol. 6, pp. 1–50. Greenwich, CT.: JAI Press.

Weiss, H.M., and Knight, P.A. 1980. The utility of humility: Self-esteem, information search, and problem solving efficiency. *Organizational Behavior and Human Performance.* 25:216.223.

Wexley, K.N., and Yukl, G.A. 1984. *Organizational behavior and personnel psychology.* Homewood, Ill.: Richard D. Irwin, Inc.

Wortman, C.B., and Brehm, J.W. 1975. Responses to uncontrollable outcomes: An integration of reactance theory and the learned helplessness model. In *Advances in experimental social psychology,* ed. L. Berkowitz, Vol. 8, pp. 277–336. New York: Academic Press.

Wylie, R.C. 1979. *The self-concept: Theory and research on selected topics,* Vol. 2. Lincoln: University of Nebraska Press.

Yerkes, R.M., and Dodson, J.D. 1908. The relation of strength of stimulus to rapidity of habit formation. *Journal of Comparative Neurological Psychology,* 18:459–482.

Yukl, G.A., and Latham, G.P. 1978. Interrelationships among employee participation, individual differences, goal difficulty, goal acceptance, goal instrumentality, and performance. *Personnel Psychology,* 31:305–323.

Zanna, M., Crosby, F., and Loewenstein, G. (in press). Male reference groups and discontent among female professionals. In *Women's career development,* eds. B.A. Gutek and L. Larwood. Beverly Hills, Ca.: Sage Publications.

Zanna, M.P., and Pack, S.J. 1975. On the self-fulfilling nature of apparent sex differences in behavior. *Journal of Experimental Social Psychology,* 11:583–591.

Ziller, R.C. 1973. *The social self.* New York: Pergamon Press.

Zuckerman, M. 1979. Attributions of success and failure revisited, or: The motivational bias is alive and well in attribution theory. *Journal of Personality,* 47:245–287.

Zuckerman, M., Brown, R.H., Fox, G.A., Lathin, D.R., and Minasian, A.J. 1979. Determinants of information seeking behavior. *Journal of Research in Personality,* 13:161–179.

Subject Index

Author Index

About the Author

Joel Brockner, a personality/social psychologist, is currently a professor of management at the Graduate School of Business, Columbia University. He earned his doctorate degree in psychology from Tufts University in 1977 and taught in the Department of Psychology at Tufts prior to joining the faculty at Columbia in 1984. He has published extensively in both psychology and management journals about a variety of topics including self-esteem, decision making, and the effects of job layoffs on remaining employees. He is also the author of *Entrapment in Escalating Conflicts: A Social Psychological Analysis* (with Jeffrey Rubin; Springer-Verlag, 1985). A member of the Editorial Board of the *Academy of Management Journal,* he has consulted frequently to industry about the management of human forces in work organizations. He resides in New Rochelle, New York, with his wife, Audrey Brockner, and sons Eliot and Dustin Brockner.